Media and Health

Media and Health

Clive Seale

SAGE Publications
London • Thousand Oaks • New Delhi

SAGE Publications Ltd
1 Oliver's Yard, 55 City Road
London EC1Y 1SP

SAGE Publications Inc
2455 Teller Road
Thousand Oaks, California 91320

SAGE Publications India Pvt Ltd
B-42 Panchsheel Enclave
Post Box 4109
New Delhi 100 017

British Library Cataloguing in Publication data

A catalogue record for this book is
available from the British Library

ISBN 0 7619 4729 9
ISBN 0 07619 4730 2 (pbk)

Library of Congress catalog card number 2002 103333

Typeset by M Rules
Printed and bound in Great Britain by
Athenaeum Press Ltd., Gateshead, Tyne & Wear

Contents

Preface

The aim of this book is to bring together the field of media studies with that of the sociology of health and illness (SHI). As a sociologist concerned with health matters, becoming interested a few years ago in media representations of illness and health-care topics, I noticed early on in my studies that SHI had not kept up with developments in media studies. For example, reviewing many small studies done on aspects of health and illness in the media, I noticed that the assumptions these made about the place of mass media in the everyday life of audiences were uninformed by the latest thinking in the field of media studies. Conversely, reading around the broad field of media studies, I noticed that there were numerous book-length treatments of certain topics – race, crime, gender, for example – but that equivalent treatments of health were rather thin on the ground and somewhat dated. At the same time, it has become increasingly clear to me that people's responses to illness, health care and health-related behaviour generally are profoundly influenced by mass media representations. This cultural aspect of experience has been inadequately recognised in numerous studies of illness experience done by sociologists relying largely on self-reports through interviews. At the broadest level, an account of media representations in this area, drawing together the studies that have been done in this field and making sense of these in terms of contemporary theories about the place of mediated experience in the everyday lives of people in late modern societies, can help illuminate the broader question (which is asked by anthropologists and historians as much as media analysts) of how cultures construct personal experiences of illness and health. An understanding of this, I am convinced, is essential for health educators, providers of health services, and students of illness behaviour. It seems to me, too, that people interested in media ought also to be concerned with the life of the body, and the place of media in influencing this, so that both fields may benefit from this work.

The first three chapters of this book outline general considerations, relevant to health and illness experience, that are helpful in understanding the role that media representations may play in everyday life experience, the form that representations of health and illness take, and some explanations for the particular ways in which media producers behave. The difficulties experienced in the relationship between media producers on the one hand and, on the other hand, health promoters, professionals and scientists are illuminated and explained in these chapters. The chapters that follow present selective reviews of research studies in the media health field, many of which are insufficiently well known, grouped around the themes of health scares, villains and threats, victimhood, professional and lay sources of rescue, and gender differences. It will become clear that an important feature of modern times is distrust of professional authority over health matters and an elevation of ordinary, somewhat narcissistic 'consumer-heroes' to a position of considerable authority. Mass media organisations play an important part in constructing – even orchestrating – this opposition, which is made more acute by considerable investment in generating fears about disease, as well as promising a variety of rewarding pleasures.

There are gaps in this book. While I have tried to indicate where and when studies have been done and which types of media are involved, readers may wonder whether a more sustained analysis of differences between countries (US versus UK, for example), between media types (television versus newspaper or radio, tabloid versus 'serious') and over time might have produced a less generalised picture of media behaviour. I can only say in defence that this is still an emerging field, with most studies being narrow in scope and not easily comparable with similar studies done on the media of other countries, or across a variety of media genres (an exception is the media treatment of AIDS, discussed in Chapter 5). It seemed to me more important at this stage to put together an argument of reasonably general scope than to attempt the kind of nuanced account that may be possible in years to come when more evidence is available. Another gap is in the area of 'new media' and health, which has only been touched on very briefly. Although the Internet is increasingly becoming a source of health information to which people turn, good studies of people's use of this are few and far between and a review must wait until more are available.

Clive Seale

Acknowledgements

I would like to thank Annette Hill for providing helpful suggestions for reading in the field of media studies, which have proven immensely valuable for the book. Both she and David Oswell have also kindly read drafts of the book and provided helpful and constructive critique. Julia Hall and Rosie Maynard at Sage have been supportive and helpful throughout. I am grateful to them all.

1 Media Health and Everyday Life

Living in the wealthy countries of the world, we nowadays experience unprecedented good health. Life expectancy is at a level higher than ever before in history, infant mortality has been reduced so far that death is largely confined to old age, and disease is subject to a host of medical interventions whose effectiveness would have appeared miraculous to earlier generations. Food is in such abundance and variety that we can all, if we choose, realistically aspire to the gluttony that once was the preserve of the privileged classes. Remedial exercise regimes and fitness programmes abound to counteract the effects of excess consumption. It is possible to imagine, for most of our early lives, that our bodies can at times be forgotten, at others can become aesthetic projects, or that even death might not exist for us.

Yet, at times, we may experience minor ailments that cause troublesome limitations – coughs, colds, aches and pains – frequently dealt with by short episodes of 'taking it easy' or chemical analgesics. Rarely, we may encounter misadventure or accidents that threaten life. If we are unlucky, more serious diseases may appear on the horizon. Typically, as we get older, this can be through experience of the degenerative diseases of affluence, such as heart disease, stroke or cancer. In late middle age, we begin to notice who has 'looked after themselves' and who has not. We may start to take an increased interest in monitoring our own state of health in order to avoid the fateful moment at which the presence of a life-disrupting disease is announced. With old age our use of health services increases.

Throughout these phases of life we are exposed to many sources of information about health matters, not least of which are various kinds of media. Television, film, radio, newspapers and magazines form a constant backdrop to our lives and contain many implicit or explicit messages about health. A starting point for this book is that health messages in popular mass media are an important influence and resource in contemporary life, in addition to specialist resources available in books or through the Internet, or the more conventional resources of professional and lay health care advice. But the media presentation of health matters is not neutral, being subject to many determining influences. Although there now exists a substantial body of information and research analysing the production, nature and influence of media health messages, I contend that health research in general has underplayed the role of popular media in constructing and influencing illness experience, and in forming expectations of health care.

An exception to this rule has been the analysis of media messages provided by health educationists and health promoters. This body of research has been important in establishing the considerable extent to which mediated images influence health experience. But, until recently, the model implicit in much health education research concerning the place of media in everyday life has been limited, in particular underestimating people's use of media for pleasurable experience rather than ascetic messages. It has also failed to investigate the full variety of audiences' readings and uses for media representations, preferring instead to concentrate on whether audiences have imbibed specific messages. After reviewing the health education perspective, and noting more recent developments in the health promotion and media advocacy fields that have attempted to address these limitations, I shall outline in this chapter an alternative vision of the place of media in constructing health experience, drawing on broad sociological theories of mediated experience and its place in the everyday lives of people in contemporary mass societies.

HEALTH EDUCATION PERSPECTIVES

The overriding aim of health educators used to be, and for many still is, to encourage individual behaviour that will result in good health. Media messages, from this perspective, are largely analysed according to whether they promote healthy behaviour by providing information and encouragement towards this goal. This has been associated, too, with a highly critical assessment of routine media coverage of health-related topics that has often (though not always) been linked with other moral or political agendas – such as feminist, environmentalist or socialist projects. As this more politicised perspective has gained ground, and the limitations of older-style health information campaigns directed at individuals have been recognised, some health educationists have shifted towards a more radical form of practice, under the rubric of health promotion, media advocacy or community empowerment. These shifts have involved changes in the way in which audiences' relationship with the media has been conceptualised. But even while these shifts have occurred, the over-riding perspective of health educators has often been that a health-promoting media ought to deliver accurate, objective information about health risks and healthy behaviour, free from any distortions of ideology, pressure from commercial interests, or obligation to entertain.

Traditional health education

A good example of this anti-entertainment, pro-accuracy, health educa-tion perspective is contained in a study by Michele Kilgore (1996) of news reporting of cancers of the female reproductive system in US news-papers between 1985 and 1993. She characterises these stories as a mixture of 'magic, moralisation and marginalization' (1996: 249). The magical category refers to the reporting of scientific developments in the diagnosis and treatment of these cancers, which, Kilgore notes, emphasises the 'amazing miracle' (1996: 252) that each of these is made to represent, using phrases like 'dawn of a new era', 'pioneering' and 'breakthrough' to excite readers with the prospects for the chosen procedure and, in Kilgore's opinion, thus raise hopes quite unrealistically. The moral ele-ments which Kilgore finds objectionable largely relate to the stigmatisation of 'career women' (1996: 254) or the sexually promiscuous that she detects in the news reports, particularly where cervical cancer is concerned. This, she observes, reflects a highly selective focus on partic-ular scientific studies (identifying multiple sexual partners or late childbearing as risk factors) that in actual fact are far from conclusive, but which fit a particular news agenda that imposes traditional standards of sexual morality and female behaviour. Kilgore's third complaint concerns the fact that useful medical information is often 'so embedded in extrin-sic material that lay readers may not be able to conduct a successful excavation' (1996: 254). For example, too many articles, for Kilgore's taste, focused on business interests affected by government decisions about whether to license particular drugs, or diverted the reader from useful health information with irrelevant information about the lives of celebrities with these cancers. 'Generally,' Kilgore concludes, news cover-age '[does] not suggest that newspapers have served as an efficient medium for transmission of medical information on [these cancers]' (1996: 255).

How does Kilgore explain this behaviour by newspapers that, we may imagine, she believes to be failing in their public duty to provide accurate and informative health education to women so that they may avoid these diseases, or deal with them sensibly if they get them? For this, she turns to Bell's (1991) analysis of the values that influence the selection and coverage of news. The preference of news media for events that are recent, factual and conveyed by authoritative sources explains the concentration on scientific discoveries, and the 'miracle' element of these is explained by a general preference for stories conveying superlative importance through their magnitude and significance. A preference for negativity and personal relevance explains the emphasis on personal risk; a preference for stories about elite people is behind the concentration on celebrities with cancer. Compatibility with stereotypes ('consonance' in Bell's terms) helps explain the sexism of the stories, and a focus on the unexpected means that well-known risk factors for cancer, such as age or smoking, are less likely to be included in stories. Kilgore's lament ends by concluding that health educators are up against some pretty powerful forces in their struggle to get newspapers to behave in a way that is conducive to good public health.

Clearly, Kilgore's overriding concern is with the health of women, and one can see how this incorporates also a feminist agenda as well as a hint of suspicion about capitalist interests (seen in the singling out of business coverage for criticism). I have chosen the piece not because it is particularly well known or original in its field, but because it is a typical example of a host of books, papers, reports and conference proceedings concerning media health that have emanated from health educators (and from media analysts influenced by health education goals) over the years. While such analyses reveal some undoubted truths about the way media operate in this sphere, I shall argue that they involve a limited vision of the relationship between popular media and their audiences.

The 'traditional' health education approach to the media, represented in Kilgore but shared by a host of other specialists in health communications (see, for example, Leathar et al., 1986), conceives of the public as ill-informed and devises a solution in terms of delivery of missing information. Too often, though, this model has led to disappointment. Thus Brown and Walsh-Childers (1994), in a comprehensive review of research on the effects of mass media health education campaigns, conclude that '[the] success of these campaigns has been mixed' (1994: 405). They point out that international evaluations of various campaigns to promote safer sex in the wake of AIDS, for example, were shown to be ineffective in influencing behaviour change in some countries. Some such evaluations concluded that fears about AIDS had been needlessly raised in low-risk groups, but had largely missed people engaging in high-risk practices.

Tones and Tilford (1994), in a similar review, note a poor record for alcohol abuse campaigns in encouraging moderation, though anti-smoking campaigns have had more success in a public opinion climate already primed for such messages. The consensus view is expressed by Naidoo and Wills (2000), who conclude that mass media health education campaigns can at times help raise consciousness about health issues and may change behaviour if other enabling factors are present, as they are in smoking campaigns, or if the media message is combined with other forms of health promotion. But for conveying complex health information, for teaching skills (such as the negotiation of safer sex) or for challenging strongly held beliefs, they are more likely to be ineffective. The individualistic orientation of the 'information delivery' mode of health education, where individuals are assumed to have the capacity to simply 'choose' a lifestyle as if there were no external constraints or influences to contend with, is a further limitation of this perspective.

Health educators will often, therefore, seek to persuade those who control media outlets to carry the somewhat ascetic messages that they wish to promote. Largely speaking, the 'entertainment' function of media outlets is seen to stand in opposition to the aims of health educators. One approach to this is to create specialist media outlets, often for precisely targetted audiences. This is done from time to time through the production of informative leaflets and newsletters, of the sort that one often finds lying around in health care clinics and surgery waiting rooms. These may be singularly lacking in entertainment value. Dixon-Woods (2001), in a review of studies of such materials, observes that the educational motivation behind such materials leads health educators to depict patients as 'irrational, passive, forgetful and incompetent' (2001: 3), concluding that '[it] is disappointing that such naïve, unhelpful, negative and patronising views of patients . . . dominate' (2001: 10). Jewitt (1997), in an analysis of sexual health leaflets and posters aimed at young people, notes that 'sex is represented in the context of sexual reproduction rather than pleasure' (1997: 4.28). These are hardly depictions likely to appeal to an entertainment-oriented media executive, concerned to attract an audience.

Edutainment, social marketing and media advocacy

A further solution has therefore been proposed, as health education has been increasingly reconceptualised as health promotion. Reflecting concern with a lack of fit between their goals and those of media personnel, health promoters have become involved in 'edutainment'. Here, there is a more realistic squaring-up to the lack of appeal that ascetic messages are likely to have, as health promoters become involved with scriptwriters to influence the health messages of popular media products, such as soap operas. In 1994 Brown and Walsh-Childers noted a number of initiatives of this sort, including the use of anti-smoking scenes in Hollywood movies, and the use of music videos and soap operas to promote the virtues of contraception in certain countries. Popular health and fitness programmes might be regarded as an aspect of edutainment, being concerned to promote healthy behaviour as fun. Sommerland and Robbins (1997) report the collaboration between health promoters and a local radio station in England to produce a weekly soap opera containing health promotion stories, linked to various other community-based initiatives. Basil (1996), in a similar spirit, advocates the use of celebrity 'endorsers' of health-promoting behaviour, drawing on the example of Magic Johnson, whose announcement of his HIV-positive status was effective in promoting concern about safe sexual behaviour amongst young people identifying with this sports star.

Edutainment initiatives reflect a shift in the position of health educators, from complaints about the limitations of a commercially oriented media system, to a compromise with the pleasure principle that drives most mass media organisations' relationship with their audiences. Another compromise is represented by an approach known as 'social marketing', which conceives of health promotion as an attempt to 'sell' a product, along lines similar to the marketing that accompanies commercial goods (Naidoo & Wills, 2000). Good health – packaged as fitness, good looks, feelings of happiness and well-being, or whatever – is promoted as something that people want, at least as much as they may want chocolate bars, beer or cigarettes. The 'problem' for health promoters working within this scheme, though, appears to lie in the intangible nature of their product (the taste of chocolate being a more concrete realisation of pleasure than anticipation of generalised feelings of well-being) and the 'cost' of getting it, which involves sometimes lengthy periods of self-denial and effort.

The frustrations of health educators with popular mass media and with a health-damaging environment, have also generated more radical solutions, based on ideas about community activism and empowerment, using the media to highlight and change social and environmental causes of ill health. These initiatives may be fuelled by the feelings of righteous anger that have always been around in health educators' analyses. One senses this anger, for example, in vitriolic condemnations of the devious behaviour of cigarette companies in order to promote their product (see also Chapter 3). A 'direct action' element may then appear, especially if community activists join with the health educators' cause. Thus Chesterfield-Evans and O'Connor (1986) give an account of an Australian consumer movement devoted to publicising unhealthy products by means of street graffiti – called Billboard Utilising Graffitists Against Unhealthy Promotions (BUGAUP). Wallack (1994) has called this and related developments 'media advocacy', involving attempts to generate media coverage of the health-damaging effects of commercial and sometimes governmental interests. This can, for example, involve sponsoring court cases in which smokers with lung cancer sue tobacco manufacturers. Wallack (1994) describes media campaigns in California to ban the sale of toy guns that mimic real firearms that were causing accidental deaths; Chapman and Lupton (1994a) describe media advocacy to enforce the fencing in of garden pools to prevent accidental drowning. Media advocacy in Australia has had considerable success in influencing media coverage of tobacco towards health-promoting practices (Chapman & Wakefield, 2001). These initiatives move away from an information-delivery model of media usage to one in which people are engaged in using and influencing media in a strategy of power. The key target audience may then become not the 'masses', but the relatively elite group of policy formers and lawmakers who may respond to such campaigns.

The dissatisfaction with the information-delivery model, which conceives of health messages as 'hypodermic needle' injections of information into a largely passive audience, has therefore led to alternative conceptions that imagine a much more active audience role, represented by edutainment, social marketing and media advocacy. These recognise, and attempt to address, the role of audience pleasure and the importance of commercial influences on media health. Too often, though, analyses of mass media health messages involve little more than a routine condemnation of biased media presentations that are felt by analysts to have health-damaging effects. In many studies in this field there remains an inadequate analysis of the complex relationship of mainstream media products with the everyday life experience of people in contemporary societies. This book begins from the position that the broader discipline of media studies now has much to offer health educators seeking greater sophistication in their conceptualisation of the relationship of media messages with everyday life. For example, the messages that health educators often believe to be so damaging may, in fact, receive a variety of readings, not all of which are health damaging in their consequences. To explore the potential of alternative models, then, I will now pursue an analysis of media health that draws on theories developed in the broader media studies sphere.

THE MEDIA HEALTH AUDIENCE

Accounts of changing models of media audiences are standard fare in introductory media studies texts. A clear and recent account is given by Abercrombie and Longhurst (1998), who also present their own audience theory (for which see later in this chapter). For the present I will use an example of a particular genre of television programme to show the variety of ways in which media health audiences can be conceptualised. The terms 'reality television', 'tabloid TV' or 'reality programming' (Langer, 1998; Hill, 2000) refer to programmes like *999* or *Children's Hospital* (in the UK), *Rescue 911* (US), *Australia's Most Wanted* and a variety of European equivalents, the common factor being a focus on dramatic, often life-threatening, 'real-life' events, filmed as they happen or reconstructed for the camera, often demonstrating successful rescues by paramedics, police, fire and ambulance services, or appealing for public assistance in the case of crime shows, or showing life-preserving medical treatments. The emphasis is on the emotions of those involved, so that audiences feel anxiety, fear and sympathy, the situations subsequently resolved when rescue efforts are successful. Such programmes may contain 'public information' sections, such as safety advice, crime prevention guidance or demonstrations of elementary first-aid procedures. There are also programmes of this sort that focus on animals, following the same format of medical emergency followed by rescue and advice on appropriate pet care.

Effects model

Let us imagine the various ways such programmes might be understood by media analysts. Firstly we may consider the original 'hypodermic syringe' model of audience effects which has been influential in traditional health education. On the one hand we could expect some endorsement of the educational elements of the programmes (indeed, this educational purpose is a major way in which both the programme makers and audiences defend themselves against the charges of sensationalism and voyeurism [Hill, 2000]). However, we might also expect to see condemnation of the focus on rescue efforts in the reconstructions of, say, health care or accident scene episodes. Patients undergoing operations in hospital for life-threatening conditions; children receiving medical care for rare diseases; and people injured in bizarre or unusual ways in accidents, stuck in lifts or mineshafts, trapped in caves awaiting the incoming tide, stranded on mountainsides – all of these, we might learn, generate fear about things which are actually quite rare, tell audiences very little about how to prevent the most common threats to health and safety (such as smoking, not wearing seatbelts), place an undue emphasis on hi-tech or institutionally based solutions to health problems, glamorise certain kinds of service worker (firefighters, doctors) at the expense of others (nurses, social workers), and in general present an inaccurate account of life's risks. It would be better for health, so this argument would go, for people to be inoculated against more important health and safety risks by a more objective and balanced approach that described statistically more prevalent threats and how to avoid them, such as the need to stop smoking, take exercise, avoid fatty foods and, for older viewers perhaps, to remember to stay warm in winter. Further, we might expect to see some moral reservations about reality TV to be aired, with eyebrows raised about the sensationalistic aspects of the programmes that appear to exploit other peoples' misfortune for public entertainment. The emphasis on success and happy endings would undoubtedly be perceived as unrealistic, misleading the audience into a false sense of security, and leaving them uninformed about the true risks of life.

What kind of research study to investigate these effects might we expect to find within this tradition? Stereotypically, we might find an experimental design in which viewers were allocated at random to view either a reality TV programme or some other 'neutral' programme, such as a documentary of space travel. All participants, before and after viewing their allocated programme, would be given a questionnaire measuring the degree to which, say, they experienced their environment as risky, trusted authority figures to protect them from danger, understood basic first-aid procedures and so on. The programme's effects, in this design, would be measured by differences in pre- and post-test scores, their magnitude being compared between treatment and control groups. Alternatively, audiences might be subjected to a cross-sectional survey in order to establish whether their views were congruent with those contained in the media messages, demonstrating the presence of a 'cultivation' effect. Perhaps, though, qualitative research would be done, to focus on the extent to which the messages gratified audiences' needs for information, and whether such information was then used and acted upon, or even to establish whether certain individuals acted as 'opinion leaders' in their local communities, relaying the messages of such programmes to acquaintances in their local community. This highly simplified account glosses over many important distinctions that exist between hypodermic, cultivation and uses/gratifications models. However, all of these approaches in their various ways may be classed as attempts to identify direct effects, in the form of a change of attitudes or knowledge in the direction expected by the dominant media message.

Active audience model

But let us now consider a different view of reality TV, and of audiences' relationships to it. Here, we can draw on conceptions of media audiences as 'active' rather than 'passive' (Hall, 1980; Morley, 1986), pursuing a variety of different readings according to their particular life circumstances (for example, their social class position, their ethnic identity) or their personal preferences. A foundational assumption in this school of thought is that varieties of 'decoding' by audiences will not necessarily align with 'encoding' intentions of programme makers (Hall, 1980). Thus, we might imagine that certain members of the reality TV audience pursue 'resistant' readings, just as Morley (1980) in his study of the audience of a news and current affairs programme discovered, when he found that, for example, trades union officials were critical of news coverage of industrial disputes. Resistant readings of reality TV are easy to imagine, since health educators are not the only people who disapprove of the voyeurism and inaccuracy they involve. In addition, some people may take entirely unexpected, bizarre things from such programmes; perhaps in certain circles there is considerable interest in firemen's uniforms as fashion statements; for others, there may be sexual or sadistic pleasures in the imagery of suffering; for others, the technology of rescue machinery may be a particular fascination. Perhaps more plausibly, men, women and children may differ systematically in their 'readings': men may be excited by the chase, rescue and heroic elements; women attracted by the health and safety or the animal cruelty issues raised by the stories; children gripped by the emotional drama of abandonment and subsequent security, or the appearance of cuddly animals. Gendered or other power differentials in families may be at play in deciding whether to watch such programmes in the first place, or in the degree of focused attention that audience members may be able to direct at the screen. Thus we might imagine that diverse readings are structured by underlying social variables, such as age, gender and social class.

This more complex picture of media health would undoubtedly require a more open and exploratory research methodology for its investigation than the hypodermic model of effects outlined earlier. Typically, audience members – perhaps grouped according to their position in social structure – are subjected to qualitative interviews or focus groups in which they are invited to surprise the media analyst with their responses to programmes. Maybe people with experience of being in similar accidents, doing similar crimes, rescuing victims, catching criminals or patching up the injured would have very divergent readings from each other, or from a group chosen at random from the general population. For all we know, just as those plotting crimes are rumoured to take tips from crime reconstruction programmes, some people could be watching medical 'docu-dramas' in order better to mimic sickness the next time they want a day off work!

Postmodern view

We have moved, then, from a linear model of direct effects to one that is concerned to explore diversity, and from a quantitative to a qualitative methodology for gathering materials to support these models. There is a third, postmodern view that has gained a degree of popularity in recent years, based on a radical deconstruction of some basic assumptions often made about the media sphere, such as the existence of an entity called 'the audience' that is separate from 'the message' or the 'producer' of the message. Instead, it may be that the 'audience is, most of all, a discursive construct produced by a particular analytic gaze' (Alasuutari, 1999: 6), and that words like the 'world', 'reception' and 'audience' ought now to be placed in inverted commas (Alasuutari, 1999: 7). This constructionist view, perhaps predictably, often ends up in an introverted pursuit of the field of media studies itself as an object for analysis and critique.

An example of the kind of research study that gets done from this point of view – although, as Alasuutari (1999) points out, empirical research may not be necessary at all to pursue constructionist ideas – is contained in Jacobs's (1996) account of producing the news in a Los Angeles television station. Drawing on an experience of participant observation, large sections of Jacobs's account are taken up with discussions of different social theories of the media. In the gaps between these discussions, Jacobs variously recounts that the TV station sometimes likes to use footage shot by 'stringers' – private camera operators who sell this to news stations; that news workers like to fit stories into a stock set of standardised narratives; that sometimes callers to the station are not dismissed as 'crackpots' but are instead taken more seriously when an unusual event (such as the Rodney King beating) has occurred; that sometimes anchor people get excited about currently 'breaking' events and read the news off scraps of paper rather than autocues, which then probably generates excitement in viewers. From these rather mundane observations the author concludes that 'processes of cultural production, cultural reception and cultural structure are never separate in concrete practice. They are overlapping moments that must be researched and theorized as such (1996: 393).

The attempt from within this third view to deconstruct divides between production representation and reception has been subjected to thorough-going critique by representatives of the second view (Philo, 1999; Kitzinger, 1999a), who argue that claims about limitless polysemy are based in a relative neglect of – or disdain for – empirical work on audiences. Additionally, the determining influence of socio-economic forces on audience experience is neglected in a social constructionist perspective that insists on seeing class and ethnic identity as endlessly mutable. Extreme constructionism, for Philo and others, consigns media studies to a drift into irrelevance because of a failure to address issues of power, since the view that representations may be biased or ideological cannot be sustained without a commitment to some form of philosophical realism (see also Seale, 1999, for a discussion of the implications of this debate for the practice of social research).

MEDIA HEALTH, SELF-IDENTITY AND COMMUNITY

The argument that runs through the rest of this book relies on a particular view of the part that health concerns play in peoples' lives in late modernity, and of the place which media representations of health issues may occupy within these, attempting to overcome some of the limitations of audience theories reviewed so far. These issues involve quite basic existential matters that must preoccupy us all, but which manifest themselves in particular forms in the social conditions of late modernity. In proposing this argument I draw in particular on earlier sociological work I have done on mortality in late modernity (Seale, 1998), as well as more general ideas that sociologists have proposed to explore the consequences of modernity, including developments in mediated communications, for self-identity.

We may draw first on Giddens's account of the conditions we face in late modernity (Giddens, 1990, 1991, 1992), which he contrasts with pre-modern social organisation. Nowadays, so this argument goes, we no longer have a strong sense of local community, in which a person's place in the world is largely determined at birth by their place in the kinship system and social hierarchy; where a sense of duty and obligation is based on respect for authority and tradition; where interaction is face-to-face and travel to distant lands is unusual; and where the world is safely divided into 'us' and 'them', with enemies who are safe to hate. Instead, we must negotiate our place in the world, puzzle out our identities in a process of reflexive self-awareness, in which the self and its story becomes a worked-on project. We perceive that a variety of 'authorities' and 'experts' exist, and that they do not always agree, so that leaps of faith and trust are required if we are to commit ourselves to becoming even temporary followers of any particular one. We have an increasingly cosmopolitan view of human variety, being aware that at some level we are part of a global 'human race' who, underneath surface features of skin colour, language and cultural difference, are 'the same as us'. Thus 'humankind becomes a "we", facing problems and opportunities where there are no "others"' (Giddens, 1991: 27). The virtues of tolerance and respect for difference become a part of official morality. This is coupled with a state monopolisation of the means of violence by means of warfare or punishment systems, so that interpersonal acts of violence to solve disputes are stigmatised in favour of talking things through. Elias's (1978, 1982) work on the civilising process, suggesting a progressive pacification of civil society, marries well with Giddens's analysis at this point.

Medicine, as an expert system to which we may turn at fateful moments, has nowadays to work harder to generate trust. Medical authority is no longer what it was, and system representatives may need to make particular efforts to adjust their demeanour in order to get clients on their side. Thus we see a plethora of training courses for health-care staff in 'communications skills', and a premium placed on what Maura Hunt (1991) has called 'professional friendliness'. In this respect, professional–client relationships mirror more intimate relationships, where commitment (to a marriage, for example) must now be generated and expressed through the display of emotional warmth, rather than relying on God-given ties of duty. Trust, Giddens argues, 'demands the opening out of the individual to the other' (1990: 121) and the philosophy of patient-centredness is precisely constituted in this way, so that it may be perceived as a 'meeting between experts' (Tuckett et al., 1985) whereby both doctor and patient co-operatively work together on the illness problem by sharing ideas. Correspondingly, relations between health-care workers in this scheme of things become increasingly democratised, so that concepts of teamwork and multi-disciplinarity hold sway, and the special expertise of nurses in the area of emotional labour is asserted (James, 1989).

Fateful moments, such as the announcement of a serious illness, initially provoke episodes of ontological insecurity as the bubble of confidence about one's place in the world, normally sustained through adherence to everyday routines that defend against the flooding in of existential anxieties, appears to have been pricked. Commonly, Giddens argues, individuals faced with fateful moments attempt to repair this damage by seeking out information. A classic example would be the cancer sufferer who searches web sites for the latest news about medical treatments: indeed, most doctors nowadays have tales to tell about patients who enter the surgery waving a sheaf of computer printouts, and demanding access to recently discovered drugs that are not yet generally available. This kind of activity, for Giddens, constitutes an opportunity for empowerment through reskilling. People may regain the skills they lost in earlier expropriations of lay expertise by expert systems. The individual with a chronic illness may thus come to know more about its aetiology, course and treatment than the doctor whom he or she consults. At the same time, there is a chronic flow of available knowledge, and complete security is never ultimately attainable in a world where knowledge claims are always contested and provisional.

For Giddens, the print and electronic media involve a tremendous increase in the mediation of experience, separating space from place and ensuring that distant events intrude into everyday consciousness. In this sense, the media are a powerful 'disembedding mechanism', lifting people and events out of their local circumstances and placing them upon a world stage. Media representations, too, are influential on behaviour: 'All individuals actively, although by no means always in a conscious way, selectively incorporate many elements of mediated experience into their day-to-day conduct' (1991: 188). In particular, this influence involves a heightened awareness of the risks of life as the media continually provide information about dangers and news of this or that disaster or threat. The individual living in a traditional society knew the risks posed by nature for life and livelihood: a sudden flood could destroy crops; a lightning bolt might strike a person down; plagues and famines were known threats to communities. Now, however, in addition to these 'external' risks, we are made aware – and most commonly through the media – of a variety of 'manufactured' risks that arise from our own technical activities and can often only be perceived with the assistance of technical knowledge. Many of these new risks are thus associated with worries about what we may have done to nature, rather than the risks posed by nature to ourselves. Global warming and the consequences of climate change are classic examples. There are many others: salmonella in eggs, BSE, pollution, acid rain, forest depletion, extinctions of rare species and loss of biodiversity, to name but a few. Giddens emphasises that awareness of the existence of manufactured risks may itself depend on expert knowledge: no one can see radiation without expertly mediated advice, but public perceptions of its risks are well known to be quite extreme and these influence nuclear energy policy. Because there is a general climate of anxiety associated with weakened commitments to fixed systems of authoritative belief, risk awareness has increased – paradoxically at a time when life-expectancy figures continue to rise, showing that the risks of life have in objective terms been significantly reduced in modern times. A state of chronic uncertainty and of crises of trust means that risk profiling is a very frequent concern, and a culture that is preoccupied with the value of safety has emerged (see also Reinharz, 1997). Increasingly, projects of self-identity become bound up with assessing the dangers of personal lifestyle choices.

At the same time, a pleasurable excitement may be had from courting risks and safely overcoming them. Modern life in urban mass societies can be, for the most part, a highly routinised affair, with the excitement produced by violence largely repressed and sexuality not only pre-packaged and commodified but accompanied by a variety of health warnings. Courting risks through engaging in dangerous sports, or by smoking against health advice, or having unprotected sex with strangers, may produce particularly poignant pleasures, reminiscent of a more authentic existence, even though some of these pastimes can themselves get recaptured by the culture of safety (as where boxers are enjoined to have medics by the ringside, mountain climbers to use stronger, lighter ropes, lone sailors to use the latest navigational equipment, motorcycle riders to wear helmets). These episodes of dangerous behaviour may be done to experience the thrill of personal mastery that comes from overcoming risks, additionally helping to construct a self-portrait of courageous celebrity. For the less adventurous majority, a 'safer' and less effortful arena for the experience of danger is, of course, the world of the imagination. Media fantasies, I argue, play a large part in enabling such vicarious thrills and have the added attraction of being available in small, predictable doses in the pages of newspapers or the half-hour slots of TV schedules.

The reflexively self-aware, risk-profiling, future-oriented actor on Giddens's stage comes across as a pretty rational, information-seeking being, even if driven by the unconscious emotional urge to find ontological security. Giddens's individual also seems somewhat disembodied, and other sociologists (for example, Turner, 1992) have pointed to the importance of the body and body projects in the formation of contemporary self-identity. The narcissism involved in late modern identity work is also an issue underplayed by Giddens. Abercrombie and Longhurst (1998) are helpful in redressing these imbalances and in relating these to a theory of the media audience. These authors take the view that media portrayals do more than just provide information at fateful moments, but also provide a resource for the (narcissistic) imagination. Thus health portrayals offer us lifestyle fantasies, incorporating an aestheticisation of ideal bodies, not merely providing information for the avoidance or cure of disease. Fitness programmes, diet and food programmes and a host of other health-related media products provide an imagined world of more or less beautiful people on which our imagination can draw.

Giddens's actor is also a fairly isolated individual, conducting negotiations with others as a matter of diplomacy, rarely standing together with others in an emotional bond that defies analysis or reflection. My own studies of death and dying in late modernity (Seale, 1998) have led me to feel that a number of opportunities for community solidarity and non-rational emotional bonding occur in late modernity, and further that these may largely be constituted in the media sphere. To understand how this can occur, we can draw productively on Benedict Anderson's (1991) conception of 'imagined communities'.

Membership of media communities

Briefly, then, Anderson points out that the advent of printed daily newspapers effectively made an imagined national community possible, whereby individuals unknown personally to each other could gain a sense of belonging, fellow-feeling and sameness to one another by knowing that throughout the land others were similarly opening their daily papers and reading the same stories, having the same feelings, sharing the same values. Thus media interpellate and, in a sense, 'construct' an audience. For Anderson, the reading of the daily paper made people feel permanent, existing within a nation-based society that had a past and was travelling forwards to a future. Applying this idea to broadcast media, Trujillo (1993) and Tsaliki (1995) have shown that nationalism can play a major part when the deaths of important leaders (J.F. Kennedy and Melina Mercouri respectively) are involved. However, the increasingly global nature of broadcast media suggests that Anderson's thesis might be modified to reduce the emphasis on nationalism and to recognise that the community memberships offered by media may be quite various. In my work on death, I have suggested that imagined communities other than those confined to national boundaries may be available to modern individuals who can, through participating in life insurance schemes, for example, or in understanding their lives in terms of statistical regularities (for example, life-expectancy tables) or through confessing their biographies into psychological discourse, gain a sense of belonging to some larger human whole that may involve a universal humanity. Additionally, I have argued (Seale, 1995a) that individuals commonly seek to construct heroic – and somewhat self-regarding – narratives of the self (an idea that is close to Anderson's notion of life as an institutional pilgrimage, and is suggested by Becker's (1973) notion of society as a structured hero-producing system). People like to feel unique even as they belong.

In late modern society, then, individuals are offered the chance for membership in a variety of potential communities, amongst which is a relatively recently formed idea of membership of the 'human race'. In addition, it is possible to understand the micro-rituals of everyday life as themselves being constituted as a continual process of negotiation of human membership, in which social bonds are routinely at stake (Scheff, 1990) even in the smallest exchanges. This is the basic insight of ethnomethodology and of micro-interactionist sociology generally (see, for example, Goffman, 1968). Minor waves of anxiety and security are involved in even the smallest conversational exchanges, in which speakers' accreditation as properly moral and competent human beings, existing in social bonds, conversant with the unwritten rules of everyday behaviour, is the subject of mutual evaluation and considerable underlying emotion. Extending this perspective – which ethnomethodologists have tended to apply largely to conversations – to the interaction of individuals with media products, seems a fruitful way forward.

Emotional bonds

With these ideas, we can begin to form a new understanding of the place of media in the lives of modern audiences. To show this I shall return again to examples such as 'reality TV'. The appeal of media material of this sort has been explained quite effectively by Langer (1998) in his commentary on the coverage of accidents, disasters and emergencies which constitutes what he calls the 'other news'. He starts from a position that rejects the 'lament' of high-minded critics of tabloid-style television, whose condemnations of its sensationalism and inaccuracy are rather similar to those of health educationists in relation to unhealthy media coverage that I described earlier. He is critical of the view that TV news ought to provide unbiased information and thus promote rational democratic debate, saying that this fails to recognise its ritual, community-forming elements that depend in large part on work done at the emotional level. The viewer's link with tabloid television is 'ritualistic, symbolic and possibly mythic . . . Story-telling, gossip, the manufacture of fame, ritual, social memory, pleasure' are important elements (Langer, 1998: 5, 25).

For Langer, the 'other news' about the life adventures of ordinary people interpellates its audience directly as 'us' in a way that news about governments, policies and social problems does not. Stories of especially remarkable acts of ordinary people, or of the unusual things that happen to celebrities to reveal that they are at root 'ordinary' people with a 'human face'; stories about victims and personal tragedies as well as disrupted communities caught up in disasters and other threats (hurricanes, fires, diseases, pollution, even alien invasions) – all of these ask audience members to identify themselves with people in the news in a direct, emotional way. Ordinary objects (a gas cooker, a child's toy, a routine vaccination) may appear in a more threatening – even animated – aspect because of their involvement in freak accidents, so that normally repressed fears about the dangerousness of the world and the malicious potential of material things can surface. When rescuers appear to save individuals or repair community damage, to explain the causes of accidents and teach lessons on how to avoid their future recurrence, a pleasurable sense of relief and security is restored. Importantly, Langer points out the link of such stories of community solidarity with Durkheimian notions of religious ritual, in which the life-enhancing energy of the group may be rapidly focused and increased through contemplation of supra-personal values and symbols; the television viewer, for Langer, therefore occupies a 'worshipful' position (1998: 125).

The 'other news' on television also contains quieter tales, reiterating fundamental truths about communal life. Langer observes that local and sometimes national community feeling is generated by less dramatic stories that emphasise the underlying continuities of everyday life, so that temporary reversals or disruptions of this are placed in a reassuring context. News of the first snow of the year, Remembrance Day, the announcement of winning lottery numbers, a reunion of the climbers who conquered Everest, a visit to war graves by veterans, the very stability with which 'bad news' is delivered within the time slots and stereotyped story formats and the demeanours of newsreaders: these things give audiences a sense of underlying permanence. These elements of 'other news' speak of stability and predictability. We seem to be a long way, now, from Giddens's isolated, scheming individual, planning a personal project of self-identity, trusting no one, divorced from communal belonging.

Television, it seems, offers viewers a safe cocoon and a sense of common purpose based on emotional appeal rather than rational evaluation of risks.

We can revisit Hill's (2000) study of reality TV at this point to observe that empirical study of audience responses appears to provide powerful support for Langer's ideas about the meaning of such media experience for people. Some quotations from Hill's diarists reveal precisely the themes raised by Langer:

> A child who had leukemia was in for a bone marrow transplant from his brother. They were both very young, nine and six years, same age as my two sons. They were so brave and courageous. My heart was crying for them both having to go through so much in their early years of life. I was so delighted when it was a success. We can all learn from different situations, and I feel I've learned a great deal about the rescue, hospital services, and how people give so much to their professions. (35-year-old student and mother, quoted in Hill, 2000: 204)

> A huge plethora of near misses and near tragedies is revealed [by such programmes]. We are aware this could be us, our family, friends. Incidents arise out of quite commonplace situations: driving, walking, DIY jobs, eating! We are helped to see how it could have been avoided and what to do should it happen to us. (44-year-old housewife, quoted in Hill, 2000: 204)

> My son is fascinated by 999, and I've watched it with him a couple of times. The reconstructions are extremely effective, and the stories, because they are true, are very moving. I think 999 is a useful program, and it also shows the tremendous dedication of our rescue services and the devotion of friends, family, or even passersby who are prepared to help, even risking their own lives. These programs are important, especially for young people. I fear too much of their viewing leads them to live in or believe in a fantasy world. (46-year-old female art student, quoted in Hill, 2000: 206)

> A small boy who fell down a hole in the hillside and got jammed, requiring very careful rescue to avoid falling further down. I have a horror of being trapped underground. So watching the program brought all my fears back to me so that I lived the program with the child and of course felt enormous relief when he was rescued. Although, of course, I felt the program would not go out if he had not been saved. (68-year-old housewife, quoted in Hill, 2000: 208)

These quotations provide obvious support for many of the themes raised by Langer, but also introduce two other features. Depictions of children facing danger are very common, and indeed I devote Chapter 6 of this book to this. Children are particularly potent symbols of vulnerability and of hope for the future, so health and safety issues concerning children are therefore rather well elaborated in media health. The third and fourth quotations show conflicting views about the degree to which the programmes reflect reality accurately. Both views, of course, are 'right': the forcefulness of the fantasies of danger and rescue promoted by these programmes depend on the 'real-life' element, which is nevertheless a selection from what is available. In this sense, the health educator's 'lament' that such programmes are unrealistic and misleading is correct in certain respects, while at the same time the programmes speak to some profound psychological realities.

The emotional appeal of media has been explored helpfully by Silverstone (1994), who manages thereby to rescue much that is of value in Giddens's analysis of self-identity. Silverstone goes a little further than Langer to explain the psychological roots of the appeal of television. He begins (in parallel with my own work on life as a defence against death) from the perception that everyday life can be understood as a continual defence against disorder. Within this ongoing daily struggle (which is not often experienced as a struggle, but may be seen to lie beneath the apparent calm of everyday routines), television often plays a role that is analogous to the security blanket or 'transitional object' that has played such a part in psychoanalytic ideas about the development of ontological security. Television, for many people, assists in the construction of daily routines, replacing the space released by earlier transitional objects, and is used in both addictive and creative ways. Thus, the weather programme, in its regular slot, provides reassurance that tomorrow will occur, and we will be OK in it, barring freak storms. Television becomes part of the taken-for-granted seriality of everyday-life routines, marking out sections of the day, using familiar storytelling patterns, generating a shared sense of community, mobilising the sacred in a new secular tradition.

Silverstone's ideas, as well as those of other media theorists who emphasise the mythic and ludic aspects of audience–media relationships, are taken up helpfully by Abercrombie and Longhurst (1998), whose ideas were briefly touched on earlier. These authors argue that the contemporary media audience is 'diffused', by which they mean that its members are often to be found treating everyday life as a performance, in which the world is constructed as a spectacle on which the narcissistic hero-self is both gazing at others and imagining the gaze of others on himself or herself. Since social life is an experience of continuous theatre, mediated images can be understood to be an imaginative resource for everyday performances, a stock of materials that we use to help us live in a world experienced as a mass-mediated conversation.

These ideas, then, take us a long way from the rational actor depicted by Giddens, and even further away from the 'attitude'-bearing actor implied in early psychological theories of media effects. Active audience theory, of course, approached these more recent conceptualisations of the media audience, but its rather exclusive focus on the degree to which dominant ideological messages were resisted now seems too narrow. Media–audience relations are more open, playful and complex than these earlier theorists suggested. In fact, to a significant extent they provide a kind of sheltering 'sacred canopy' to channel the emotions, fears and fantasies of modern individuals in a secular age that was once supplied by religious faith (Berger, 1973).

Religious rituals

I am prompted to this last statement because some analysts have identified an emotional component in media consumption by analysing media events as religious rituals. Bauman (1998), for example, observes that nowadays we can all have 'peak experiences' by engaging in acts of consumption of various sorts, rather than going to church or engaging in ascetic spiritual rites. Karen Becker (1995) shows how such exciting effects are made available to a mass audience through coverage of public 'events', such as royal weddings, men landing on the moon, and annual parades. Notably, editing of camera footage at public events concentrates on 'peak moments' – the first step on the moon, the ring being placed on the finger, the arrival of the head of the parade at its destination. Other shots show 'liminal' moments, where people are seen moving in and out of the ritual performance arena. Expert commentators are frequently brought in to tell viewers about the broader significance of what they are seeing. Dayan and Katz (1992) have pointed to the community-building effects of such media events, aligning media commentators and a reverent general public with official meanings.

Coverage of sporting events and of crime stories can be understood similarly as ritualised enactments of dramas that address basic existential concerns at an emotional level and thus speak to the themes once the province of religious authorities. Sport is a form of safely contained warfare (Elias, 1978, 1982), a human activity in which fundamental concerns about sheer survival are clearly at stake. The language of the sports journalist is strikingly similar to that of the war correspondent. Jansen and Sabo (1994; Sabo & Jansen, 1998) have noted this interrelation at the level of shared language and metaphor. These authors studied the language used in US television reporting of the Gulf War, finding that this reflected 'the multiple intersections of sportive and military cultures' (1998: 203). Reporters spoke of US soldiers as the 'home team'; air pilots described their actions as being 'like a football game'; and Norman Schwarzkopf was described in terms similar to those used by sports commentators for US football team coaches. At the same time, Jansen and Sabo point out that sports journalism is redolent with military language, so that there is a 'convergence and conflation of the vocabularies of sport and war' (1994: 2).

Charteris-Black (2000), studying war metaphors in sports journalism, finds that the underlying concepts on which these metaphors depend 'evokes notions of species survival'. The concept 'football is war' is supplemented by two further concepts: 'sport is a struggle for survival' and 'success and failure in sports is a biological condition'. These, for example, underpin references in *The Times* to the 'haemorrhaging' of the confidence of Wimbledon football club players as their league performance in the 1999–2000 season declined, or the reported exhortation by the manager of Chelsea to players to 'die on the pitch for the club'. In the light of this it is worth noting that some commentators have observed parallels between mainstream sporting activity and religious experience, analysing sport as a civil religion. Sport, like religion, thus contains rituals of sacrifice and asceticism, testimonies to courage, ceremonies recognising achievement and a capacity to assist participants achieve other-worldly mental states, so that sport – like religion – can be understood at one level as an imaginary defeat of death (Prebish, 1993). Clearly, if sports journalism can so readily recruit the language of bodily trauma, life and death, in a neo-religious context, the conditions exist for illness experience to be compared with sporting struggles, and I show how this does in fact occur in Chapter 8.

Crime stories have been analysed from this point of view by Sparks (1992), who outlines a Durkheimian view of this area of the media. Stories about the risks posed by crime serve to uphold the strength of the community, with a sense of membership and certainty offered in tales of the capture and punishment of criminals. It is essential, of course, for crime tales first to present a heightened sense of risk so that the moment of pleasurable relief when the crime is condemned and justice is done can be experienced fully. Emphasis on violent crime is a quick way to produce such sensations. Heroes and villains emerge rapidly in crime stories, to represent the opposing poles of security and danger. In this book I show that some very similar things occur in health coverage.

Through feeding narcissistic fantasies of personal heroism, much media coverage of health issues encourages a belief that reversals, losses, bodily limitations and perhaps even death itself can be overcome, contributing to a culture in which there is a widespread desire to avoid disappointment, a condition analysed extensively by Ian Craib (1994). Hoping for a great deal, we are encouraged to see the opportunities for personal growth in numerous areas of life; reversals to our expected good fortune frequently result in a search for villains who, like criminals in relation to the crime problem, can be blamed for the situation, so that such negative events may 'never happen again'. Mediated images of the route to good health, while often dealing with 'real' events and addressing psychological 'realities', are also profoundly 'unreal' at a certain level, since – as I shall show at various points in the rest of this book – they often encourage individuals to imagine that they possess super powers.

CONCLUSION

We can return, then, to the complaints of health educationists regarding the inaccuracies and distortions and damage done by media health representations. The epidemiological accuracy, scientific objectivity and political correctness of media health have all been shown to be at fault by the health education lobby, failing to transmit health-promoting information in a host of areas. Yet the 'hypodermic needle' model of health education that conceives of audiences as somewhat passive receivers – or perhaps more often 'forgetters' or 'misinterpreters' – of media messages is a limited one, something that has been recognised in more recent health promotion initiatives that conceive of audiences and communities as more active, and that are willing to compromise the ascetic agenda of health education in recognising the entertainment priorities of mass media. Thus community empowerment, media advocacy and edutainment initiatives have developed with a more sophisticated image of the media health audience.

Beyond the issue of whether media portrayals promote or damage the health of audiences, reality TV is helpful in demonstrating some of the main themes that I want to emphasise as running through a variety of media health areas, since this genre conveniently gathers these together into a single format. Such programmes address basic anxieties about the security of individuals in the world, while at the same time reassuring audiences that they are surrounded by an effective community rescue service, in a society where we can all – as long as we contribute through keeping a watchful eye out for danger – feel rather safe. In a world where there is increased distrust of single-source claims to have authoritative expertise, media audiences are encouraged to think of themselves as individual adventurers – albeit bound together in a vaguely perceived community based on common underlying humanity. Self-identity is tied to the construction of increasingly 'heroic' narratives of individually crafted biography, even though these personal stories – felt to be so unique by their bearers – from an outside view may appear strikingly conformist. Aestheticised body projects are also supported in media health representations, speaking to the more playful elements of the relationship between everyday life and the media. Media health representations assist in providing the raw materials for such stories – in the form of information about risks to avoid, pleasures to aspire to – and in organising a generalised denial of ultimate disappointment, since good health is associated with an inevitable progress towards personal fulfilment and psychological actualisation. In this respect, media health representations, like coverage of sport and crime, work on emotions and feelings abut community membership in a ritualised way, in a manner reminiscent of religious ceremonial.

Having established a framework for understanding the complex place that media health representations can have in people's lives, then, we can now turn to a consideration of the forms that these representations take. The chapter that follows describes some of the rhetorical effects that media analysts have uncovered in their studies of a variety of media spheres. It will become clear that a sense of the meanings audiences draw from health stories, which I have tried to give in the present chapter, is important in understanding why particular rhetorical forms prevail.

2 The Forms of Media Health

In reviewing studies of media health representations in preparation for this book I have been struck by two things. Firstly, there is a large number of studies of individual media health 'stories', and only a very few attempts to summarise media health *across* different health stories. Thus, there are individual studies of, say, the BSE scare story, AIDS, cancer, sexuality, violence, drugs, suicide, and mental illness as treated by a variety of media channels and formats (news, soaps, television, radio, for example). These are very helpful in elucidating the dynamics of those individual stories, and much of this book draws upon these single-topic studies. But it seems to me that audience experience is not confined to single stories or themes, instead being composed of collages of elements taken from many of these. The channel-hopping viewer, whose level of attention to any one programme is likely to be variable, is increasingly representative of actual audience experience. I take the view that an adequate understanding of the forms of media health therefore requires an analysis of how a variety of stories may interact from the point of view of audience experience. A viewer may see a news report of an environmental scare at one moment, then switch to a medical soap emphasising medical heroism at another. Reading a magazine article about diet and fitness may be followed by viewing a 'reality television' accident-rescue show, interspersed with advertisements for headache pills. Analysis of the forms of media health requires recognition that there are cumulative effects of such juxtapositions, with opposing elements not necessarily being presented within the confines of a single story or programme. Another way of putting this is to say that audience experience is intertextual.

Secondly, the few attempts that have been made to summarise the media health field as a whole have been striking in their omission of the broad range of theoretical perspectives and analytic approaches developed in the general media studies field. There appear to have been no sustained attempts to conceptualise media health as a case study within larger media processes, or to compare media health coverage with that in other areas, such as sport or crime (see Chapter 1). Karpf (1988), for example, presents an account of British media health coverage, concentrating mainly on the broadcast media and focusing on the issue of whether medical rather than alternative perspectives are dominant, following the concerns that then preoccupied media analysts with the degree to which dominant ideology was influential. Because of this overriding purpose, also derived from the preoccupations of medical sociologists with documenting the declining professional authority of medicine as an institution, she pays more attention to portrayals of the medical profession than to portrayals of the lay experience of illness. While her study provides a wealth of detail about the institutional history of health broadcasting by the BBC, its analysis of media representations is largely based on common-sense commentary and reviews of a small number of descriptive content analyses of particular programme genres.

Signorielli (1993) presents an overview that is again focused on broadcast media, and on US television in particular, deriving much of her material from studies done within the tradition of the Cultural Indicators project, set up by George Gerbner, with whom Signorielli has a long-standing professional collaboration. While this research tradition has contributed a great deal in documenting the facts of media health coverage through systematic content analysis of media output, it is driven by an overriding concern to compare media health representations with health 'reality' and a limited theory of the media audience. Thus Signorielli's work is situated firmly within the lament of health educators, described in Chapter 1 of this book. This involves criticism of media bias, pointing out that coverage of cancer, physical disability, death, doctors, nurses, sex, AIDS, smoking, drugs, alcohol, food and the environment presents information which too often is inaccurate or damaging to health. Some analyses of the factors that may lead to this is presented, in terms of the news values of journalists and the entertainment agenda, which is understood to have led to the selection of sensational stories and produced the resultant bias. The overriding implication is that the sorry situation thus revealed ought, in a more responsible society, to be put right.

There are other book-length treatments of media health – Turow's (1989) and Dans's (2000) studies of doctors in medical soaps and Hollywood movies, and a similar treatment of portrayals of nurses by Kalisch et al. (1983). Klaidman's (1991) *Health in the Headlines* turns out to be a chatty account by a journalist of the underlying events in newsrooms that lead to coverage of certain health stories (AIDS, a pesticide scare, greenhouse gases, cholesterol, radon, and smoking) that presents a distorted estimation of risk. Each of these books is written largely from a common-sense point of view, sometimes driven by a concern to point out injustice or inaccuracy, as most powerfully shown by Kalisch et al., whose concerns revolve around redressing demeaning images of the nursing profession on US television. At other times, as in Dans's *Doctors in the Movies*, the agenda is simply that of the film buff taking a childlike delight in telling readers about the relevant movies the author has enjoyed. Apart from Signorielli's use of content analysis, none of these studies draws on systematic methods for analysing representations of forms that have developed outside the health area in recent years, and there is only a minimal engagement with broader ideas about the place media may play in people's lives.

In this second chapter, then, I shall outline a variety of approaches to the analysis of media forms, with a view to highlighting aspects of these that are the most helpful in understanding the rhetorical effects of media health portrayals. In particular, this chapter will outline the way the media set up and deploy a variety of oppositions to generate the entertaining tensions involved in media health portrayals. Heroes and villains, pleasure and pain, safety and danger, disaster and repair, life and death, the beautiful and the ugly, the normal and the freak, cleanliness and dirt, are all examples of such dichotomies, exploited in media health portrayals. In particular, I shall argue that this can be detected when an overview of different media health stories is taken, rather than focusing on single stories alone.

OPPOSITIONS AND NARRATIVE STRUCTURES

The account given by Propp (1968) of the structure of Russian folk tales has rightly become a central document for the analysis of narratives. Propp argues, as a good structuralist, that the apparent diversity of folk tales can be reduced to a small number of functions and stock characters. The characters are somewhat interchangeable in terms of the purpose they serve. Thus an evil force may be represented by either a dragon or a witch; a ruler by a king or a chief; a loved one by either a wife or a daughter; a disappearance by a kidnap or magical vanishing. The deeds of heroes, helpers and villains figure large. The phase in which the story is set up, or prepared, may involve a rule or prohibition for the hero, or the villain's learning something about a victim. This situation may then be 'complicated' by a further twist – the villain may harm the victim, or the hero may be sent on a quest, involving leaving home or use of some magical agent, eventually leading to a struggle between hero and villain. Struggles, either with a villain or with some seemingly impossible task, are very common features of such tales. Victory is normally followed by events such as a hero's return, acclaim and recognition for the hero, or punishment for the villain.

Others who have shown the importance of fundamental oppositions in narrative structures include Todorov (1977), Lévi-Strauss (1968) and Barthes (1975), and these ideas have entered the field of media studies. Todorov charts the common development of narratives from a state of harmony, through disruption of this equilibrium (often involving a villain), to a final state of restoration (often brought about by a hero). Lévi-Strauss pays particular attention to the notion of binary opposition, with wet and dry, raw and cooked, good and evil being symbolically represented in stories that place real-life contradictions on public display, making these into objects of contemplation so that they can be more readily lived with. James Bond stories can thus be understood as setting up a series of oppositions, such as that between the role of fate, luck and chance in uncertain enterprises, as opposed to the part played by forward planning and modern technology (Eco, 1966). Barthes's notion of codes has been applied by Fiske (1987) to indicate, once again, the structure of many narratives: an enigma or mystery captures the audience's attention, and the tension continues as the struggle to resolve the problem is displayed, ending with a solution in which tension is dissipated. As Abercrombie comments:

> Todorov, Propp, Lévi-Strauss and Barthes all articulate theories which claim considerable generality of scope in suggesting that narratives are to do with very fundamental ways in which societies see themselves. They are not simply stories; they deal with basic conflicts, events and relationships that characterize human societies. In this sense, narratives of all kinds, including television narratives, have a *mythic* quality. (Abercrombie, 1996: 23)

Abercrombie further points out that application of these ideas to the understanding, say, of television has centred around the issue of whether all elements of narratives may be detected in particular media products. It is here that I depart from Abecrombie's judgements, since I believe he too easily dismisses the applicability of a general theory of oppositional elements. For example, Abercrombie says that serials and soap operas may not contain resolutions to storylines as the plot must continue from week to week and commercial breaks disrupt the action; sports presentations and game shows are 'difficult . . . to imagine . . . fitting in easily to any of the narrative schemes' (1996: 25). He cites Lewis's (1991) study of news programmes to argue that 'This form has very few of the narrative conventions' (1996: 26), with resolutions or 'punchlines' being presented first, before dramatic tension has had time to build up. Thus the 'news' may be that a criminal has been convicted for a crime that has previously received no coverage.

The mistake made here is to take individual programmes and search for all elements of, say, a classic fairy tale in them. Television coverage of a sports event may show a struggle, a victory and a defeat, but it does not show an initial state of harmony which the struggle seeks to resolve. A convicted criminal is not shown plotting his or her crime; the struggle of the police-officer heroes to catch the criminal is not displayed; the acclaim that sportspeople and police personnel receive from their families, colleagues or superiors for winning their struggle may not be shown. The spread of an infectious disease may be newsworthy when it is threatening, yet by the time of its eventual containment by public health agencies the fickle interest of news reporters may have moved on to other topics. Yet all of these stories, if put together with others, with due recognition that there are many opportunities for audiences to 'fill in the gaps' by the power of imagination, based on prior knowledge that is made generally available in a media-saturated culture, can be understood as presenting elements of a more general mythic form.

Benthall (1993), in his account of images and narratives of disaster relief, has made this point well, analysing these with the aid of Propp's (1968) scheme. A hero (for example, a foreign correspondent, an Oxfam worker, the surgical team), a villain (for example, Pol Pot, Saddam Hussein), a donor (the charity giver or the viewer), the magical agent (a sack of grain, an aeroplane), a princess (Diana), and a false hero (the charity accused of spending too much on its own administration) are all likely to be evident in such stories. Benthall observes:

> Even when only a part of a narrative relating to disaster is shown on television – for instance, pictures of starving babies, or an aeroplane setting off from a familiar airport bringing supplies, or an ambassador thanking the public for their generosity – viewers come to recognize it as part of the total narrative convention. (1993: 188–9)

If we take media health coverage as it occurs across a variety of stories and genres we may see how this can work. Let us take it that an important overall 'story' told in media health coverage is the life of the body, its struggle against the evil of death, its search for an admiring gaze, its elevation of Everyman or Everywoman to the status of hero or victim. Helper-heroes may take the form, say, of doctors or research scientists bearing magical cures, nurses behaving like angels, or fitness gurus pointing the way to beauty. Villains may take the form of disease, disease carriers, pollution of the environment or of food supplies, wicked or incompetent doctors, commercial interests selling foodstuffs that damage both health and appearance, and the like. We can then begin to see that all of the elements that occur in narratives generally occur from time to time in the big story told by media health representations. Clearly, these are not available in a single episode, although 'reality television' shows come close to this (see Chapter 1). But where such elements or fragments crop up, a media-wise audience can be reliably assumed to know the rest of the story, just as we know that convicted criminals will have planned their crimes, that police officers get promoted when they catch criminals, or that a football team's victory may be a struggle to restore the sense of well-being and harmony that flowed at the end of the last victorious match or previous season when the team came top of the league. The essential point here is that modern audiences already 'know' a lot, in a way that – perhaps – the more childlike audiences of fairy tales might not. Media health is a sophisticated and fragmented form compared with Snow White, because it addresses a skilful audience, but we may yet detect similar stock characters, routinely available plots, and familiar oppositions if we look hard enough.

Prior knowledge

Analysis of news texts (Bell, 1991; Fowler, 1991) suggests that these 'work' by triggering audiences to 'fill in' the gaps in stories from a considerable reserve of prior knowledge. This suggests a rather different conceptualisation of audience activity from that contained in the politically focused work of 'active audience' theorists (see Chapter 1). In fact, it is remarkably similar to interactionist notions of how people bring a stock of common-sense knowledge to everyday encounters in order to manage these. Bringing off a successful interaction so that both parties are mutually recognisable as competent within a given culture depends on rapid processing of this knowledge, acquired originally in the socialisation process. It consists of layers of understanding about how the world can be expected to work, and a part of this involves knowledge of how stories are usually told in contemporary mass media. Kitzinger's (2000) notion of 'templates', used to identify the stock story forms, as well as elements of content, that journalists use to construct news accounts, can be extended to apply to audiences as well. Audiences in significant respects share with media producers the capacity to recognise templates.

Bell (1991) analyses news stories using the scheme of narrative analysis for verbal storytelling developed by Labov (1973) in which an initial abstract that summarises the central action is followed by an orientation, then a complicating action, an evaluation of this, a resolution showing how the sequence of events has been concluded and frequently a coda that wraps up the action and returns the speaker to the present. In this respect, we can see similarities with the schemes of Propp, Todorov and the like. Bell finds that this scheme can be applied to news stories but in modified form. The headline, he points out, is an abstract of the abstract; the outcome of the story is frequently told first, the chronological sequence following later. Resolutions are not always presented, as news stories frequently occur in series, with updates to the story occurring as the news event 'develops' over a period of time. Implicit in Bell's analysis, however, is the notion that news stories are indeed stories, and that these are somewhat like the other stories people have traditionally told each other, and that where they are not like these, allowances can be made so that they do in the end draw upon the same kind of general cultural competencies that we all acquire.

Fowler (1991) takes this several steps further. Firstly, he describes in considerable detail the way in which newspaper language – particularly the tabloid style – attempts to mimic conversational modes of interaction:

> The fundamental device in narrowing the discursive gap is the promotion of oral models within the printed newspaper text, giving an illusion of conversation in which common sense is spoken about matters on which there is consensus. (1991: 47)

Drawing on the notion of 'modes of address' (Hall et al., 1978), Fowler notes that a journalistic objective is to negotiate a style with readers that feels like a natural extension of everyday speech. Here, of course, both Fowler and Hall are concerned with the politics of this negotiation, as it is seen as a device for promoting ideological consensus. Whether one takes a critical view of the political element or not, it is clear that Fowler's analysis allows us to understand the media usage of an oral mode of address as an appeal to a jointly shared stock of common knowledge. Readers are being invited to share in discursively producing a version of the world. The life of the media text depends on pre-existing frames, templates, stereotypes or common constructions between producers and audiences, which involve a process of active construction of meaning by audiences, though usually within the confines of dominant scripts. The prior knowledge of audiences bestows a degree of order and structure on media products that otherwise may appear fragmentary. The tragic death of a celebrity is followed by news of a breakthrough cure for leukaemia; news of a doctor who has murdered his patients is followed by a documentary about the miracles of heart surgery; a food scare story is followed by a rescue drama; a public inquiry into a transport disaster is juxtaposed with news of an outbreak of infectious disease in farm animals. None of these stories on its own contains all of the elements of a completed narrative, and even if followed up in subsequent stories may never do so. But in the imagination of the media audience these fragments can make a more coherent sense. The audience may be exposed to all of these things in a single night of viewing, or in a copy of a daily newspaper. People are thereby invited to reflect on themes of danger and security, good and evil, and so on, forming for themselves an overall narrative that speaks of the anxieties and pleasures of existence.

Standard story forms

Langer's (1998) study of the 'other news' was touched on in Chapter 1, where I argued that it has many points of applicability for an understanding of media health stories. Importantly for the present chapter, Langer makes it clear that an important rhetorical device in constructing 'other news' is the framing of stories as a confrontation of opposing forces, a stock device in the construction of a relatively standardised set of story frames in which most 'news' can be reported. Thus, as Galtung and Ruge (1973) observed, 'news', in fact, is really 'olds': new car crashes, muggings, suicide bombings, and sex scandals that have happened today are in fact mere examples of endlessly recurring similar events, reported according to familiar formats, so that they simply become 'another one of those' stories (until, of course, a really big one comes along, such as the World Trade Center incident). Just like folk tales, repeated telling reflects a continual striving to find a 'good one'.

Langer identifies several broad story forms and these find significant parallels with the analyses of fairy tales described earlier. Heroic deeds are contrasted with the ordinariness of everyday life, victims are pitched against villains or fools, and community safety is disrupted by a variety of threats, often then opposed and resolved by community rescuers. The vulnerability of victims is stressed through reference to their smallness, helplessness or innocence – thus children do well in this role. The unexpected nature or magnitude of the threat that victims face is emphasised by a variety of devices. Ordinary objects like kettles, cars, trees and paper-knives become suddenly malignant without warning as they are implicated in accidents or wielded in the wrong hands. Best of all, devices that are intended to enhance safety turn out to be dangerous, as where a seat belt traps a car passenger underwater or a crash barrier impales a driver.

Medical threats work well if they are exceptionally rare or 'terminal'; thus the terminally ill child with a rare form of cancer will always signal news value. The goodness or innocence of the threatened person is contrasted with the sheer malignance of some enemy, whose evil must be beyond understanding; the enemy must be placed outside the sympathies of the reader and thus become thoroughly bad. Thus the subjectivity of the child abuser, abductor, paedophile, terrorist or infection carrier is deleted, and replaced with a devil's image. The incapacity of ordinary people to predict or control such threats or resist such evil is emphasised by these devices that contrast the ordinary experience of security and routine goodness with sudden episodes of devastation or wickedness at its most extreme.

The ease with which such stories become part of a common stock, so that new examples are added to a standard frame or template, involving a hardening of oppositional motifs, is shown in Stallings's (1990) account of the reporting of bridge collapses in the *New York Times*. This rash of stories began when, on 5 April 1987, some vehicles fell from a disintegrating highway bridge in upstate New York, the flood waters below sweeping 10 occupants of these vehicles to their deaths. Much of the subsequent coverage focused on competing explanations by those charged with discovering the causes of the accident. Typically, monocausal, simple explanations were preferred by news media, since complex multicausal explanations made it harder to allocate blame completely and threatened readers with the prospect of 'good' people sharing responsibility for the bad event. Scapegoating by the media, of course, is the frequent complaint of captains of sunken ferries, drivers of crashed trains, surgeons in botched operations, forensic experts in miscarriages of justice and so on. Yet the urge to concentrate blame seems almost irresistible.

More importantly for the argument here, though, is the phenomenon noted by Stallings whereby new bridge collapses were discovered to be 'news'. Sometimes this involved resurrecting news of past collapses that had not, originally, been reported. Subsequent to the 1987 disaster, for a while every reporter in the State was alert to possible bridge stories so that every crack, groan or sign of dilapidation became evidence of a pattern, which was now the story, involving a quest for a single explanation for all these events. In reality, experts might argue, one bridge collapse is not the same as another. After all, bridges have different designs; some collapses are caused by floods, others by traffic, yet others by heavy winds. But for a while bridges had captured the journalistic and popular imagination, which designated all bridges as being alike and all collapses as having, potentially, the same cause. Debates could then be ranged around which single explanation was going to hold sway, with political interests clearly playing a part in seeking to influence the outcome of this hunt for a cause. Bridge collapses and their cause thus became a public issue, a scandal, around which a media-orchestrated public opinion was mobilised to urge that something ought to be done. Phenomena that were previously disregarded and unconnected were, through the alchemy of the media, noticed, their significance heightened, and ultimately classed as instances of a pattern.

As I argued in Chapter 1, crime stories are an important vehicle for generating anxieties and their resolutions and they do this through juxtaposing opposites in stock story formats. As Muncie (1994) has put it, crime stories allow for an 'easy identification of opposing factors: young people versus adults, hooligans versus police, black people versus white, "violent" protestors and "innocent" victims. In this way crime is depicted in terms of a basic confrontation between the symbolic forces of good and evil' (1994: 176). Sparks (1992) bases his analysis of crime stories on Klapp's (1954) account of the role played by heroes, villains and fools in popular stories that identify scapegoats and affirm core values, heroism being a key device for the countering of danger and insecurity and the restoration of order in the face of threat. Importantly, Klapp's original article stresses the stereotyping that is involved in placing heroes on their pedestals and the making of villains and fools. Through 'gossip, rumor, propaganda, journalism' the 'imputation of such types occurs through an impression conveyed by a drama or story rather than a mere matter of fact' (1954: 59). Inevitably, this means that 'Public figures usually eventually find that they have been simplified or typed in some way . . . as genius, saint, criminal, man of the people, or clown' (1954: 60).

There are direct parallels here with health stories, which tend also to present extrematised contrasts. The appeal of medical soap operas, for example, has been analysed by Turow (1989), who argues that the historic concentration on doctors (rather than nurses) in such series is due to the fact that life/death decisions – clearly the ultimate 'opposition' – could not be as effectively hung around the role of a nurse as they can a medical role. Doctors can be easily shown to do things that rescue people from death, so that their heroism is beyond doubt. (However it should be noted that contemporary medical dramas have partly moved away from this exclusive focus on doctors – see Chapter 9.) While not all medical soap storylines need to involve life/death dramas, a proportion of these must do so if audience appeal is to be retained, and those that do not are enhanced by the knowledge that such powerful figures are involved.

In this analysis of the importance of oppositions in the generation of standardised story forms we may turn, finally, to the idea that media health has many parallels with children's pantomime shows. Hartley

(1987) presents an important argument here, beginning from the view that media producers 'imagine' their audiences as having 'childlike qualities and attributes' (1987: 127). This is particularly the case when really large audiences are imagined, so that the 'paedocratic regime' increases as the target audience size rises. Hartley quotes from a study of US television producers to illustrate this, one producer saying:

> Our audience is the guy who's used to walking around and getting a beer. We've got to reach him. He's the guy who hasn't made much of a commitment to give his rapt attention to what we're offering, right? We're going for the eighty million who will watch something. An infant in a cradle likes to watch things that move. So there you are. We go in for close-ups and we try to find the conflicts. (Gitlin, 1983, quoted in Hartley, 1987: 128)

In particular, Hartley says, 'narrative suspense is constructed according to the conventions of children's theatre' (1987: 128). Citing the pronouncements of the 1977 Annan committee, which conceived of the British television audience as fundamentally childlike, he also quotes a US television executive explaining the methods of Aaron Spelling, producer of such shows as *Starsky and Hutch*, *Charlie's Angels* and *Dynasty*:

> The villain walks out onstage and says 'Heh-heh-heh! I have the secret matchbook, and I am going to hide it. I am going to put it behind this basket, and the heroine will never find it. Heh-heh-heh!' And he walks off. Now the heroine comes out and says, 'Where oh where is the secret matchbook?' And all the kids in the audience say, 'It's behind the basket! It's behind the basket!' That's what Aaron does. He believes that's what the American audience is, you see. (Gitlin, 1983, quoted in Hartley, 1987: 128-9)

Media producers' conceptions of what children are like may, of course, be fantasies themselves (Buckingham, 2000), quite apart from whether a mass audience of adults may be 'like' such imagined children. Nevertheless, the explanation fits the finding that oppositions, stock storylines and standard characters are deployed by media producers, effecting a simplification of issues that may in other discourses (for example, those of 'experts') be complex. Scapegoats, stereotypes, heroes, fools, victims, and villains are lined up in a pantomime-like collage of fragments to create an emotional drama. In the media health sphere, as in some others such as crime, this drama entertains by generating a tension between feelings of anxiety or fear, and security or pleasure. For Hartley, at least, this constitutes a paedocratic regime in which audiences are constructed as children being told a fairy tale. At the same time, however, there are twists and twitches to standard plots which media producers like to use in order to stimulate audiences' appetites. After all, once a media feeding frenzy for a particular story has become exhausted, there is still the need to produce something 'new' for tomorrow.

Reversals

Hartley may be right about media producers' conception of audiences as childlike, but fear that these children will become bored with the same old presentations appears also to drive story formats and plot lines. If the media audience is childlike, then it would seem to be a slightly older child that has passed beyond the earliest stage of appreciation of finding 'Snow White' entertaining every time it is read, seeking only comfort from routinely repeated phrases. Media producers, in Langer's (1998) phrase, like to 'twitch' the plot from time to time in order to retain audiences' interest. Commonly this involves a system of sudden surprises that (safely) challenge ingrained expectations of media narratives (providing further evidence of the dependency of media producers on the 'prior knowledge' brought to media consumption by audiences). A stronger version of the twitch, in my view, is the reversal, in which polarities previously set up may suddenly be reversed, so that evil and good swap places to provide an entertaining disruption of expectations. Quickly, however, one can see such reversals settling down into new standard forms, so that there is a continuing – indeed chronic – need for twitching and reversing, with some of these switches even involving revivals of played-out forms, once these are judged to be sufficiently 'forgotten' by audiences.

Several examples of twitches are given by Langer. A celebrity portrayed doing an incongruously 'ordinary' thing, as where Princess Anne was reported to have taken her driving test, or Queen Elizabeth and Prince Philip visited a theme park and 'took a ride in the tunnel of love' (1998: 60), are effective in disrupting expectations. The news value of stories about the activities of ordinary people or the status of ordinary things may depend on the presence of a twitch. Thus a schoolboy (rather than an engineer) is reported to have built a hovercraft, or comic books are surprisingly designated as not being childish when an academic conference is held to discuss them.

Such plot devices surprise and entertain like a ripple on the surface of a pond. Larger waves, however, are also sometimes needed, and this is where reversals come into play. 'Stigma champions' (Seale, 1995b) emerge from time to time in such reversals, as where Princess Diana began, in the early years of the AIDS pandemic, to be pictured shaking the hands of the previously untouchable. Another area where significant reversals have occurred is in the reporting of child abuse (discussed at greater length in Chapter 6), where the reversal took the form of a 'backlash'. The media 'discovery' of child sexual abuse in the early 1980s involved a classic feeding frenzy, juxtaposing extreme stereotypes of childhood innocence and stranger danger. As Kitzinger (1988, 1996) has pointed out, sexually knowing children and parental abusers were largely ruled out of this frame since they constituted uneasy anomalies, difficult to fit into a simple story of opposition between good and evil. 'Templates' (Kitzinger, 2000) were used in which to fit each new event, so that in the British press 'Orkney' became 'another Cleveland' just as in other areas of media we hear of a war being described as 'another Vietnam', a national leader as 'another Hitler', a nuclear accident as 'another Chernobyl', and a police beating victim as 'another Rodney King' (we saw this phenomenon earlier with bridge collapses). Heroes, villains, scapegoats and fools were established.

Yet the story could not last for ever, and anyway there were considerable tensions involved, with male journalists being distinctly uneasy with the feminist slant of the story (Kitzinger, 1998). Orkney and Cleveland, where social workers and doctors were accused of overzealousness in removing children from suspect families, constituted the beginning of the reversal of automatic sympathy for victims of abuse, a theme which achieved its full reversal when the 'false memory syndrome' story broke, juxtaposing vindictive (adult) children and their misguided (or at times evil) therapist helpers making false accusations against innocent fathers. Previously popular confessional accounts of childhood abuse were then potentially discredited, and the victim was transformed into a villain. Previously framed as good 'helpers', selected doctors, therapists and social workers could then be subjected to vilification. As yet, however, no significant stigma champions have emerged on behalf of paedophiles, who remain a secure category for media-orchestrated hate. This is entirely understandable in a culture preoccupied with maintaining childhood innocence.

Metaphors and numbers

Metaphors and numbers are also of considerable importance in creating rhetorical effects in media representations. By placing disparate things together, metaphor plays an important part in generating the stock stories used to frame media health products in familiar form and to draw parallels with other areas so that a sense of underlying order in the world is created and the unfamiliar can be presented as already known. Thus the cancer experience may be considered as being like a battle (Sontag, 1991) or a race or other sporting struggle (Seale, 2001a), thereby allowing the language of sports reporters, war correspondents and health writers to merge at a certain level. Inevitably this allows overdrawn contrasts between oppositional elements to be drawn. As Dwight (1997) has pointed out, treating health issues as sporting contests is evident in the reporting of male infertility, where sperm are imagined to be swimming races towards eggs, beating their competitors. Economic metaphors (sperm as money, stored in a 'bank', or a declining sperm count represented as a 'diminishing asset') may also be used. Descriptions of new drugs as 'magic bullets' or 'breakthroughs' sensationalise and simplify otherwise complex science stories (Nelkin, 1995). Media templates, mentioned earlier, often depend on similes (for example, Saddam Hussein is 'like' Hitler, AIDS is like a plague) and their potential for stereotyping and overdrawing oppositions is clear. Metaphor, of course is not unique to media narratives, being something that we all 'live by' (Lakoff & Johnson, 1980), but an alertness to the effects created by the use of metaphor is helpful in analysing media health representations.

Numbers, too, are important devices for creating extreme contrasts. Classically, they are used to exaggerate effects as either very tiny or, more usually, very large and important, so that news value is automatically enhanced. The rarity or uniqueness of a disease is emphasised by a statistic of the 'one in a million' sort; the magnitude of an epidemic's threat is conveyed by 'millions' talk. The monetary damage caused by a disaster is normally calculated in media reports ('billions of dollars' worth of damage'), the magnitude of an injury being emphasised through reporting of 'record' compensation figures for victims. The extreme importance of some new risk to health and safety such as child abduction (Best, 1987), crack usage by expectant mothers (Kline, 1996) or the number of eggs infected by salmonella (Fowler, 1991) is emphasised by the use of big numbers. The scandal of charities wasting donors' money on useless research can be extrematised by contrasting a very large number of incurables with a very small number of curables (Potter et al., 1991). Debates may then occur about numerical accuracy, fuelled by outraged parties in the debate, feeding further stories. Numbers, as Bell (1991) observes, work by enhancing the facticity of reports, appearing to be objective to a credulous and somewhat innumerate public. Clearly, they can, like metaphor, play an important part in generating oppositional extremes that enhance emotional engagement, so any analysis of media health must be alert to their presence.

PRODUCTION

One can ask, then, why oppositions, overdrawn contrasts and stock storylines and characterisations are so popular in media forms generally, and in media health in particular. It is helpful here to examine the standard accounts of news values in order to answer this. The well-known analysis by Galtung and Ruge (1973) is a good start. A story will make the news, these authors say, if it is negative, recent, close to home, compatible with dominant stereotypes, unambiguous, novel or unexpected, superlative (for example, the biggest, most destructive, most dangerous), relevant to an audience's daily life experience, personalised, involving important people or sources, and containing certain kinds of hard facts such as places, numbers, names and so on. Thus AIDS was treated as news in the 1980s. AIDS was implacably negative, threatening a widespread epidemic that brought almost certain death. It was happening 'now', and some analysts say (Check, 1987; Klaidman, 1991) that it was only when it came close to 'home' (threatening the heterosexual community) that coverage intensified. Dominant stereotypes about homosexuals, drug users and prostitutes figured large and 'unexpected' communities, such as haemophiliacs, became involved, so that searching for the next risk group (mothers and babies, as it turned out) was for a time the newshound's task. Scary 'discoveries' involving transmission through spittle and toilet seats could be trumpeted (and then condemned as irresponsible 'scares'). The potential size of the eventual 'epidemic' could be hyped and here numbers and authoritative sources played a major part, as well as a metaphoric connection with the plague. Stories of people affected by the disease made for a plentiful supply of personalised 'human interest' material, made even more exciting if that person was already a celebrity.

Bell (1991) expands Galtung and Ruge's list to note that once a story is in the news, further instances of the story will get printed, until the feeding frenzy of journalists is over. Additionally, other stories that are tangentially related to the current journalistic enthusiasm will have enhanced newsworthiness. Because of the efficiency with which news organisations work, prefabricated stories in the form of well-written and judiciously timed press releases are likely to meet the news agenda. Clarity and brevity are attractive in both press releases and in reporting itself, where the skills of writing lead paragraphs that succinctly summarise key issues are at a premium. Of course the ultimate example of this art lies in the construction of eye-catching headlines.

It is evident that this account explains the nature of newsworthiness without really assessing why these values dominate rather than others. To understand this we must recall the discussion in Chapter 1 regarding the place of media messages in everyday life. Emotional engagement of audiences is the key task for news, advertising, fiction and other media forms. Media organisations are largely driven by the need to acquire, keep and expand their audiences, so media producers seek out ways of stimulating appetites for entertainment that may be somewhat jaded. The drive towards sensationalism and the 'tabloidisation' of serious news has always been present in mass media, but some commentators feel that it has intensified across many media in recent years (Kimball, 1994; Sampson, 1996) as a response to the enormous expansion of media channels. An atmosphere of fear, danger, and excitement followed by secure resolutions creates a roller-coaster effect that keep the customers signing up for more. Media health stories can quite easily lock into this ride, as dangers to bodily integrity and their potential resolution by powerful hero-helpers (including the heroic sufferer himself or herself) can quite readily be told.

The sensationalist agenda leads to overdrawn contrasts when compared with the mundane nature of everyday life. People who talk about their war experiences will often emphasise, when in a reflective mood, that a lot of the time this involved hanging around, training, polishing boots, and cleaning kit, punctuated by short episodes of terrifying drama. This is similar to the relationship of everyday life experience to media-dramatised experience. Complexity and uncertainty rather than simple truths; lack of sufficient information to make a firm decision; periods of boredom and waiting; people who are neither clear enemies nor absolute friends, neither wholly weak nor totally powerful but who, instead, are a perplexing mixture; long stretches of routine maintenance; and experiences that are neither particularly pleasurable nor significantly painful are all characteristics of daily experience which contrast with the lurid worlds of mediated experience. The world is not black or white, but many shades of grey. Indeed, one of Bell's (1991) factors affecting the news value of a story is called 'colour'.

The creation of colourful contrasts and oppositions that enliven the emotional experience of audiences can involve the generation of stereotypes, whose potential for damaging effects is often pointed out by critical media commentators. The creation of categories of all sorts is a fundamental procedure for media storytelling, with stigmatised categories being an important component of the power differentials thus involved. Stigma, as Goffman (1968) has observed, involves the branding of a person, or category of person, with an overarching master status, so that the quality chosen for stigmatisation is used to explain every action. Thus a mentally ill person has no legitimate reason to get angry except that he or she must be exhibiting signs of mental illness; the prostitute has no reason to speak to a man in the street except for the purpose of sex; the drug user cannot possess a syringe for any 'good' reason; a woman will cry more readily than a man. Because of these spoiled identities, considerable effort is needed to escape from them, or efforts may be made to control information so that the individual can 'cover' or 'pass' as 'normal'.

Much media analysis has concentrated on exposing negative stereotypes that arise from the tendency of the media to prefer overdrawn contrasts. For example, stereotypes about gender, race, and sexual identity are very easy to find, forming the stuff of numerous undergraduate essays on the evils of the media, as well as a rather large number of impassioned publications by righteously angry media critics. A somewhat more sophisticated critique of media stereotypes is provided by Fowler (1991), whose practice of critical linguistics identifies power issues at stake, whereby the oppositional divisions preferred by the powerful tend to be aired more frequently than their alternatives. Thus he notes that in the UK in the 1980s a series of conceptual oppositions underlaid Thatcherian public policy rhetoric, so that oppositions between strikers versus non-strikers, and appeasement versus peace through 'defence' spending, for example, were emphasised. In another example, Fowler shows how 'patients' are depersonalised as 'cases' or 'numbers' in news reports of NHS policy, suppressing patients' perspectives even as the journalists involved positioned themselves as the voice of the people, in exposing cover-ups. Storytelling, as Franzosi (1998) has pointed out, involves prioritisation of the perspective of the storyteller, which tends to exclude and suppress alternative voices. In view of the dominance of official perspectives in the production of media reports, such 'bias' is inevitable and, if we accept the view that audiences then believe such messages, it works in favour of the interests of people already powerful.

There is considerable current debate about the phenomenon of 'tabloidisation', which many feel accentuates the tendency towards stock oppositions and stereotypes as the media appear to prioritise an entertainment agenda. Firstly, there are voices opposing the view that it is actually an increasing tendency in contemporary media, or questioning easy separations between 'serious' and 'tabloid' forms (Sparks & Tulloch, 2000). There is also argument about how to judge tabloid forms, particularly in so far as they influence the quality of political debate in the public sphere. These depend on contrary visions of the audiences for these products. Should these be regarded as 'dumbing down' the serious news agenda, or providing a low level of opportunity for previously silenced voices to enter public debates? Livingstone and Lunt's (1994) study of popular afternoon talk shows suggests limited support for this positive view, as they argue that 'experts' and officials are confronted with the experiences of ordinary people on such shows and must thus adjust their views. Dovey's (2000) account of 'freakshow' television, such as the *Jerry Springer Show*, is a much more unrestrained celebration of the audience empowerment provided by this tabloid form. Franklin (1997, 1999), on the other hand, is in no doubt that the tabloid agenda damages the quality of public debate over important social issues, such as the coverage of child abuse.

This debate over media stereotyping and tabloidisation, fuelled at times by a somewhat conspiratorial view of production processes in media organisations, seems destined to continue unresolved without more adequate evidence about the actual relation of media forms and everyday life. While not wishing to detract from political analysis of the causes and possible negative effects of tabloidisation and stereotyping, I believe it is necessary in the case of media health stories to enquire further into the reasons for the popularity of media storytelling that depends on overdrawn contrasts and the depiction of extreme behaviour. Clearly, it is possible through such means to highlight some rather basic anxieties and tensions through dramatising existential issues of life and death, good and evil, and so on. I have explained in the previous chapter that these anxieties may then be pleasurably resolved in various ways to produce feelings of comfort, security and belonging. At this level, tabloid oppositional devices and stereotyping can be seen as entertaining rather than oppressive, perhaps through this means building an enveloping sense of community by producing pleasures rather than simply taking away important democratic rights.

CONCLUSION

Building on the analysis of Chapter 1, I have argued here that the continuing place of media health stories in the everyday lives of audiences is ensured by the adoption of particular forms, many of which are shared with other kinds of media coverage. Amongst these I have emphasised the role played by oppositions, stock storylines or 'templates', and standard characters that bear some similarities with the generic characters present in most folk tales. I have emphasised that one should not expect to see all of the constituent elements of classic folk tales in a single media health story, since the presentation of these is inevitably fragmented, with audiences using prior knowledge of story forms to fill in the narrative gaps. In this respect, audiences' relationships with media presentations draw on resources that are similar to those that we all use in everyday interaction, 'filling in the gaps' or 'bestowing' meaning on what faces us in order to understand the world as an orderly place. Media health fragments can invoke whole stories by implication, in a situation where audiences have long been socialised into an understanding of storytelling conventions and are well-schooled in intertextual readings.

Further, I have pointed out the appeal of the argument that media products are tailored to an audience imagined to be childlike (itself based on an imagined view of children). This is an important explanation for the dominant oversimplification, stereotyping and juxtaposing of opposites that one sees in much media output. This leads to an understandable lament about the intellectual limitations of popular media and, more specifically for our concerns, their health-damaging effects. Yet I have argued that twitches and reversals occur, suggesting that the imagined child may be an impatient one, in need of continuing stimulation. Of course, this also opens up the possibility that more complex stories get told through accumulative effect as familiar oppositions are reversed and stories adopt new configurations dissonant with previous versions. Metaphors and numbers play a part in the toolkit of the media health storyteller, assisting with the business of overdrawing contrasts and blurring fine distinctions. Potentially, this leaves the audience with a more subtle appreciation of issues, as awareness of contradiction grows. Audiences may be treated like dupes, but they do not necessarily behave like them.

These are the concepts, then, that form a backdrop for the analysis that follows. In the next chapter I shall look more closely at inaccuracy in media health representations, using the concepts of extrematisation and oppositional elements to understand the causes of this. I shall also enquire further into explanations for inaccuracies by investigating further the influences on media producers. Following this are chapters that centre around some of the stock characters and core emotions in media health stories – the heroes, the innocent victims, the villains, the helpers, the magical cures, the fools and the false heroes, the fears and anxieties, and the pleasures. Through the regular deployment of these things, media health stories assist in asking and answering basic existential questions that are related to the life of the body.

3 The Production of Unreality

Many commentators on health in the media are concerned with the degree to which media portrayals of health matters are accurate in relation to some alternative, preferred measure of reality (for example, epidemiological statistics). In practice, this is often associated with a view that inaccurate messages will have direct and harmful effects on audiences (although the issues of inaccuracy and of effects are, logically, separate). This chapter, then, will first demonstrate this 'problem' of inaccuracy in media health portrayals as this is often described by health educators and the producers of scientific knowledge. There are parallels to be drawn here with the 'lament' about the 'tabloidisation' of TV news, identified by Langer (1998). The explanations provided by critics for media distortions and oversimplifications will then be assessed, drawing on studies of media production and the influences experienced by media organisations to portray issues in a particular light. I shall contrast relatively apolitical explanations for media bias that emphasise the role of sensationalism in the entertainment agenda, and the differing culture of journalists and scientists or health educators, with more political analyses that invoke larger forces such as capitalism, patriarchy or medical influence as explanations. I begin this analysis with consideration of evidence for inaccuracy in selected areas.

EVIDENCE FOR INACCURACY

The collection of evidence for inaccuracy has ranged over many topics within media health. Here, I focus on three broad areas – death, illness experience and health care. Other topics where inaccuracy has been an issue for media analysts appear in later chapters.

Death

The sequestration, or hiding away, of death in late modern societies so that witnessing dying or handling bodies is no longer a part of the average adult's experience, being dealt with by specialist professionals and institutions, is an important feature of contemporary societies (Blauner, 1966; Seale, 1998). Under these circumstances, media images of death acquire a particular importance as sources of information about what causes death and what it might be like to die. It is therefore disturbing to see that death in media representations is not at all realistic and, further, that this really does seem to influence audiences into mistaken beliefs.

Lichtenstein et al. (1978) studied the beliefs of college students and citizens in Oregon concerning the frequency of 'lethal events', comparing these with mortality statistics, and found that:

> Even though stroke causes 85% more deaths than all accidents combined . . . only 20% of the students and 23% of the [citizens] judged stroke to be more likely . . . Tornadoes were seen by the student subjects as more frequent killers than asthma, even though the latter is 20 times more likely . . . Death by lightning was judged less likely than death by botulism even though it is 52 times more frequent . . . Death by asthma was judged only slightly more frequent than death by botulism . . . even though it is over 900 times more frequent! Accidental deaths were reported by the students to be about as likely as death from disease despite a true ratio of 15:4 for diseases over accidents . . . death by a motor vehicle accident is only 1.4 times as likely than death from diabetes . . . not 356 times more likely (the students' [estimate]) or 100 times more likely [citizens' estimate]. (1978: 555)

Sensational events (botulism, tornado, flood, homicide, accidents and cancer) were amongst the most overestimated causes of death; the 'undramatic, quiet killers' (1978: 575) of asthma, tuberculosis, diabetes, stomach cancer, stroke and heart disease were underestimated. The authors propose the media as a chief source of these beliefs:

> the media have important effects on our judgements, not only because of what they don't report (successful plane trips or [nuclear] reactor operations), but because of what they do report to a disproportionate extent. (1978: 575)

The authors then recommend 'that these biases be recognized and, if possible, corrected. Improved public education is needed before we can expect the citizenry to make reasonable public policy decisions about . . . risks' (1978: 577).

Two of the authors of this paper subsequently published another paper (Combs & Slovic, 1979) looking more closely at the media representations judged responsible for these erroneous perceptions, examining coverage of the causes of death in two US newspapers in a systematic content analysis. The results were in line with the earlier audience study:

> All forms of disease appeared to be greatly underreported while violent, often catastrophic events such as tornadoes, fires, drownings, homicides, motor vehicle accidents and all accidents stood out as being overreported . . . Although all diseases claim almost 1,000 times as many lives as do homicides, there were about three times as many articles about homicides than about all diseases . . . The most underreported causes [were] stroke, all diseases, stomach, lung, and breast cancer, diabetes and tuberculosis. (1979: 841–2)

Some years later, Singer and Endreny (1987), again concerned about misperceptions of risk, reported a study of US broadcast as well as print media, assessing whether there had been any changes in reporting between 1960 and 1984. They found no significant changes over time, noting that 'the *amount* of media attention to a hazard . . . appears to be unrelated to the number of deaths it causes in a year' (1987: 14), concluding that 'The media do not report on risks; they report on harms' (1987: 14).

Other studies have focused on US television. Gerbner et al. (1981) summarise 10 years of monitoring television drama shows as a part of the Cultural Indicators project, noting a preponderance of violence and 'mayhem', with daytime serials being particularly concerned with health themes, where the principal causes of death were 'homicides, car accidents and heart attacks' (1981: 903), a finding supported by Cassata et al. (1979, 1983a), who also note that 'bad' rather than 'good' characters tend to die in soaps, although death itself is rarely portrayed as involving significant suffering. In fact, the portrayal of suffering in such soaps usually enhances a character's chances of survival. Signorielli (1993), summarising continuing work on the Cultural Indicators project, notes that 'hardly anyone dies a natural death on television' (1993: 6). Cassata et al. (1983a) found that where death from disease did occur, it was likely to happen to women rather than men, no doubt reflecting their lesser involvement in action and adventure plots.

In the UK there has been little analysis of the newspaper coverage of death, although Kristiansen (1983) noted no correlation between mortality statistics and the frequency with which British newspapers in 1981 reported diseases. Since many common diseases rarely cause death, however, this is not a true comparison. A later, direct comparison with

Kristiansen's study (Entwistle & Hancock-Beaulieu, 1992) found that diseases resulting in death were more likely to be reported than non-fatal diseases, no doubt reflecting news values emphasising the dramatic and the negative.

Death on British television has been more recently analysed. Crayford et al. (1997) examined mortality in four popular soap operas, *Coronation Street, EastEnders, Brookside* and *Emmerdale* from 1985 to 1997, comparing them with average mortality rates for different age groups as well as known 'dangerous' occupations. The death rate for characters in these television series was very high:

> Characters in these soap operas lead very dangerous lives . . . Their lives are more dangerous even than those of Formula One racing drivers or bomb disposal experts . . . People suffering from many forms of cancer and other serious diseases have better five year survival rates than do these characters. (1997: 1649)

Additionally, the causes of death were disproportionately violent, these being three times more likely than non-violent causes, which themselves contained a high proportion of obscure causes, such as 'mystery' viruses. The authors say that 'characters in these serials would be advised to wear good protective clothing (designed to withstand sharp implements, sudden impacts, and fire) and to receive regular counselling for the psychological impact of living in an environment akin to a war zone' (1997: 1652).

Characters in television dramas are also commonly portrayed as being at risk of death, nowhere more so than in the dramatic cardiopulmonary resuscitation (CPR) events that are a staple scene in programmes such as *ER, Chicago Hope, Casualty* and *Cardiac Arrest*. Gordon et al. (1998) found, in contrast with similar studies of US serials, that British television dramas depicted a realistic proportion of initial survival from CPR (about 25 per cent), with survival in US equivalents being disproportionately high. However, a focus on young people and traumatic causes in CPR scenes was unrealistically high, as the procedure in reality is most commonly experienced by elderly patients and the conditions that lead to it are normally connected with illness. The focus on the lives, illness and deaths of younger people to the exclusion of coverage of older people is a theme we will encounter later.

Studies of suicide in the media (for example, Stack, 1987; O'Connor et al., 1999; Hawton et al., 1999; Platt, 1987; Wasserman et al., 1994) have focused less on inaccuracy than on attempts to discover an imitation effect. Walter's (1991; Walter et al., 1995) studies of bereavement and grief in the media analyse representations, but not in relation to inaccuracy. Instead, Walter focuses on the social construction of appropriate grief responses, without regard to some assumed standard of accuracy, in a departure from the usual realist critique.

In general, the media biases identified by the other authors reviewed are explained by these authors as the result of the media's need to entertain through presenting audiences with sensational events, in both news and fictional coverage. The feeling that underlies this can range from mild amusement to condemnation. Thus Crayford's study of British soaps appeared in the Christmas edition of the *British Medical Journal,* an annual issue where traditionally a number of joke items appear, and there is a generally light-hearted tone to the piece. Gordon's study of CPR, however, adopts a more serious purpose, observing that the findings have important implications for health-care workers talking to patients about resuscitation, who may have unrealistic expectations of the procedure. In general, a serious and critical rather than light-hearted tone is adopted by the media analysts reviewed above, accompanied by some evidence of media effects in the direction assumed by their critique. This affects research, though it does not enquire into the more playful and variable readings that audiences also may bring to these media tales.

Illness and health behaviour

Many studies have shown that the kinds of illness experienced by characters in fictional portrayals, and reported in news or documentary programmes and articles, are different from those experienced by the general population of the relevant countries. For example, the depiction of illness in soap operas tends towards the acute illness rather than the chronic, to the young and middle-aged rather than the old, and so on. Negative and potentially stigmatising portrayals of health problems in old age, women's health issues, disability and mental illness have been particularly well documented (see Chapters 5 and 9 for a fuller account).

As early as 1948, James Thurber noted that soap opera series in the US never mentioned cancer or infantile paralysis (polio), diseases that were widespread at the time, instead inventing such strange illnesses as 'island fever' or 'mountain rash' so that audiences were not disturbed by illnesses that came too close to home. In 1981, after a decade of monitoring health and medicine on US television, Gerbner and colleagues noted a variety of distortions and biases. For example, there were few depictions of disabled people, and mentally ill characters were almost always depicted to be violent or evil in some way, or to be the victims of violence, this last being particularly the case if they were women. Signorielli (1989) notes that mentally ill characters were also more likely to be depicted as failures or bad at doing their jobs.

Signorielli (1993), in a later report on US media, notes a variety of other distortions in the depiction of illness. For example, there is an under-reporting of news about environmental influences on health, or on occupational health (see also Raymond, 1985), leading to a focus on individual solutions to health problems rather than collective or political action. Heart disease is more likely to be associated with men rather than women. Women's magazines focus excessively on diet, fitness, and emotional and reproductive health at the expense of stroke and heart disease, which are major health risks for women. These same magazines have been charged with treating menstruation and premenstrual tension in excessively alarmist ways. Portrayals of cancer experience are biased towards stories of people who adjust successfully to the disease or are cured.

Henderson (1999) has examined British soaps, focusing particularly on the recent phenomenon of the presentation of serious 'social-message' storylines, which often involve health issues such as HIV, mental illness or breast cancer. 'Realism' is a frequent claim made by producers of these programmes, and interest groups representing people with the relevant conditions will often be involved in advising the programme makers in the interests of accuracy. Nevertheless, Henderson identifies many points of inaccuracy. For example, the 'long-term process of recovery of characters from trauma is rarely seen' (1999: 77) due to the need to condense stories in favour of dramatic interest. The need to present medical jargon in accessible form introduces a degree of unreality to health-care scenes. There is continuing negative stereotyping of mentally ill characters.

The depiction of health-related behaviour has also been identified by media critics as notably unrealistic. Characters eat unhealthy foods, yet stay slim and fit, have multiple sexual partners, yet rarely suffer from sexually transmitted diseases, and drink excessive amounts of alcohol without suffering ill effects. The review by Gerbner et al. (1981) makes this and other points. Obesity, for example, is rarely portrayed in dramatic series and obese female characters are extremely rare. Car transport rather than public transport is shown most often and the wearing of seat belts is rare. Significantly, Signorielli (1993; Signorielli & Staples, 1997) reports research showing that people who watch a great deal of television programmes of this sort also exhibit the unhealthiest diet, exercise and other health-related behaviour. Signorielli concludes:

[The overall picture] gained from the media and particularly the world of entertainment television . . . is a somewhat unrealistic vision of health and what one must do to be healthy . . . the overall picture of health on television minimizes or ignores the societal, political, or economic factors of disease ... The television world's view of health is medical: Illness is treated with drugs or machines, which seemingly are available to everyone with little thought as to the cost and availability. (Signorielli, 1993: 26)

Health care and health professions

Signorielli's mention of medical bias is a familiar complaint, too, in studies that focus on the inaccuracies of media portrayals of health care and health professions. In general, critics note that there is excessive glamorisation of acute, technically oriented medical care at the expense of community and public health initiatives, or the contributions made to health care by non-medical people such as nurses, paramedics, alternative therapists and lay carers. Once again, the report by Gerbner et al. (1981) is a good way into this literature. Doctors, these authors say, are commonly depicted as positive characters, and most often as males, while nurses play lesser roles and are more often female, so that 'The work of the television doctor is one of personal and almost mystical power over not only the physical but also the emotional and social life of the patient' (1981: 902). As well as exhibiting more unhealthy habits, high viewers of such programmes also exhibit unusually high levels of faith in doctors and medical solutions to health problems. Signorielli (1993), adding to this, notes that medicines are overwhelmingly portrayed in a positive light, and that socio-economic problems that lead to limited access to health care (a particular problem in the insurance-driven US health care system) are rarely portrayed.

The depiction of health care as an unlimited resource is also evident from studies of British media. Entwistle (Entwistle et al., 1996; Entwistle & Sheldon, 1999) analysed coverage of the 'Child B' case in which a child with cancer was denied expensive treatment by health authority officials on the grounds that the cost was unjustified in the light of the potential suffering the treatment might inflict on the child and the low prospects for success. Coverage focused on the parental struggle to fund treatment through charitable sources that then ensued. As with many other stories about health-care rationing, the media juxtaposed the emotional appeal and human interest of the person at risk against the harshness of the decision made by health officials, thus stigmatising them as faceless, unfeeling bureaucrats. Entwistle et al. (1996) present compelling evidence to the effect that there was inadequate depiction of the hopeless clinical situation, in favour of a story that hyped the chances of cure. In other work Entwistle and Sheldon (1999) have commented on the significance of more recent coverage of the medical profession that has emphasised scandalous or unprofessional behaviour by particular doctors. Such stories modify the view that the medical profession is portrayed in an exclusively positive light, and such coverage in the British media has strengthened the hand of the government in promoting closer regulation of doctors' activities. I shall return in later chapters to the significance of such negative portrayals of the medical profession.

At the risk of overstressing a point that ought to be continually in mind when considering such studies of misrepresentation, I may add that the majority of these analysts premise their criticism on an assumption of direct effects, without presenting much evidence for·this. An alternative reading might, for example, claim that viewers regard such media stories with a healthy scepticism, or that certain groups generate oppositional readings, or that it is well understood by viewers that media realities and everyday reality are distinct. More audience studies exploring the consequences of inaccuracy are needed.

EXPLAINING INACCURACY

The concern of realist critics of health in the media, then, is focused on lack of accuracy and the potentially health-damaging affects of unrealistic portrayals or, in the special case of suicide, the potential for imitative effects. We have also seen, in the example of grief, that a realist perspective that searches for bias may be contrasted with a cultural or constructionist perspective on media health that does not involve concern about accuracy. So far, in this chapter, we have only seen explanations for bias that are couched in terms of an implied theory of news values (which applies to drama as much as news, although genre differences are somewhat under-explored in media health research). This implicit theory emphasises the mission of media producers to entertain by stressing the sensational and the negative, differing from the objectives of scientists or health educators, who are supposed to be more concerned with accurate reporting. In this section, this 'two cultures' explanation will be contrasted with more political analyses of the forces that lead to distortion and bias.

Two cultures

When interviewed about how they choose particular stories, journalists covering health issues reveal a cultural difference from scientists, who, at one level, are engaged in a similar enterprise: representing knowledge of the world through writing about it. Entwistle (1995), for example, found British newspaper journalists saying that information deemed medically worthy is not necessarily newsworthy:

> They said they were more likely to cover currently topical subjects; common and fatal diseases; rare but interesting or quirky diseases; those with a sexual connection; new or improved treatments; and controversial subject matter or results . . . they were aware . . . that if they were too cautious their stories would not get printed at all, and if they could find a recognised expert to speak with enthusiasm about the latest results his or her comments were considered fair game. (1995: 921)

The area in which the 'two cultures' explanation has been furthest developed is in studies of the production of science news. This, of course, can at times cover stories outside the sphere of health and illness, but science news equally contains much that is relevant to health, and the 'two cultures' explanation for bias, with which we are concerned here, can and often is applied to coverage of health news. Nelkin (1995) has provided a review of this area, on which I rely considerably in this section.

Nelkin begins from the perception that media reporting of science tends to oversimplify, extrematise and therefore distort the true nature of scientific research and the content of scientific findings. Extrematisation, of course, is a core aspect of the juxtaposition of opposites identified in Chapter 2 as an important media health format. Tensions between the worlds of scientists and journalists result from this. The solution to this problem proposed by many who work within the 'public understanding of science' tradition is identified in a bringing together of the disparate occupational cultures of the two groups. Programmes of education aimed at mutual understanding and compromise are advocated, so that the public will then be served with better quality (in other words, more accurate, more understandable) scientific information. All of this rests on a somewhat functionalist model of media institutions in their relation to other institutions, and a belief that communication processes between media messages and audiences will be pretty straightforward once their content is correctly presented. In spite of these blind spots, interesting empirical work on media production processes has been conducted from within this tradition that deserves attention.

Firstly, there is a considerable body of work that details in rather precise ways the nature of the different inaccuracies that arise in science reporting, and these in themselves are quite revealing. Singer (1990) is a good example of work of this sort. She analysed US news and television media for four months in 1984, monitoring reports on hazards, and eventually collecting 42 stories of which 15 related to illness (the largest group). Departing from the methodology of previous studies, in which scientists were asked to report on the extent to which media stories reporting their work was accurate (which introduces the problem of scientists making mistakes about this!), Singer collected the original scientific papers that had led to each story and made her own assessment of the extent to which media reports were congruent with these, comparing her ratings with those made independently by a research assistant. Singer's classification of inaccuracies in the news reports includes the omission of important results, treating speculation as fact, rewording involving loss of precision, overstating the generality of results or their causal implications, and failure to report on the methods of scientific studies, so that extreme positions creating an impression of certainty, and oversimplified and dramatic results were generated where they did not exist in the original scientific reports. Only two of the 42 stories were judged to have contained no errors. Examples of errors include

> a *Newsweek* story that reports on an experimental treatment for Alzheimer's disease [implying] that a new treatment is at hand when in fact it is at the earliest stages of clinical trials . . . a *Wall Street Journal* story that omitted all authors' statements about the limitations of the study, which involved only six AIDS patients and no control group . . . (1990: 107, 110)

Such studies of 'inaccuracy' in media reports are generally unquestioning of the scientific point of view. However, some analysts interested in the 'two cultures' explanation have made telling points about the limited extent to which scientists appreciate the journalistic agenda, or about the undue influence which scientists may themselves bring to bear on reporters. Peters (1995), for example, notes that scientists increasingly belong to organisations that may employ public relations consultants to hype scientific results inordinately to the press. Scientists themselves, in comments to journalists, may succumb to the temptation of exaggerating the significance of their studies. Scientists, Peters claims, commonly do not appreciate the legitimate concern of many journalists with the reasons why research is done on some topics rather than others, on the power and justice issues involved in science stories, and on the politics of scientific knowledge and its application.

Nelkin (1995) supports many of these criticisms of the science establishment, devoting much space to analysis of the public relations efforts of scientific organisations over the years. Promotions by scientists and doctors of artificial heart surgery, heart transplantation, the Human Genome Project, cold fusion, and so on are all examples where it has been in the interest of medical and scientific groups to make too many promises about benefits, encouraging inaccurate reporting. Yet it is clear that excessive dramatisation of science stories pre-dates such efforts, being a part of the inevitable dynamic of media organisations whose existence depends on fulfilling an entertainment agenda on behalf of an audience that is somewhat illiterate in relation to scientific knowledge and procedures. The result, Nelkin feels, is considerable disillusion of scientists over the adequacy of media organisations for creating accurate public understanding.

Political analyses

It would be unfair to say that work done within the 'public understanding of science' tradition ignores the influence of larger social forces on media production, but there are writers on media health inaccuracies who prefer a much more political explanation than does Nelkin. These have tended to focus on the influence of capital and big business, of patriarchal authority or of medical power which are seen to influence the media agenda in different ways. For these writers, the existence of 'two cultures' is not an explanation for media bias, but something that itself needs explaining by reference to the larger things that hold it in place. Solutions couched in terms of increasing levels of education and co-operation between scientists and journalists are seen as inadequate in addressing the roots of the problem, which lie in broader social structures.

Clearly, the influence of powerful economic and political interests on media coverage is a large topic that ranges beyond that of health reporting, being a general feature of Frankfurt School analysis of cultural forms. For example, the Glasgow Media Group studies of news coverage of industrial disputes and other topics (Glasgow University Media Group, 1976) was an important moment in the development of this argument in the media studies field as a whole. In relation to health topics, perhaps the clearest example of the influence of capitalist interests on generating inaccuracy is that exercised by tobacco manufacturers, wielded largely through their advertising revenue. Economic and political interests have significantly diverged on this topic in recent years as the critique of smoking has now locked into a wider official agenda that involves the general promotion of a culture of safety (see Chapter 4). The critique begins from the observation that it is in the interests of cigarette manufacturers to suppress stories that remind people of the link between smoking and disease. Other stories are also suppressed: tobacco companies try to cast doubt on the notion that advertising tobacco products causes consumption to rise, and to promote instead the view that causal links for both of these are unproven, or that advertising merely encourages brand loyalty without affecting overall consumption, or that they are not promoting smoking aggressively in poorer countries where populations are unprotected by health-minded governments.

Altman et al. (1987) show how cigarette advertisements in US magazines in 1960–85 promoted ideas that, for them, were wholly inaccurate: that for women, smoking was glamorous, erotic or romantic, and for young people that it was an adventurous sign of vitality. Kennedy and Bero (1999) show how coverage of passive smoking in US papers in 1981–94 gave, for them, what was excessive prominence to tobacco industry views that the underlying science was controversial. Chapman (1989) has shown that positive coverage of smoking in Australian newspapers is more likely if a paper is owned by Rupert Murdoch, a proprietor known for his links with business interests. Warner's work (1985; Warner et al., 1992) as well as that of Whelan et al. (1981) makes it quite clear that pressure has been brought to bear on magazines (a major outlet for tobacco advertisements since the banning of such advertisements on television) through threats to withdraw advertising revenue. Fear of economic reprisals, it seems, has been particularly influential on women's magazines, where the negative correlation between cigarette advertising revenue and mention of the health hazards of smoking is particularly strong (Amos et al., 1991; Kessler, 1989; Warner et al., 1992). Clearly, the source of this inaccuracy does not lie in the differing cultures of scientists and journalists but in the machinations of powerful third parties.

There are other examples of direct influence by powerful economic interests to influence health reporting. Power (1995) describes San Francisco newspaper reporting of the 1900 outbreak of bubonic plague, analysing 'how macro level relations affected the media content regarding the plague and its carriers' (1995: 90). The issues centred firstly on whether the plague existed at all in San Francisco, and then on whether quarantining the city – which would have damaged economic interests through restricting trade – or expelling the Chinese would control the outbreak. Reluctant to acknowledge the existence of the disease, the San Francisco Board of Trade, Chamber of Commerce and other business interests recruited medical supporters to the view that other conditions (septicaemia, tuberculosis) were in fact being misdiagnosed. This view was also supported by the Chinese community, who sought to hide evidence of plague. This was understandable, since in the later phase of reporting (by which time evidence of plague had become incontrovertible) the stigmatisation of the Chinese population was encouraged to new heights by media reports. In both phases – initial denial and then stigmatisation of the Chinese – business interests were strongly reflected in news reporting. It was only when a second outbreak occurred outside Chinatown after the 1906 earthquake that the true carriers of the disease (rats and their fleas – as had been conclusively demonstrated by Yersin in 1894) were identified in press reports. Power quotes the *Journal of the American Medical Association* of 1900 reflecting on San Francisco press coverage:

> There is no other city in Europe or America that has met the peril of plague in the way San Francisco has done, there is no place where press and public have so persistently fought the necessary measures in the desire to prove that plague did not exist among them. (Quoted in Power, 1995: 89)

In this case, economic interests are not the whole story, popular prejudice also playing a part in fuelling news reports, and the plague story bears points of resemblance with that of AIDS (see Chapter 5). In fact, this mixing of influence is usually identified in political analyses of media production; the influence of economic interests on media reports also is not always direct. The explosion of Ritalin prescribing for attention-deficit hyperactivity disorder (ADHD) in children is a case where both economic interests and other forces are seen by some media analysts to have combined in promoting inaccurate, health-damaging media accounts. Lloyd and Norris (1999), for example, note that UK press coverage of this topic over a five-year period has contained a large number of articles about 'parents describing difficulties they had faced with their children prior to diagnosis, many very critical of the lack of support they had received from professionals' (1999: 506). Another group of articles represent professional views, many of which feature the views of Ritalin enthusiasts. Critical views, where they do occur, tend to be those of doctors rather than other professions, such as teachers. All of this, for Lloyd and Norris, generates the impression that ADHD is a medical problem rather than a reflection of more general human behavioural issues, and creates a climate that is generally favourable towards a drug-based solution: Ritalin. A similar analysis has been presented by Diller (1996) for US media, noting that overwhelmingly favourable press and television reporting encourages 'biological determinism in which only heredity and brain chemistry determine behavior rather than interactions with the environment' (1996: 15).

Unlike coverage of smoking, where particular incidents of manipulation of media organisations by business interests have been identified, no such direct evidence is adduced by these media analysts. However, the financial interests of pharmaceutical companies are clearly involved and can be damaged by adverse media coverage, as was shown by Safer and Krager (1992), who charted a local decline in prescribing rates after media reports in Maryland of a lawsuit initiated for damaging side-effects. Drug companies in the US, say Lloyd and Norris, have produced 'massive funding' (1999: 511) for parents' organisations, identified as key lobbyists of media organisations. Drug companies pursue 'aggressive marketing' (1999: 511) campaigns to promote Ritalin with doctors, recently encouraging the view that adults would benefit from the drug as much as children. Clearly, these are routes for indirect influence on media coverage. The views of concerned family pressure groups and representatives of the medical profession are always high on any journalist's list of heavily used, authoritative sources of stories.

Marketing of drugs by pharmaceutical companies to the medical profession has long been a way of influencing medical opinion and practice, which in turn has a knock-on effect when doctors communicate their opinions to mass media organisations. Analysis of these promotional efforts is an interesting but rarely explored sub-genre of media health studies. Chapman's (1979) account of advertisements for psychotropic drugs in Australian medical journals is revealing in showing the techniques employed to persuade doctors that a drug solution, rather than some lengthier treatment programme associated with a 'healing' approach, is appropriate. Of course, there are considerable restraints placed on drug companies so that they do not make claims for efficacy unsupported by research, but this does not stop an element of mythic unreality entering the advertisements, particularly through their visual elements. Chapman's semiotic decoding of advertisements shows a structure in which a problem is juxtaposed with a promised solution. The problem may, for example, be the doctor's guilt about being a 'buck passer' or employer of a 'quick fix' in the form of a drug, or possessing inadequate authority over patients. The 'promise' may involve positive and appealing visual images of the drug-supplying doctor, portraying him or her as a detached and skilled 'scientist', for example, an image that is in tune with drug-based solutions. Alternatively, the fantasy of wielding a solution so powerful that respect will inevitably occur is played upon. Thus, analysts have shown both direct and indirect influence exerted on the form and content of media health messages by commercial interests.

Patriarchy

One of Chapman's advertisements shows a young, slim woman ready for bed, challenging the (assumed to be male) doctor's potency by complaining that the current sleeping pills do not work. The promise of this advertisement, Chapman argues, is that 'Dormicum will make his patients respect him, they will take his drugs in good faith and will find him sexually appealing . . . He will be the inspirational healer he wishes himself to be' (1979: 760–1). This introduces another element of the political explanation for inaccuracies and distortions in media representations of health: that of patriarchy. Many media analysts are inspired by feminist theories of media relations (Van Zoonen, 1994) and this line of analysis, while rarely producing the kind of direct evidence of media influence by large organisations that has become available in relation to the tobacco story, nevertheless has adduced persuasive evidence of indirect influence. As with the influence of business interests, a few examples will suffice, as the rest of this book will frequently contain further discussions of these factors affecting media health coverage (see particularly Chapter 9).

Darling-Wolf's (1997) analysis of the *New York Times* coverage of the breast implant controversy in the early 1990s starts from the position that mass media promote an oppressive cultural environment in which unhealthy depictions of female beauty predominate. Generalised hegemonic processes underlie the social relations of media production, so that there is a shared discourse and collective interpretation between journalists and powerful interests in society. Additionally, the occupational structure of journalism tends to be male dominated and male values are particularly influential in newsrooms (Van Zoonen, 1994). More specifically, Darling-Wolf observes that the financial interests of the cosmetic and diet industries influence women's magazines to create a 'close tie' (1997: 79) between editorial content and beauty product advertising.

When silicone breast implants began to go wrong (leaking, causing infections, etc.), the *New York Times* ran stories that almost exclusively relied on 'official' sources, such as Federal Drug Administration (FDA) spokespeople, representatives of the implant manufacturers, doctors and lawyers. Only 13 'non-official' sources (such as women with implants) were used, compared with 219 official sources during the period covered. Lay people were only interviewed if they belonged to pressure groups. The debate was framed as a struggle between the FDA on one side and plastic surgeons and implant manufacturers on the other. There was almost no space given to views that were critical of patriarchal interests in keeping women dependent on implants for their self-esteem (although one editorial mentioned this) and no discussion of the profit motives that drove the cosmetic industry: instead, the issue was framed in terms of women's right to choose. The FDA view that these cosmetic devices could be equated with life-preserving devices such as heart valves, so that implants were by implication assumed to be a medical necessity, went unchallenged. Darling-Wolf concludes that coverage was 'affected by professional and business practices, as well as by larger social and political forces' (1997: 92). Powers (1999), in a later analysis, notes that the breast implant manufacturers gradually succeeded in getting the press to shift coverage away from the health risks of implants and instead towards the possible financial ruin that manufacturers faced.

Gender bias in media health coverage, as in other areas of the media, is not hard to find. Differential depictions of doctors and nurses, overly thin body images reflecting stereotypes of female beauty, the tendency for female characters to be portrayed as victims rather than perpetrators of violence, the negative stereotyping of elderly women, and biased coverage of women's reproductive and sexual health experiences are all example that are discussed at various points in this book. Many such studies rely on analysis of media images themselves, inferring (usually quite plausibly) the underlying production processes. Only rarely are media producers themselves interviewed or observed to provide direct evidence of what goes on in production.

An exception to this is the study of the reporting of child sexual abuse, a topic which I show in Chapter 6 is related to the media health agenda. Skidmore and Kitzinger have reported on studies of production processes that lie behind a coverage that is generally defensive of the interests of men, particularly fathers, who are nevertheless major perpetrators of abuse (Kitzinger & Skidmore, 1995; Skidmore, 1998; Kitzinger, 1998, 2000). Skidmore (1998) quotes several female journalists covering the story:

> I would have constant arguments in the office with reporters that just think – well, male reporters probably don't want to think about child sex abuse . . . I would sit in the office and come out with these arguments in a very matter of fact way, because I was always desperately trying not to get angry – there was one particular occasion where I was saying all of this and the *chief reporter* was being hysterical about it all and *I* was told that *I* was probably too involved with the case! (interviewee's own emphasis). (1998: 213)

Another journalist said, 'I have never known the whole office to be so divided along gender lines as over that issue' (1998: 213). Some years later, when false memory syndrome (FMS) (discussed in Chapter 2) became a hot news topic, Kitzinger (1998) interviewed journalists, one of whom conveyed the macho atmosphere of her newsroom when she:

> described the 'total glee' with which editorial staff responded to her own article attacking psychotherapy. In their view, she commented, 'therapists are kind of weak-minded and they're in the business of feelings, which in journalism is the bloody last thing you would ever express in the office.' (1998: 196)

A last example comes from the field of cancer reporting. Quite consistently, studies of cancer reporting in the media find that a distorted picture of the prevalence of different cancers is given, with breast cancer being featured more often than its epidemiological prevalence, and other cancers, such as lung and colorectal, being under reported (Sarna, 1995; see also Chapter 8). While tobacco company interests are clearly served by the under-reporting of lung cancer, gendered notions of the audience for 'soft' and 'hard' news effectively explain the breast cancer phenomenon, as Henderson and Kitzinger (1999) have shown through interviewing journalists involved in breast cancer genetics stories. As one journalist put it:

> [It is] a way of talking up the women's vote, if you like. Let's play the female card. Women are bound to want to read this and let's make the newspaper more female friendly is the big drive. (1999: 569)

Thus women are considered by editors to be attracted by such 'soft' news (abortions, lost babies, relationships, etc.) and less interested in matters of State or hard science news. Henderson and Kitzinger conclude by invoking the health educator's complaint about inaccuracy: 'This is all good news for the media, but the implications may be less welcome for those seeking to promote public understanding of cancer' (1999: 570).

Both direct and indirect influence by business interests and patriarchy as a general background to media production have been implicated in creating inaccurate or distorted accounts of health and illness. The 'two cultures' view begins to look a little limited in the light of these more political analyses which expose forces that maintain bias in media organisations. In particular, the view that increasing journalists' and scientists' understanding of each other's cultures so that the two might be brought closer together seems naïve. The influence of capital and patriarchy on media health is only a part of the story, however: the influence of the medical establishment is another major factor that deserves attention.

Medical influence

Commentators on the gulf between scientists' and journalists' cultures tend towards the view that media organisations owe an obligation to report scientific views accurately, being relatively uncritical of the scientific agenda itself (although the sociology of science in general has adopted a far more critical approach in recent years – see, for example, Conrad [1996], Nelkin & Lindee [1995]). This is not the case with medical influence on media health representations, where the voice of critical sociologists concerned about the negative effects of medical power, and the cultural dominance of biomedical ideas, has been prominent. The depiction of medical influence, then, drawing on this broader, critical agenda, will be discussed in considerable detail in Chapter 7, where I shall also assess the competing view that medical influence is declining. For the present chapter, I shall simply present some case studies that demonstrate how this influence has suppressed alternative accounts that might otherwise have achieved more media prominence.

Perhaps the most sustained analysis of this sort is presented by Anne Karpf (1988) in her book that focuses largely on the British broadcast media: *Doctoring the Media*. As the title of her book suggests, this is a critical account of medical dominance, distancing her from the conventional 'lament' of health educators that if only more accurate medical information were reported in the media we would all be better off. Karpf argues that:

> in spite of greater diversity in the media's reporting of health and medical issues over the past decade, medical definitions and perceptions still prevail, and squeeze out more contentious, oppositional viewpoints which take an environmental approach and look at the politics of health . . . By excluding or marginalising other perspectives – notably, a more explicitly political analysis of the origins of illness – the media play a significant part in narrowing public debate about health, illness and medicine . . . medicine as a social and ideological force is fortified and amplified by the mass media . . . (1988: 2)

Although, as she points out, doctors and scientists are often critical of the inaccuracies that enter journalists' reports, in broad terms the media promote a medical agenda and therefore sustain the larger 'inaccuracy' of which Karpf complains. There was a time when medical organisations were reluctant to get involved in 'popularisation', being concerned that this might be construed as advertising. As Ziporyn (1988) has shown in her study of relations between the US medical profession and the media, this stance had largely been abandoned by the 1920s as the opportunities for health education through media influence, as well as the chance to enhance the cultural authority of the medical profession, proved irresistible. Turow (1989) charts in considerable detail the relations between medical authorities in the US and the producers of television medical soaps, in which medical interests pursued the twin agenda of ensuring that stories enhanced medical prestige and preserving opportunities for private practice through resisting any hint that socialised medicine might be a better way.

Karpf's story charts medical influence over broadcasting in Britain from the late 1920s, describing the close relationship between the government Ministry of Health, the British Medical Association (BMA) and the BBC. These relationships were subject to a degree of negotiation over the years, but the exigencies of wartime meant a considerable emphasis on fitness and disease prevention in programmes designed to educate the public towards healthier habits. From the 1950s, though, there was a significant shift of emphasis towards the depiction of medical technology and the wonders of science, meaning that preventive medicine messages gave way to curative, often hospital-based dramas, documentaries and news reports. Although the 1970s and 1980s saw an increased interest in the representation of patients' views, this consumerist orientation, in Karpf's view, did not seriously challenge medical dominance. Consumer issues were couched in terms of the right of people to choose, as individuals, between different medical options. Even the resurgence of interest in prevention, seen, for example, in the growth of media interest in fitness programmes and 'look after yourself' messages, was highly individualised, failing to pay significant attention to social structure and class culture in causing ill health. When medical interests were threatened by budgetary reductions, health service finances rapidly became news.

Karpf is particularly concerned with a continuing media emphasis on the benefits of costly curative procedures, such as heart transplantation, at the cost of low-technology alternatives that might bring greater benefits to larger numbers of people, as well as the failure of the media to take alternative or complementary medicine seriously. Heart transplant stories, milking the human interest angle for all it is worth, follow a stereotyped pattern or template,

> producing perfect replicas of previous reports. They stress the desperation of those waiting for a heart, and the fear that time will run out. The fatal alternative is made plain. The operation is depicted as offering the chance of a new life or future, an opportunity to vanquish death. Grief and joy are voiced, and the press conference following the operation is an aria of hope. (1988: 149)

The media is also often used to mount campaigns searching for transplant material (livers, bone marrow, etc.), commonly for sick children (see also Chapter 5 in this book), so that the public is mobilised to support services for very rare conditions at the expense of more common conditions. There is strikingly little coverage of the failures of such procedures – transplant patients who die, for example. The false hopes thus generated, in Karpf's view, stand in remarkable contrast to coverage of alternative medicine, which, while increasingly sympathetic to the cause of complementary health practitioners (in line with a softening of the medical view on this), is overconcerned to issue 'health warnings' that stress the limitations of alternatives in achieving cures.

Karpf's account of medical dominance now has a slightly dated feel to it, arising from the concern of medical sociologists in the 1970s and early 1980s to chart the negative impact of medical dominance. This itself had originated with the powerful influence of Marxist and neo-Marxist perspectives on medical sociology. Now, of course, this unified political stance has become diversified into a greater variety of academic projects that do not always have clear political implications (Foucauldian perspectives, postmodernism, for example), and the growth of media studies as a discipline means that we can perceive a greater variety of influences on media health than Karpf's monocausal emphasis on medicine. Additionally, the media itself has changed somewhat since Karpf's day – heart transplants are no longer 'news' but routine; fitness and diet programmes have become less overtly concerned with promoting health, and more with pleasure and beauty; 'alternative' therapies are less clearly distinguishable from 'orthodox' medicine. Nevertheless, the work of Karpf as well as others (for example, Ziporyn, 1988; Turow, 1989) is significant in identifying an important source of influence on media health.

In addition to these points about the limited relevance of the 'medical dominance' thesis, it is also worth noting that the depiction of medical influence as harmful to health may be a particularly biased view. This can be shown through brief consideration of the media treatment of AIDS (see also Chapter 5). Here, as is well known, media accounts of the disease in the 1980s have been subjected to a barrage of hostile criticism from media analysts concerned to counter stigmatising messages. Phrases like 'gay plague', religiously inspired messages about immorality, sexual prudishness, homophobia, and hostility towards injecting drug users have been condemned by such critics as Watney (1997) as profoundly damaging aspects of media coverage. Occasional 'rogue' doctors who have surfaced in the press to promote alarmist or right-wing agendas are cited by critics as evidence of a medical conspiracy.

In the light of this critique, which bears some points of similarity with

Karpf's (1988) account of the negative effects of medical dominance, it is instructive to turn to the work of Berridge (1991) and Williams (1999). Berridge notes that the impact of the media on small groups of elite policy makers may be more important than their supposed impact on mass opinion. Furthermore, she noted that the highly charged lament promoted by critics like Watney ignores the fact that the media, as well as containing stigmatising messages, has been a forum for other views too. In practice, in Britain, HIV carriers have not been banished, quarantined, imprisoned, sterilised or otherwise cast out as a matter of policy or practice. Instead, the social policies that have held sway have been precisely those advocated by a liberal public health lobby (needle exchange schemes, public education, etc.), consisting of members of the medical profession who share the view that stigmatising media coverage is a bad thing. In particular, television coverage (rather than that of the tabloid newspapers) was considerably more 'responsible' in promoting a non-stigmatising, public health view, being subject to considerable influence from an alliance of governmental and medical influence. Williams (1999) adds the further note that different sections of individual newspapers contained conflicting messages, with general reporters engaging in 'gay bashing' and health reporters promoting the public health line. Medical influence on media health, then, may suppress alternative voices (in this case, those of the far right), but this may promote rather than damage health or democracy.

CONCLUSION

I have reviewed four major explanations for the inaccuracies and distortions that concern many critics of media health, having begun the chapter with the case study of death in the media, and continuing on from this with an account of important biases that have been identified in the reporting of illness, health behaviour, health care and the health professions. The account of bias is consistent with the analysis, presented in Chapter 2, of media forms, in which it was argued that the juxtaposition of opposites and the extrematisation of complex matters, so that they appear more simple and certain than they really are, are important features of media health portrayals.

Explanations for media distortion range from the somewhat functionalist, but nevertheless revealing, account of the differing cultures of scientists and media people, to the more political analyses that emphasise the role of big business, patriarchy and medical power in influencing the media health agenda. The charge of functionalism may, in fact, be a little unfair. Studies of newsroom culture, such as those conducted by Entwistle (1995) and Kitzinger (1998), might more accurately be termed interactionist, focusing on the daily negotiations by journalists with people in their immediate environment (sub-editors, sources and so on). Such small-scale, microlevel studies perhaps cannot be expected also to present fully worked-out analyses of macrolevel institutional relations, whether these be system-maintaining functionalist accounts or conflict-emphasising Marxist or feminist accounts. Schudson (1989) points out that interactionist studies of media production might be regarded as filling in the gaps left out of Marxist analyses, pointing to the degree to which room for negotiation exists even in a highly determined social system.

Clearly, all of these explanations have some force in explaining the production of media health representations, and this multicausal influence will be demonstrated further from time to time as this book progresses. It is now time, though, to turn from these preliminary three chapters, which have successively focused on the place of media health in everyday life, the forms of media health, and the phenomenon of inaccuracy and explanations for it, to the first of several chapters that analyse media health representations themselves. Production and reception issues will be touched on in the course of these chapters, but the vast majority of work in this area has been done on representations themselves, so this book reflects this emphasis. Additionally, we can now turn to a more 'constructionist' approach that is less concerned with accuracy, as compared with some alternative version of reality, than with the nature and form of the media health story itself. This, in fact, is Schudson's (1989) third method for analysing media production, which contains the potential for seeing how media health stories relate to broader cultural myths. We will also be reminded, from time to time, of the need for much fuller evidence about audience responses to media health portrayals than is currently available. In particular, there is a continuing tendency amongst media analysts critical of representations to assume a direct, usually negative effect. Such analysts tend to underplay the oppositional, narcissistic or just playful readings that have been identified in studies of media in other areas, and are conceptualised more fully by the media theorists discussed in Chapter 1.

I start with an account of media health scares, since this initial arousal of the emotion of fear is often the starting point for subsequent moves in the overall story told in media health representations. Disruption to normal patterns, notification that something unusual is afoot, and signals of approaching danger are common devices in folk tales and storied entertainments of all kinds, presaging an adventure, a journey or perhaps the opportunity for some heroic trajectory. Who knows what may happen next?

4 Danger, Fear and Insecurity

An important task of many media health representations is to emphasise the riskiness of modern life for audiences. A stress on imagined danger may provide a ripple of disturbance to the basic security of viewers and readers so that an entertaining effect is created, stimulating further media consumption, and making the resolution of insecurities doubly pleasurable. In this respect the media allows participation in dangerous activities at the level of the imagination, a low-level version of the active courting of risk that Giddens (1991) has identified as a feature of modern risk mentality. The actual courting of risk (gambling, roller-coaster rides, dangerous sports activities, and so on) generates both thrills and a sense of mastery, being an experiment with trust in which the routines of everyday life, normally acting as a protective cocoon for the individual, can temporarily be disrupted. Strategies for managing real-life risk are, most of the time, hidden from consciousness by routine. The stimulation provided by mediated images hints at confrontation with existential terrors, though for the most part in such small, 'safe' doses, and so is commonly juxtaposed with resolutions – promises of safety, heroism or rescue – that the viewer can sleep sweetly at night. (Resolutions, of course, may or may not be ones that logically relate to the particular threats that precede them in the collage-like world of media experience.) This chapter describes a variety of media health scares that have achieved prominence in recent years. Initially, though, I assess the broader issues of the media's role in supporting the 'culture of fear' that some commentators have identified as an important feature of modern times.

THE CULTURE OF FEAR

In spite of the apparently innocuous nature of media health scares if taken one at a time, it is nevertheless the case that the media has contributed to a culture of fear that has gradually been generated in the past few decades. The continual drip-feeding of violent or frightening images and stories, which are the essential first part of the scare-resolution couplet, creates a cumulative effect in which consciousness of safety issues has reached chronic levels. This has offended some sociological commentators who hanker after what they feel is a more authentic way of life involving acceptance of life's dangers, with all the disappointments and losses, as well as pleasures and creativity, that this is felt to have involved. Furedi (1997), for example, refers to

> society's fear of taking risks . . . warnings of doom [such as the Millennium Bug] have little to do with the real scale of the problem, and a lot to do with a predisposition to panic in a society that lives in fear of itself. (1997: v)

Furedi notes that a continual cycle of food panics mean that 'virtually every aspect of eating has been transformed into a risk' (1997: vi), supported by government programmes of warning, prevention and control. Fears about predatory adults mean that fewer children are free to play unsupervised in public spaces; fears of technology gone haywire fuel concerns about nuclear and other accidents; fears about addiction mean that such pleasures as television watching or computer gaming are curtailed. An army of counsellors and safety advisers has arisen to prevent or deal with the consequences of accidents, so that new illness labels (post-traumatic stress disorder, for example) have to be generated in order to keep these people in business. Furedi feels that powerlessness is accentuated in a climate of diminishing trust and increasing isolation, since almost any human action can be interpreted as potentially dangerous. The result, he argues, is that every human experience is transformed into a 'safety situation' (1997: 4). Finally proposing that 'passive living can damage your health', Furedi condemns these attempts to 'ban risks' since this 'has the effect of undermining the spirit of exploration and experimentation' (1997: viii).

Reinharz (1997) presents a similar, if more light-hearted, analysis of the pervasiveness of warnings in everyday life, conveying the chronic nature of the anxieties thereby produced:

> I would like to get through the day without being assaulted with warnings. I find this barrage of dire information intrusive, pervasive, and depressing . . . signs, newspaper articles, radio reports, and labels tell me to 'watch out'. They let me know that life is dangerous. It's almost foolhardy to be in the sun, to be in a car, or to take food (poison?) from a supermarket shelf. Do I buy margarine or butter, knowing, as I have learned, that both are

bad? . . . warning signs have become extraordinarily repetitive. Can't we assume that everyone already knows that 'smoking is dangerous to one's health'? Can't we assume that I know 'the 10 danger signs' without having to open a cookbook sponsored by the American Cancer Association and find warnings related to many body parts. You can lose your appetite! (1997: 31–2)

Advocating a programme of resistance to this over-amplification of the dangers of everyday life, Reinharz suggests that respect for science and, in particular, the medicalisation of life problems lie behind the phenomenon. Additionally, she cites the (American) trend towards litigation as a solution to disputes, as well as the emergence of political advocacy around illness and other social problems (for example, campaigns to fund breast cancer prevention). Increased safety consciousness, though, must also be a product, at least in part, of the safe, secure and well-fed conditions of daily civil life in most Western industrialised countries. Mediated images then fill in for the absence of real dangers by supplying vicarious thrills. Awareness of danger, paradoxically for populations living in objectively quite safe conditions, is thereby encouraged to grow to extremes, being free of any requirement to relate to 'reality'. This leads in turn to generalised support for warnings and safety policies, designed to defend against imagined threats.

Altheide and Michalowski (1999) provide empirical confirmation of an accelerating trend in the use of fear as a theme in the US media. Tracking the use of the word 'fear' in the headlines and body of news articles of the *Arizona Republic*, they found a doubling of incidence between 1987 and 1996 (in headlines, for example, the increase was from 123 times in 1987 to 232 times in 1996). These authors also studied coverage of fear in 10 other major daily US papers during 1994–96. There was some variation between papers, the 'prestige' titles (*Washington Post, New York Times*) giving somewhat less prominence to 'fear' stories. But where it occurred there was a consistent pattern for such stories to be particularly focused on fear of crime, violence in general, threats to the community, neighbourhood or schools, drugs, youth gangs and threats to children. Thus crime, particularly if this threatened children, provided the major content for such stories, with dangers to health from cancer or the environment also featuring as a secondary threat. The result, Altheide and Michalowski say, is the construction of a culture of surveillance that targets children above all, together with punitive penal policies to deal with crime. Scaring the audience, then, is a major preoccupation for media producers, and a study by McNaughton-Cassill (2001) confirms that such negative news coverage is positively related to levels of stress and anxiety in viewers.

Before proceeding to analyse particular scare stories, we can note that there are two broad areas of threat that generate media health scares. Firstly, there are stories about harmful substances, practices or features of the environment that threaten health and safety. Stories of medical products gone wrong, contaminated food, or harmful natural events (climate, radiation) that may themselves be the consequence of human interference are examples and will be covered in the present chapter. Secondly, there are stories about people who are held responsible for damage to health and safety through evil, incompetent or thoughtless behaviour. Villainy is often best revealed by contrasts with the purity or innocence of victims, and here the identification by Altheide and Michalowski of children as a primary focus for anxieties about safety is significant. Children are a focus for media-fuelled concerns with health, as well as safety in general, and therefore feature large in both crime and health stories. Chapters 5 and 6 focus on villains and innocent victims in order to complete the coverage of media health scares. For the moment, though, we shall focus on stories that for the most part do not stress the direct effects of malevolent human agency, beginning with the coverage of food scares.

FOOD SCARES

The depiction of ordinary objects turning out to be dangerous is a popular device in tabloid television (Langer, 1998; see also Chapter 1) and in media generally. Thus the news value of the car crash where a safety barrier (supposed to save life) impales a driver, or the domestic fire caused by an activity as apparently innocent as using a frying pan. What could intensify this effect? The depiction of ordinary objects whose ingestion is essential for life, yet nevertheless reveal themselves as threats to life, presents a highly entertaining juxtaposition of opposites for the media health producer (second only, perhaps, to stories associating sex with disease). Additionally, food in recent years has been presented by a variety of media in increasingly pornographic terms as cookery programmes have turned away from the traditional approach of giving practical help with recipes, towards glossy magazine formats that provoke audiences' appetites with mouth-watering dishes. News about the dangers of food therefore attracts a good deal of media interest, creating a thrill of fear that can be compared with responses to similar news about the dangers of sex. Additionally, such stories enable the exploration of deeper themes of national identity and belonging since, in more senses than one, what we eat is what we are.

The British media coverage of two major food scares – salmonella in eggs and bovine spongiform encelphalopathy (BSE) ('mad cow disease') – has been rather well documented by media analysts, who have explored both the form and rhetorical features of the stories themselves as well as the conditions under which the stories were produced and received. Chronologically, the salmonella story preceded the BSE story, and it can also be understood as having set up a 'template' (Kitzinger, 2000) for subsequent BSE and other food scare stories. It was the first food scare to hit the British headlines since one in the 1960s that involved contamination of canned corned beef, and it led to a series of other such scares that have incorporated a variety of concerns about the industrialisation of food production and, more broadly, the environment. In part, too, as Miller and Reilly (1995) point out, changes in food journalism away from the exclusive focus on providing healthy recipes have created conditions under which stories about the politics of food are likely to attract attention. The growth of environmental pressure groups was partly responsible for this change, linked with generalised concerns about the ethical capacities of business interests and their associated scientific advisers, whose activities came increasingly to be distrusted in favour of media concern to be seen as championing consumer rights. Indeed, an important theme of the BSE scare has been the capacity of a critical media to position itself as the voice of ordinary people who have lost their faith in official expertise (Brookes, 2000).

Salmonella

Fowler's (1991) analysis of the salmonella story (and the related listeria story that developed in the late 1980s at around the same time) is instructive, suggesting that its development involved the incorporation of many other topics. Other dangerous organisms or substances (pesticide residues in cereals), concerns about food hygiene in public places, food production practices such as the feeding of animals with hormones, other kinds of 'poisoning' (for example, Legionnaires' disease) and eventually a whole spectrum of environmental concerns could be related to the core story. The effect of this was to enhance the symbolic resonance of salmonella in eggs, so that mention of the topic could stand for a range of other concerns about the way the world was going. This symbolic status in which the 'reality' of the problem was of secondary importance may be appreciated by noting that, after 1989, coverage of the story had died down to almost nothing, yet the number of cases of food poisoning in the country due to this agent actually increased from 12,931 in 1989 to 16,151 in 1990 (Eldridge, 1999: 124).

In particular, Fowler notes that coverage was 'hysterical in terms of its high emotive content, the massive scale of Press reporting and its extraordinary generalization to the "poisoning of our world"' (1991: 148). Triggered by mention of the high prevalence of salmonella infection in eggs by a junior government minister, the story grew exponentially in a classic press feeding frenzy. Fowler's close analysis of the language of the reports is effective in pointing out the clustering of words around the 'scare' theme: words like 'scare', 'anxiety', 'confusion, 'threat', and 'hazard' were used frequently. The bacteria themselves were treated as if they possessed cartoon-like personalities, being maliciously animated 'killer bugs' or 'germs' that 'invade', 'erupt' or 'penetrate' their hosts in their 'millions'. The 'housewife' was portrayed as the first line of 'defence' in the war on this enemy, but also as its first (somewhat sexualised) victim. Particular stress on the magnitude of the threat was achieved through the use of large numbers, the story providing many opportunities for counting things such as the number of cases of infection, of germs that could breed in a particular time period, of hens and eggs in the country, of eggs consumed per day, and so on. The argument that numerical estimates of the size of the problem ought to be upgraded due to 'under-reporting' by overcautious officials was also a theme to be found in numerous other scare stories (see later chapters of this book). It led to speculative statements whose chief feature was the use of very large numbers indeed ('The total figure could be as high as 2,500,000' (*Daily Telegraph*, quoted in Fowler, (1991: 167) as well as words to indicate growing numbers: 'grow', 'mount', 'jump', 'proliferation' and 'rampant rise'.

Terms common in press coverage such as 'the salmonella outbreak' or 'the egg crisis', Fowler argues, displace the name of the bacteria or the problem (salmonella, eggs) to the position of a 'subordinate modifier'. This arrangement, he says, 'is a good indication that the real subject of the discourse is not objective phenomena such as salmonella or eggs, but abstractions and subjective states such as crisis, danger, alarm' (1991: 172). Such formulaic linguistic patterns helped incorporate a diversity of other things as journalists seized the opportunity to generate linked stories. This meant that it became possible for the topic to be generalised, as in a *Daily Telegraph* reference to 'toxicity of chemicals in food, consumer products and the environment' or in the *Guardian*'s promiscuous listing of areas of life now implicated in the scare: 'changes in agriculture, food production, food technology, distribution, catering, and handling in the home' (1991: 178). On occasion, journalists demonstrated reflexive awareness of what they had been doing: 'a Pandora's box of food hygiene scares . . . have kept the headline writers busy in an otherwise dull political winter' (*Sunday Times*, quoted in Fowler, 1991: 174). Such episodes of ironic self-consciousness in non-tabloid outlets, in which the story-making itself becomes a 'story', function as minor 'twitches' (see Chapter 2 and Langer, 1998) to retain the interest of readers whose 'educated' identity might otherwise be threatened by total immersion in the rather pantomime-like proceedings of the scare story itself.

BSE

Analysing the political dynamics influencing the media production of both the salmonella and BSE stories in the British media, Eldridge (1999) notes that in both cases influence was sought by two opposing lobbies: that of food producers (farmers, agriculture officials) versus that of food consumers (represented at government level by health officials). The producer lobby 'won' in the case of salmonella, successfully mounting a claim to disparage the risk (leading to the dismissal of the government minister who had triggered the scare) and reducing coverage at a time when, as we saw earlier, infection cases were actually rising. A similar victory for producers (in spite of 'beef is safe' campaigns by the government in the early days) was not available in the case of BSE, where beef was eventually shown to be unsafe, and massive damage to the economic interests and reputations of food producers resulted. This was in part due to the press scenting a government 'cover-up', itself a good news story, when agriculture officials were cautious about issuing firm guidance because of underlying scientific uncertainty, and when food industry spokespeople decided that the best policy for calming things down was silence. Journalists then turned to other sources, including vets and dissident scientists, to fill the news vacuum, finding a plentiful source for scare stories in these. When, in 1996, after a lull of several years, the BSE story was revived by news of the government admission of a link with human CJD (Creutzfeld-Jakob disease) the producer lobby was finally and thoroughly discredited and the media/consumer voice vindicated.

Journalists sometimes like to claim, when faced with evidence of their own scaremongering, that audiences are really rather sensible and know how to distinguish serious scares from those that are purely aimed at entertainment. Perhaps in doing this they are encouraged by media audience theorists who argue against the assumption of direct effects. Thus Radford (1996), science editor of the *Guardian*, argued in a *Lancet* article that 'people are discerning and seem able to spot the dangerous rubbish, happy to be entertained and unlikely to be misled by the things that will really alter their lives' (1996: 1533). Evidence from the few studies that have been carried out on the effects of the BSE story, however, suggests otherwise.

Reilly (1999) has charted the effect of the BSE story on audiences, revisiting focus groups so that views before the final discrediting of the 'beef is safe' line could be compared with views after the events of 1996. In the initial 1992 BSE scare, Reilly found that most people dismissed it as 'crying wolf' in a way that Radford might recognise and students of active audience theory might celebrate as evidence of 'resistant' reading. Following from the salmonella in eggs story (where, as we saw, the producer lobby successfully discredited the scare), many people reported that they were simply tired of such warnings, additionally being somewhat reassured by government statements about the adequacy of anti-contamination measures. After the 1996 coverage of the link with CJD, though, many changed their views. For example, one man said in 1992:

> It's all a lot of nonsense really. I mean, to think that the government would allow us to be put at risk from such a thing is ridiculous. The media are just playing things up again and trying to scare us. I don't believe a word of it, and I certainly haven't stopped eating meat. (Quoted in Reilly, 1999: 131)

In 1996 the same man said:

> I couldn't believe it when I saw it on the TV. It was such a shock to think that all these years I'd completely believed that there was no risk because I thought it was all just a scare. I watched everything I could on the TV and realised that so much information was kept from us, that risks were taken with our health for purely economic reasons. I put everything with beef in it in the bin straight away and won't touch the stuff now. (Quoted in Reilly, 1999: 131)

Food scares, then, can be both resisted and accepted by media audiences, although most affect consumption patterns to some extent, as has been shown also by Wigand (1994), who has reviewed a number of parallel scares as well as the impact of nutritional advice in the US media. For example, a 1989 scare about the use of the chemical Alar on apples led to a decline in apple sales of more than 12 per cent, putting many orchard owners out of business. This was in spite of attempts to play down the size of the risk by the government agency that had unwittingly sparked the story when it had reported the effect of the chemical in huge doses on laboratory animals.

The BSE story, like the salmonella story, contained opportunities for the incorporation of a wide variety of other themes. Reilly, whose focus groups were conducted in Scotland, found that there were some individuals who based their dismissal of the scare on the grounds that BSE was an 'English disease'. As one man put it: 'we don't eat English beef' (quoted in Reilly, 1999: 143). Brookes (1999) has pursued the theme of nationalism in media coverage of BSE, observing that the crisis provided many opportunities for newspapers, in particular, to construct an imagined national community under threat. Through addressing readers as 'we' or 'us', newspapers like the *Sun* or the *Daily Mail*, Brookes feels, generate a sense of national togetherness. This reached xenophobic levels when European countries instituted a ban on the import of British beef, as evident in a 1996 *Sun* editorial:

> Anyone who believes British beef is less safe than French beef is crazy. We appear to have more cases of BSE because we are more honest about it ... If Brussels has the power to stop Britain from selling a product anywhere in the world, then we are no longer an independent sovereign nation with control over our own affairs. We are just one of the herd. John Bull has been neutered. (Quoted in Brookes, 1999: 260)

Food scares, then, contrast the innocent familiarity of routinely available substances essential for life, or which elsewhere are promoted by the media as sources of intense pleasure, with the prospect of hidden dangers lurking within these same substances. This basic juxtaposition of innocence and danger, routine and its disruption, pleasure and punishment, is effected by rhetorical devices that journalists use in a variety of contexts. Large numbers emphasise the size of dangers, as we saw in Fowler's account of the salmonella story (noted also by Brookes as features of media accounts of BSE). The glossy magazine coverage of the tempting dishes of food pornographers contrasts with images of cattle being incinerated. Oversimplification of complex scientific information in order to create unambiguous storylines is also a feature of such scare stories (noted by Eldridge [1999] and Wigand [1994]). We also see the phenomenon of initial stories (for example, salmonella) setting up 'templates' into which new stories can be fitted (BSE), as well as the incorporation of a number of themes that might otherwise have been considered extraneous to the original story, such as nationalism or generalised environmental issues, whose effects may have been to generate a sense of shared imagined community in viewers. The environment, of course, is potentially the source of a number of threats to health, and it is to such stories that we can now turn.

ENVIRONMENTAL DANGERS

Sociologists specialising in the study of health and illness often like to say that a narrowly biomedical perspective dominates the popular cultural discussion of illness causation, neglecting social and environmental causation. It is often implied that such bias, which involves an emphasis on individual rather than collective and politically challenging behaviour, is in the interests of a medical profession that is, in some loosely specified sense, implicated in an oppressive governmentality. This, for example, is the line taken by Karpf (1988) when she writes that her

> central argument is that, in spite of greater diversity in the media's reporting of health and medical issues over the past decade, medical definitions and perceptions still prevail, and squeeze out more contentious, oppositional viewpoints which take an environmental approach and look at the politics of health. (1988: 2)

Brown et al. (2001), in their study of US print media coverage of the causation of breast cancer, also pursue this line, arguing that a 'dominant epidemiological paradigm' keeps the focus of both press and scientific interest away from environmental causes, as well as deflecting attention from 'corporate and governmental responsibility' (2001: 747). Instead, genetic causes, or ones that involved individual responsibility for breast cancer, were stressed by frequent stories about, for example, the role of diet or the age at birth of the first child. Admitting that 'human studies of environmental pollutants and breast cancer have been mostly negative in the late 1990s' (2001: 749), they argue nevertheless that coverage of these ought to be given higher priority since breast cancer 'activists and committed scientists' (2001: 748) believe that future studies are likely to reveal environmental causes to be important.

Brown et al. are clearly influenced by pre-existing political commitments, thorough though their content analysis of media is. When general media coverage of environmental threats to health is considered, however, it becomes clear that this has become (perhaps increasingly since Karpf was writing) an important area for the stimulation of anxieties, and that this is associated with a media-sponsored critique of governmental authorities as well as commercial interests. Particular interest is shown by media producers in environmental threats that can be constructed as the result of human activities 'gone wrong', allowing powerful moral themes to be rehearsed. Floods, tornadoes and the like are rarely, then, simply 'natural' disasters, but the result of human interference with nature, often involving inadequate care exercised by people in authority.

Comparison of the reporting of different environmental threats has focused, like much of the literature on the communication of risk information, on purported inaccuracies. Thus Klaidman (1991) and Signorielli (1993) both say that such communications are rather inaccurate when it comes to environmental threats to health, concentrating on the dramatic and the sensational at the expense of risks that actually may affect more people, but are more boring for the media audience. Klaidman (1991), for example, complains that coverage of pesticide scares and nuclear power accidents is exaggerated when compared with the dangers of radon, which potentially affects many more people. The way in which statistical estimates are presented is often seen as being at fault for this, leading to such irrational behaviour as continuing to smoke while refusing to eat beef.

Bell's (1994) work on the reporting of climate change in the New Zealand media is a good example of work done with the identification of inaccuracy as a primary goal, and is revealing in demonstrating that biases are generally in the direction of increasing fear-provoking elements (although some inaccuracies, such as the conflation of ozone depletion with the 'greenhouse effect', were due to journalists' inadequate understanding of scientific complexity). Bell used a methodology common in this study genre: sending scientific and professional sources of news stories relevant news clippings and asking them to comment on their accuracy. In headlines, 'the main problem was overstatement' (1994: 263), so that the 'minute contribution of New Zealand's domestic refrigeration' was judged to be exaggerated by the headline 'Fridges Threatens Ozone Layer' (1994: 264). Overstatement, however, could sometimes be combined with other inaccuracies, such as misquotation, omission and distortion. Thus, the lead paragraph of one story stated alarmingly that 'New Zealand could face a water shortage similar to Israel's by 2030 if world temperatures continued to rise.' The original source of this story commented: 'The reference to Israel is quite extraordinary, since what I said is that the dry areas would need to learn to use their water more efficiently, just as Israel has done' (1994: 265). Significantly, Bell found that where units of measurement were misreported (for example, centimetres rather than millimetres), all were in the direction of exaggeration, and none in the direction of reduction. Bell concludes from this that 'inaccuracies are at base caused by the news values which journalists ... work by ... If the cause was purely technical, such inaccuracies would be similarly distributed between exaggeration and reduction' (1994: 271). Bell feels that scientists and journalists should work more closely together in order to reduce these errors, revealing a somewhat functionalist orientation to the problem of inaccuracy (see Chapter 3).

In a delightful commentary on media reports of the causation of childhood cancers by high-voltage power lines ('Fear of frying: power lines and cancer'), Chapman (2001) shows how exaggeration of fears leads to significant distortion. Media people who believe in this are 'like the plucky, armless black knight in Monty Python's *Quest for the Holy Grail*: they just won't give up' (2001: 682). Headlines like 'Pylons are cancer risk – official' (*Sunday Times*) and 'Power lines double cancer risk' (*Sydney Morning Herald*) contained, as Chapman puts it, 'one tiny problem-ette' (2001: 682), in that the report from the UK National Radiological Protection Board on which the story was based did not in fact support this interpretation, containing conclusions like 'such levels of exposure are seldom encountered by the general public' and 'it has not been possible to detect this increase'. Chapman reports that cancer agencies in Australia have received many calls from anxious parents as a result of the alarm, and observes that even the worst case scenario that can be extrapolated from the (inconclusive) report is that of three extra deaths in 50 years in a population the size of Australia. This compares with 10 childhood deaths every year that are caused by drowning, including those in unfenced residential pools. 'Would that these could get such headlines,' he concludes (2001: 682).

The reporting of adverse health effects arising from exposure to electromagnetic fields (EMFs), such as are emitted in the operation of ordinary household appliances, has been the subject of particular criticism in relation to the US media. This topic also reveals the role that 'rogue scientists' can play when their extreme views coincide with the need of media organisations to produce scare stories. Jauchem (1992) has documented the media reporting of Paul Brodeur's views on this topic, which began with a 1989 book and a series of articles in *The New Yorker* magazine, in which he stated his view that EMFs constitute a serious health hazard. Jauchem regrets the media's dissemination of these views and devotes the majority of his article to a point-by-point scientific refutation. Wartenberg and Greenberg (1992) are similarly critical of press coverage of this controversy in a survey of US national newspapers over a three-year period, in which the results of three epidemiological investigations detecting small effects of EMFs were reported. They identify a failure to place the risks of exposure to EMFs in the context of the risks of other kinds of exposure, a tendency to report the findings of the original investigators without critical evaluations from other scientists or from the journalists themselves, and a lack of advice on how to avoid or remedy exposure. Distortion of numerical information in favour of exaggeration is a feature that should be familiar to us by now. One news report stated:

[the investigator] found exceptionally high rates of breast cancer among male technicians who work on telephone switching equipment in central offices. Her study found two cases of breast cancer among 9500 central office technicians; ordinarily the incidence rate for males would be about 1 in one million, she said. (*New York Times*, quoted in Wartenberg & Greenberg, 1992: 387)

Wartenberg and Greenberg point out that epidemiological data would predict 1.4 such cases in the time period involved, a rate of two not representing a statistically significant excess.

Not all studies within the risk communication tradition, however, agree with the simple line that inaccuracies exist or that they should be corrected: Dunwoody and Peter (1992), for example, observe that such charges are often made by scientists who may themselves be biased and trying to influence the media agenda their way. Lichtenberg and Maclean (1991), while agreeing that coverage may be sensationalistic, note that it is unrealistic to expect media organisations to report on topics that make dull reading. The risk communication field, then, appears to be moving towards acceptance of such communication involving a social construction of reality. Such construction can be appreciated by understanding the conditions of media production. A case study by Mazur (1987) regarding coverage of the radon hazard is illuminating here.

Radon is a naturally occurring gas that, when it decays, produces radioactive elements that adhere to dust particles, which may be implicated in raised rates of lung cancer in areas where housing is built over concentrated sources. About 5,000–20,000 excess deaths from lung cancer occur per year in the US, Mazur reports, basing this on estimates from the Environmental Protection Agency (EPA). Coverage of this hazard in the media, though, is generally at a low level since the fact of causation has not been subject to significant dispute and there is no strong argument that a lot can be done about it. This scenario changed, however, in the mid-1980s when a series of incidents brought the issue into a prominent media position. Efforts had been made to alert media interest by a campaigning group in the early 1980s, but the triggering of radiation alarms by a nuclear power worker whose high dosage was found to have originated in his home rather than workplace provided the 'human interest' angle that sparked what was, initially, a local media interest and then a national one once the *New York Times* took up the story. Once politicians got involved, a feeding frenzy ensued as more and more stories could be related to radon. A national radon protection plan emerged, new legislation was passed, and controversy entered the picture in an entertaining way when residents of one area objected to contaminated soil being moved for temporary storage nearby, in transit to a more permanent dump in a remote area. Coverage of this 'dumping war' then proceeded apace, with nearly half of radon-related coverage in the *New York Times* being devoted to it in the second half of 1986. Mazur explains that the rise in coverage was the result of many factors converging, so that a hazard that was previously ignored was subsequently constructed as unusually dangerous, perhaps to the point where the 'real' level of threat radon represented was now being exaggerated.

'The environment', then, has been constructed by the media in recent years as a significant source of danger. Stories appear to work particularly well if some loosely specified human agency can be detected, often associated with official or expert sources, a popular theme being also the castigation of humans in general for their profligate or destructive use of technology. Thus the moral component of warnings about risk is highlighted in such stories. The radon story is unusual in this respect, being a 'naturally occurring' danger, and it required a special combination of circumstances (involving a loose parallel with the dangers of nuclear power, a 'scare' that involves human agency) to get prominent coverage. The threat of infectious disease also has great scare-carrying potential, which does not always require human agency (bugs and germs, after all, can be personified), although, as the next section shows, stories of this sort also run further when it is possible to implicate human error, malevolence or foolishness.

INFECTION

With the decline of infectious disease as a major cause of illness and death in affluent countries of the world, media stories about such illness inevitably evoke imagery from a somewhat mythicised past. Classically, this involves references to 'plague' in the attempt to evoke these distant folk memories, word about these threats spreading in part as media sponsored 'urban legends' (Weldon, 2001). Chronic infectious diseases that debilitate and weaken human hosts (for example, bilharzia and malaria) are not major news items in Western media, even though they are important in world health terms. Instead, media excitement is generated by dramatic events, however insignificant in epidemiological terms these may be, this involving a considerable degree of manufacture, as the brief but intense coverage in 1994 of the 'killer bug' that causes necrotising fasciitis shows.

Killer bugs

Military metaphors reify 'germs' or 'bugs' as malevolent entities threatening media audiences, who are thereby encouraged to mobilise defences in a state of apprehension and alarm. These may be combined with the gothic themes common in horror or science fiction stories. Gwyn (1999) has charted the necrotising fasciitis story in these terms, noting the use of maps to chart the spread of the bug (like military campaign maps), and the addition of horror film imagery in the form of 'a creeping, flesh-eating superbug, which literally devours its victims, killing them within hours' (*Today* quoted in Gwyn, 1999: 338–9). A few headlines convey the flavour of this coverage:

Independent:	'Killer bug may become even more virulent'
Sun:	'Curse of the killer virus'
	'It devours in 1 hour flat'
Guardian:	'Return of the killer bug'
Daily Telegraph:	'Flesh-eating bug claims sixth victim'
Express:	'Squad to beat killer bug'

(adapted from Gwyn, 1999: 338)

Two newspapers (*The Times* and the *Sun*) appealed to readers 'not to panic' while at the same time encouraging readers to do just that. Thus the *Sun* stressed that 'the bug is a mutant strain', one version of which has 'no known cure and can get into water supplies' (quoted in Gwyn, 1999: 241). Medical authorities did their best to calm down the scare, but for a short while the feeding frenzy was irresistible. A journalist caught up in it conveys the atmosphere of the newsroom:

> I felt a bit like Peter O'Toole playing Lawrence of Arabia in that scene when the Bedouin suddenly charge off and massacre the retreating Turks, shouting no, and oh god, and don't, and then thinking what the hell and getting out the sword and digging in the spurs. Thinking the harder we went for it the sooner it would be over. I was right. Within about 3 days someone from the features department wandered up and said wasn't everybody making too much fuss about necrotising fasciitis; weren't there many more serious diseases to worry about?' (Quoted in Radford, 1996: 1534)

In fact, the extremism of press behaviour could then itself become a 'story' in some media outlets – particularly those appealing to an educated audience and reminiscent of the similar 'twitch' in food scare stories (see above). Thus the *Guardian* (28 May 1994) ran a piece listing a number of other more common yet troubling diseases that received no media cover-age. This theme began to link up with efforts of medical officials, as where *The Times* quoted the government Chief Medical Officer saying he was 'doubtful that some of the cases reported in the media were *necro-tizing fasciitis* and [he] repeated that nationwide figures had not exceeded the normal incidence' (quoted in Gwyn, 1999: 342).

In another development of the story, the *Today* newspaper compared unfavourably the research effort devoted to necrotising fasciitis with the much larger amount of government money being spent on AIDS research at the time, suggesting that this was because 'The Government has let itself be browbeaten by the militant gay lobby, with its powerful, politi-cally correct pals' (quoted in Gwyn, 1999: 343). Compared with necrotising fasciitis, AIDS contains particular opportunities for stigmati-sation, as will be shown in Chapter 5. Human agency in the form of 'carriers' of necrotising fasciitis could not be so readily constructed as it was for AIDS and this, together with the consistent medical line that in fact the infection was not a serious problem in epidemiological terms, meant that this scare was relatively short-lived.

Just as food scares juxtapose in a poignant tension something desir-able – indeed, essential for life – with the prospect of this same thing turning dangerous, so sexually transmitted infections are used in media stories to demonstrate the dangerousness of human desires. At the same time, though, it is obvious that the pleasures of sex are commonly dis-played in media outlets of all sorts. This area of media has been subjected to considerable analysis and the field cannot be summarised here, but one consistent finding that is of relevance to media health deserves mention: sexual activity is commonly portrayed as having few health-damaging effects. In order to concentrate attention on the pleasurable side of life, sex is therefore made 'unrealistic' in this sense and this has attracted the condemnation of media critics concerned to promote health education goals who believe that audiences directly adopt such media messages.

Thus, for example, a variety of studies monitoring the portrayal of sex in US television soaps have been summarised by Greenberg and Woods (1999). The incidence of sexual activity in these programmes has increased over the past few decades as media producers have exploited relaxations in censorship, in part fuelled by the proliferation of interna-tionally available television channels. Above all, heterosexual activity between unmarried people is portrayed in soaps. Lowry and Towles's (1989) and Sapolsky and Tabarlet's (1991) studies of US prime-time tele-vision have shown similar patterns, also noting that portrayal of contraception is rare. All these analysts have found that sexually trans-mitted diseases are rarely portrayed as a consequence of sex, although

Olson (1994) detected occasional discussions of safe sex practices in US television soaps, whereas a decade before there has been none. In a rare study of the effects of these portrayals, Greenberg and Woods (1999) found that viewers' estimates of how frequently people have sex rise as a result of these programmes. An associated concern has been that of Zillmann (2000) with the potential of mediated erotica to create high levels of sexual callousness in viewers.

While sex is portrayed, in general, as a danger-free area, this is sharply reversed when sexually transmitted diseases and infections are the focus of media stories. The unreality of sexual pleasures, it seems, is then contrasted with an equally unreal opposition: the idea that all sex could be dangerous. The AIDS story (covered in detail in Chapter 5) is an obvious candidate for this, containing the additional theme of the extraordinary dangers of 'abnormal' sex. Yet the AIDS story has been shown to build on previously popular images and themes, in particular by Gilman (1988), who points out the continuity between AIDS imagery and that of syphilis in the nineteenth century. Gilman also notes that media interest in herpes shortly before the explosion of interest in AIDS enabled the rehearsal of many of the themes that were eventually to be fully developed in the AIDS story, chief amongst which was the capacity for these diseases to frighten people about the free expression of sexuality that elsewhere in the media they were encouraged to embrace.

Genital herpes, Gilman argues, was treated during the 1970s as a possible replacement candidate for syphilis as a primary symbol indicating the dangers of unbridled sexuality, images of which had occupied a prominent place in popular culture for centuries until the 'taming' of the disease by antibiotics. But because the symptomatology of herpes was 'too trivial to warrant this association over the long run' (1988: 258), it dropped out of the picture when AIDS came along. All the same, media organisations, as in the case of necrotising fasciitis, did their best to boost what could have been an insignificant story to public prominence. Mirotznick and Mosellie (1986) and Roberts (1997) have both described the progress of the herpes story in the US media, analysing magazine and newspaper coverage. The massive rise in coverage between March 1982 and February 1983, argue Mirotznick and Mosellie, was accompanied by six types of inaccuracy, all of which were in the direction of sensationalising the reports. Firstly, the idea that herpes had reached epidemic proportions was a recurrent claim, so that news of an 'alarming epidemic' that had 'erupted' in a 'runaway increase' was accompanied by the use of the largest numbers that could be extracted from fairly flimsy anecdotal data and somewhat limited epidemiological studies.

Secondly, Mirotznick and Mosellie note that the disease was

constructed as one that particularly affected the middle classes, a story originally derived from a single survey of members of herpes self-help groups rather than a random sample representative of the population. In my own experience I have found that the claim that social problems affect people from 'all walks of life' is a common journalistic device to exaggerate the level of threat that a problem poses. Such claims are generally based on unsophisticated surveys, or incorrect interpretations of good surveys, the journalist ignoring evidence of differential rates in social groups, for example. In this case, the distortion appears to have occurred in spite of better evidence pointing to the opposite conclusion: serological surveys showing the prevalence to be higher in lower socio-economic groups. The claim to be a 'middle-class' disease, of course, brings the problem closer to 'home', since the majority of readers are likely to identify themselves with this group in a media world where the 'working' or 'upper' class lives are usually constructed as exotic.

Thirdly, coverage exaggerated the physical effects of the disease, even to the point of its being portrayed as life-threatening. Thus a piece in *Newsweek* suggested that an episode involved 'so much fever and pain that [one] had to go to bed . . . It was like scraping your knee and someone putting salt in it' (quoted in Roberts, 1997: 277). The 'incurable' nature of the disease was often stressed, the repetitive usage of this term eventually acquiring connotations of terminal disease. Roberts found only one passage in 99 articles which seriously challenged the image of a pain-racked experience, so that 'the preferred reading was that the herpetic body had been transformed from a locus of hedonistic sensual gratification to an orgy of pain' (1997: 278).

The other three features of herpes coverage identified by Mirotznick and Mosellie relate to the psychological reactions of herpes sufferers and those at risk of the disease. Firstly, the depiction of sufferers implied that the disease was psychologically devastating, rather than the minor irritant that it actually is for most people. Once again, evidence for this was based on anecdotes and self-selected samples of people who had had particularly bad experiences of the illness. Thus a sufferer was quoted in one magazine article: 'For the first year that I had herpes, I was essentially depressed the whole time. My attitude focused entirely on herpes – it became the center of my life' (quoted in Roberts, 1997: 276). Condemned otherwise to a gloomy group life in herpetic support groups, some sufferers were portrayed as taking a vengeful way out, deliberately infecting others: 'Some people act out their fantasies of revenge,' a *Time* article claimed, citing 'A Midwestern woman [who] says she has infected 75 men in three years' (quoted in Mirotznick & Mosellie, 1986: 8). People free of the infection were depicted as fearfully reconstructing their behaviour. The overall effect of this fear-inducing coverage was indeed to promote a paranoid culture of surveillance and exclusion, reflected in a string of stories about parents demanding the exclusion of children with cold sores from school.

The herpes story is instructive in showing the constructed nature of media-fuelled panics about infection. Anyone with even a cursory familiarity with the media coverage of AIDS will be able to detect direct parallels. Both herpes and AIDS have been effective symbols of the dangerousness of sexual promiscuity, replacing syphilis in a chronological sequence. The herpetic character, as Roberts points out, was either a stereotypically 'promiscuous' person, who therefore could be seen to have brought the disease upon himself or herself, or someone who had once, but disastrously, made a 'single mistake'; this is familiar territory for those conversant with the distinction between the 'guilty' and the 'innocent' in AIDS stories. The seriousness of herpes as a disease, though, is so clearly of such lesser magnitude that we can now look back on this coverage and perceive the features of press treatment that contributed to the hyperbolic effect, which were later to be deployed with far greater force in the case of AIDS. This new disease made the herpes story redundant, so that the absence of media coverage would seem to indicate that a disease that was once so devastating no longer exists.

Cancer as 'infection'

The final case study in this section on infectious disease is cancer, which is not in fact an infectious disease but which has at various points in time been constructed as if it were one. The key device that has enabled this to occur is that of metaphor, and in particular the use of military metaphors involving invasion and spread, as has been famously pointed out by Sontag (1991), who showed the parallels between images of cancer and TB (which is an infectious disease) and later applied the same logic to popular representations of AIDS. Sontag argued that:

> The disease . . . arouses thoroughly old-fashioned kinds of dread. Any disease that is treated as a mystery and acutely enough feared will be felt to be morally, if not literally, contagious. (1991: 6)

Treating cancer as if it were an enemy invasion, declaring war on cancer cells, invoking battle imagery in descriptions of treatment and, finally, equating cancer with death itself, are themes that have permeated the popular culture of cancer according to Sontag. Studies of media representations provide considerable support for this view (though not in all respects, for which see Seale, 2001a, and Chapter 8). Historically, women's magazines have been shown (Black, 1995) to have participated in the popular idea that cancer is in fact contagious up until the 1930s, though direct claims of this in such media outlets were not made in the post-war years. In general, though, the elevation of cancer as the disease to be feared above all others has involved the media in cultivation of the idea that everything, potentially, causes cancer, as well as exaggeration of the extent to which it causes death, so that cancer has been constructed at the very least as a 'contagion', in a sense similar to that of a miasmatic cloud permeating everyday objects, from which the disease may be 'caught'.

Sontag herself criticised the popular conception of cancer as being caused almost entirely by environmental damage associated with modern indus-trialised societies, yet this mythology is quite persistent in media accounts. This perspective is fuelled by media-wise environmentalist organisations such as Greenpeace, who use fear of cancer as a way of raising concerns about a variety of ecological threats (Driedger & Eyles, 2001). Greenberg et al. (1979) found in a survey of 50 major US daily newspapers that over 800 carcinogenic substances were mentioned across 700 news items in a three-month period in 1977. While smoking constituted 15 per cent of these mentions, equal coverage was given to pesticides, insecticides, water pollutants and food additives 'even though the evidence linking these other substances to cancer may be less conclusive and their impact on cur-rent cancer incidence rates far less important' (1979: 652). Headlines often seemed to suggest, these authors conclude, that 'everything causes cancer' (1979: 652). In this and in another report from this study (Bratic & Greenberg, 1979), the authors note further an emphasis on dying rather than coping with cancer, and an underemphasis on what individu-als can do to control their risk of getting cancer, in favour of articles depicting uncontrollable risks or showing risks that are only amenable to government action (for example, radiation risks).

A later study of US newspapers in 1980 (Freimuth et al., 1984) found similarly that stories about dying from cancer predominated, and noted that approximately half of the headlines for the 1,466 stories were judged to be 'fear-arousing', examples being 'No Way To Avoid Cancer-Causing Agents' and 'Tap Water Linked to Cancer' (1984: 70). Where drugs, chemicals, additives in cosmetics, household cleaners, clothing, pesticides, and air and water pollutants were mentioned in articles, 60 per cent of associated headlines were judged to be fear-arousing. Clarke (1986), in a study of US and Canadian magazines between 1961 and 1984, followed trends over time in the extent to which cancer was equated with death, finding a decline during 1961–65, in which 74 per cent of articles associated death with cancer, to a figure of 61 per cent by 1976–80, though still concluding that this was an inappropriately high proportion. She also noted a 'promiscuous listing of innumerable possible causes for cancer', ranging from 'Chlorination Threat?' to 'Breast Cancer and Virus' (1986: 189).

Breast cancer has been selected for special media treatment in recent years, most studies showing that it is reported in the media much more frequently than might be expected from epidemiological prevalence data (see Seale, 2001a, for a review). An account given by Lantz and Booth (1998) of the social construction of breast cancer as an 'epidemic' goes some way to explaining this. These authors point out that epidemiological data did show a 30 per cent increase in incidence during the 1980s and 1990s, but that this was largely an artefact of improved mammography screening, meaning that more cases came to medical attention at an early stage in the disease. Predictably, Lantz and Booth find in their study of popular US magazine articles between 1980 and 1995 that media coverage focused on the supposed increase rather than the artefact explanation. They chart a 'tremendous increase' (1998: 912) in the incidence of articles on breast cancer during the study period, with 52 per cent involving mention of the increase in breast cancer incidence. Where increased screening was mentioned as a possible cause of this, the majority of articles gave this as one of many possible explanations. Thus the increase was portrayed as 'mysterious' and 'alarming' rather than, as Lantz and Booth feel, 'fairly well understood' (1998: 913) by the artefact explanation. Phrases such as a 'disease that is out of control', 'mysterious reasons', 'insidious rise' and 'unexplained upsurge' are judged by Lantz and Booth to be 'dramatic, sensational [and] frightening' (1998: 912). A bias towards stories of breast cancer in younger, white women (also found in other studies of breast cancer in the media) was a further distortion, clearly designed to increase the relevance of the pieces for the readership.

The danger with this exaggeration of risk, these authors feel, is that as incidence apparently declines when the effects of screening programmes 'catch up' with the statistics, journalists and readers may believe that the supposed 'epidemic' is in decline, thus relaxing such sensible precautions against breast cancer as can be taken (such as mammography itself). Johnson (1997) has found that frequent readers of articles on breast cancer in magazines are more scared of the disease than people who do not read these pieces. In this climate, media reporting of the deaths of celebrities from breast cancer can result in sharp increases in anxiety (Boudioni et al., 1998). The epidemic of breast cancer fear that has been fuelled by such media reports has raised other concerns. Press et al.

(2000), for example, worry that decisions consequent on genetic testing for a propensity for the disease will be adversely affected (towards excessive rates of prophylactic mastectomies, for example). Whiteman et al. (2001) have misgivings about excess media reports of scientific studies showing positive links between hormone replacement therapy (HRT) and breast cancer, which ignore studies that show no such link.

The treatment of infectious diseases, or the construction of some diseases as 'epidemics', draws on deeply rooted folk memories. Infections also allow horror film imagery in the form of evil, predatory bugs to be mixed with science fiction images of monstrous invasion, as the 'killer bug' tale of necrotising fasciitis shows. If the threat can be constructed as arising from a basic human pleasure, such as the desire for sex, themes of innocence and blame can be rehearsed to provide entertaining effect, as the example of herpes demonstrates. The imagery of epidemic invasion, threatening loss of control as defences are overwhelmed by the forces of death, can be recruited in order to construct non-infectious diseases as infectious, generating profound fears about survival in a world perceived to contain hidden dangers about which very little can be done, as the case of cancer, and particularly breast cancer, shows. Later chapters of this book will show that scares are commonly juxtaposed with tales of rescue and security, but such rescue is not always readily at hand. Chapter 7 will show that those charged with saving people from health threats can be portrayed, from time to time, as the source of threat themselves, adding to the climate of fear that is the first move in the fear–security couplet. In the next section I turn to the part the media plays in the arousal of fear about the direct harm done by medical and scientific activities gone wrong.

MEDICAL AND SCIENTIFIC ACTIVITY

The portrayal of scientists in popular films has been dominated by Frankenstein-like imagery, stressing the dangers of science more frequently than its benefits. In one review of 1,000 horror films made between 1931 and 1984 (Frayling, 2000), 31 per cent featured mad scientists or their creations as villains and 39 per cent of the threats depicted were produced by scientific research. Of 6,000 films reviewed in *Variety* up to 1993, Frayling reports that fewer than 20 depicted real-life scientists in (usually positive) 'biopics'. For the most part, obsessionality combined with excessive ambition was commonly depicted as leading to failed and dangerous experiments, requiring ordinary people (or their military representatives) to mobilise every available resource of courage to overcome them. *Jurassic Park* is a classic example of such a film, depicting the disastrous consequences of genetic engineering in combination with the crazy fixations of an ideologue dreamer (who is suitably devoured by his creations in a final scene of retribution). Biopics of scientists, while portraying the benefits of science in idealistic terms, nevertheless portray their heroes in obsessional terms, as sacrificing normal human relationships for their calling. The magical power of science for good, or more often evil, is thus stressed in lurid tales that feed the fears of audiences.

Turning to media reports of 'real-life' scientific activity, and the medical sphere in particular, it appears that these contain similarly monstrous creations. We saw in Chapter 3 how the breast implant story perpetuated gender stereotypes; the story was also an opportunity for audiences to contemplate 'implanted' bodies gone wrong. Artificial substances lodged deep beneath human tissue could be imagined, and were sometimes shown, to be scarring and leaking through the body's surface, juxtaposing beauty and ugliness in poignant opposition. The breast implant story prompted much anxiety in women (Anderson & Larson, 1995), and the same is true for coverage of the harmful effects of another quasi-medical product in the toxic shock syndrome story. Here, tampons were implicated in the development of a life-threatening infection, whose symptoms include 'the sudden onset of high fever, vomiting, shock, body rash and peeling skin' (Cheek, 1997: 185). Cheek's (1997) analysis of the Australian media coverage of this issue between 1979 and 1995 reveals some similarities between this and the sensational treatment of necrotising fasciitis. Thus the causative bacterium was described in a variety of magazine and newspaper articles as a 'killer germ' and 'death in a packet' that 'sounds hideous and it is'; other terms were a 'horrible disorder', 'shocked', 'shocking' and 'scary' (quoted in Cheek, 1997: 186). Irwin and Millstein (1982) showed that US coverage resulted in significantly decreased usage of tampons amongst adolescents, the population at greatest risk of the disease.

Periodic 'pill panic' stories about the dangers of contraceptive pill usage have also been demonstrated to create significant changes in levels of anxiety and behaviour, including raised rates of unplanned pregnancies reflected in abortion rates. Thus Wellings (1986) reports on a 1983 panic resulting from coverage of two *Lancet* papers suggesting links with cancer, judged by Wellings to be part of a 'long line of epidemiological studies which have sometimes produced quite contradictory and conflicting findings in the past two decades' (1986: 109). A report published a week earlier in another medical journal suggesting a protective effect of the pill on breast cancer received a single mention in the UK national press; the 'bad news' papers, by contrast, generated 34 articles in the national press and 161 in local papers. While much of the reporting Wellings judges to have been of 'a fairly high standard' (1986: 110), in that the findings were not generally presented as definitive, the mention of a link with cancer, because of the independently fearsome reputation of this disease, she feels to have been inflammatory. Where numbers to indicate risk were reported, these were usually accurate, but did not include estimates of relative risk (for example, juxtaposing the raised risk of cancer with the risks of abortion or pregnancy). As with reports of sexually transmitted diseases (for which see earlier in this chapter), a note of moral retribution entered some reports. For example, the *Belfast Telegraph* stated 'there will be those who'll believe that it's the wrath of God finally bearing down on the promiscuous' and the *Sunday Telegraph* contained similar sentiments, beginning with 'Perhaps it is puritanical, but . . .' (quoted in Wellings, 1986: 110).

The scare did not result in raised rates of health service consultations by worried women, which Wellings feels is due to initial reports being quickly followed by media reports of official 'don't panic' messages, which led women to believe that such consultations would be regarded negatively. Opinion poll data, though, showed that many women's anxieties had been raised, and the rate of pill prescription dropped by 14 per cent. Subsequent abortion rate data show a 'particularly marked' (1986: 113) peak which, on further investigation, was entirely due to an increase in abortions in the age group identified in the press reports as the one most likely to suffer adverse effects from pill usage.

Wellings refers to similar impacts of past pill scares, and it is clear that this is a story that surfaces periodically. Allison et al. (1997), for example, report on the increased levels of disquiet experienced by women as a result of an October 1995 'pill alert' in the UK press, reporting a link with thromboembolism. Hammond (1997) reports on both this story – which involved the familiar 'panic' message – and one in 1996 regarding links with breast cancer, which, by contrast, was dominated by 'don't panic' messages. Assessing explanations for the difference, Hammond puts this down to handling of the news release by government sources. The 1995 story was released in an emergency press conference at the Department of Health, with inadequate accompanying reassurances about the small size of the risk and warnings to doctors that this news was about to break arriving too late. Pini (1995) explains that this sequence of events arose from official fears that news of the study had leaked to the press before an agreed embargo date. A health correspondent describes how this led to front-page hyperbole:

I had to ring the newsdesk and tell them the strength of this story, which I thought was huge. I said at the time and subsequently nobody disagreed, this should be on the front page; it's the main story of the day . . . and then everybody starts jumping up and down as they do in newsrooms and wanting to make it a huge story. Then it was part of an exercise of rowing back and trying to stress just how small the additional risk was. But of course by then the news editors, and the editors, and the backbench, and all the people that really run the paper get less and less interested in caveats, and more and more interested in health alerts. (Mihill, quoted in Hammond, 1997: 65)

The 1996 story originated as a leak as well, but this was to the *Sunday Times*, a paper which for a variety of complex reasons, concerning its editorial control and general line, many journalists at the time distrusted. Additionally, government sources moved rapidly to stress that the original study had also found beneficial effects of the pill (protecting against ovarian and endometrial cancer, for example, which successfully dampened the flames of press interest.

The imagery of injection contains considerable potential for fantasies about invasion by harmful substances, made particularly poignant if children are involved. In the case of vaccine scare stories, press interest has been fuelled in recent years by the lobbying of pressure groups, organised to oppose mass immunisation campaigns by public health authorities. Leask and Chapman (1998) report a study of 40 months of press coverage in Australia, focusing on the kinds of argument ('discourses') that were put forward to oppose immunisation. These included accusations of official covering up of evidence about adverse effects; a view that this was the result of an unholy alliance for profit, or an aspect of totalitarianism; a 'back to nature' theme; and a view that vaccines are 'poisonous chemical cocktails' (1998: 17). The anti-vaccine movement, many public health representatives claim (for example, Begg et al., 1998), paradoxically gains particular force from the fact that past immunisation rates have led to a decline in the incidence of, for example, measles, mumps and rubella (MMR), so that people are less often exposed to their adverse consequences. Begg et al. document a 1 per cent drop in MMR vaccine coverage resulting from a media scare about a report of possible links with Crohn's disease (subsequently felt to be unfounded), and show data designed to counter the anti-vaccination case, demonstrating raised death rates from measles in European countries with low vaccination coverage, and recalling the 100-fold increase in death rates in some countries from pertussis, following media reports that lowered the uptake of vaccination for the disease.

CONCLUSION

As with coverage of food, environmental and infectious disease issues, stories about the harmful potential of medical and scientific products contain considerable potential for creating scares. News and current affairs reports may invoke imagery that is shared with the more lurid treatments available in horror movies, which themselves have mined a rich source of themes that involve mad scientists, monstrous creations, and experiments gone wrong, commonly followed by attempts at heroic rescue. While most of the evidence reviewed in this chapter relates to the content of media stories, some reveals underlying production processes and some provides evidence that, on the whole, scary stories do indeed generate fear and influence behaviour in the negative ways imagined by those who criticise such portrayals. However, researchers have not made great efforts to seek out other aspects of audience responses that relate to divergent readings, pleasurable excitement through the courting of risk, or the role that scares might play in the moral regulation of audiences' imagined communities.

The scares reviewed in this chapter are those that do not involve malevolent agency on the part of the creators of the various products shown to do harm. Rather, they are constructed as mistakes, the unpredicted consequences of excessive human ambition or greed, at times made worse by bungling officials seeking to cover their tracks, or by business representatives seeking to deny evidence of harm, thus delaying the progress of rescue efforts. The imputation of purposely harmful intent adds an extra dimension to scare stories, and this is the subject of the next chapter, which concerns the identification of villains and freaks whose sinister purpose in causing destruction is felt to be a much more naked affair, resulting in media-orchestrated calls for retribution, and relating more directly to the construction of an imagined community of viewers encouraged to identify boundaries between self and other.

5 Villains and Freaks

Ideologues who take on the task of forming imagined communities, shaping these for tribes, races or nations, have generally found their burden considerably eased when they can find an enemy that is safe to hate. Sentiments of this sort and the events to which they give rise (wars, massacres, oppressive colonial systems, and so on) litter the pages of history books, and the group psychology that is involved in racism, xenophobia, we-versus-us talk, and designation of the Other is well understood (Seale, 1995b). The urge to stigmatise is also generally condemned in official morality as leading to divisiveness and suffering, so that the interesting feature of our present time is perhaps not so much the progress of various regimes of hatred, but the fortunes of stigma champions who argue for the reversal of basic urges towards violent feeling, in favour of more enlightened, inclusive and tolerant sentiments that recognise universal human rights. Pity may then replace hatred, itself containing weak currents of stigmatisation and stereotyping, but having the potential for including the pitied in the imagined community. Thus there is an appeal to a sense of membership in a generalised 'human race', sustained by a loose sense of what it is to be counted as normal.

Media health representations reflect the difficulties that are generally experienced when trying to create a sense of imagined community that potentially includes the entire human race. Such inclusiveness appears to be, in fact, an impossible task; it is an aspiration, rhetorically invoked by media representatives as an ideal at certain moments, but in practice rarely reached. Media health representations alternate, then, between the construction and deconstruction of stigmatised categories, often allowing for popular feelings of anger at some group to be aired for a while, or in certain areas of the media, only to be restrained by official moral pronouncements urging greater tolerance. Media analysts themselves are often implicated in this cycle, commonly as stigma champions, pointing out the bad behaviour of the press or television with regard to some unfortunate group, often couched in terms of a generalised lament about inaccuracy and its assumed direct effect on audiences. While this has led to some new insights into media behaviour, it can also become pretty repetitive when a social issue inspires particularly strong passions. The case of AIDS in the media reflects all of the above considerations, so this chapter will begin with an account of this, before moving on to consider representations of people with mental troubles, disabled people and others with unusual bodies, and elderly persons. These have all been subject to particularly powerful forms of media stereotyping, as well as impassioned arguments for the reversal of this. It will become clear that while these topics have ensured the media a steady supply of villains and troublemakers to add to the scare stories reviewed in the last chapter, none of them have been without their champion. It is only when the most innocent are considered that the most irremediably wicked also appear – an enemy that is truly safe to hate – and that will be the subject of the chapter that follows this one.

AIDS

After the disappointing performance of the herpes story (see Chapter 4), AIDS provided an ideal opportunity for media imagery that could replace syphilis as the disease to represent a moral warning about the dangers of free sexuality. Indeed, it surpassed syphilis in this respect, since injecting drug users could also be included in the list of stigmatised people, as well as the sexually deviant. The contours of stigmatising media coverage were subjected to a fierce critique that itself gained considerable media publicity. Thus AIDS provided an opportunity both to construct villains and to counteract and debate these constructions as media analysts themselves became players in this drama. The story also reveals that an analysis of effects based on logical extrapolation from the media messages themselves was inadequate in picking up some 'unintended' and sometimes quite health-promoting effects. I first summarise work from around the world that emphasised the stigmatising messages constructed in media reports, assuming that these had direct negative impact on audiences, before turning to analyses that claim a more complex picture.

Stigmatising coverage

The media treatment of AIDS is unusually well documented across a variety of Western countries, revealing considerable similarity from one place to the next. Firstly, the disease became an opportunity to heap oppro-brium on the gay community for generating a 'gay plague'. Thus Wellings's (1988) analysis of the first two years of reporting in the British media found that up to 1984 the term 'gay plague' was a virtually universal descriptor across all sections of the press. Stories of heterosexual trans-mission, and the possibility of an African origin, only began to appear in British tabloids in March 1985. The stigmatisation of gay male sexuality has been documented in some detail by Watney (1997), whose judge-ment of this is given below:

> Sympathy goes to mothers and children, to haemophiliacs and those who contracted Aids through blood transfusions which were contaminated before the virus was even isolated. But for gay men with Aids there seems nothing but hatred, fear, and a thinly veiled contempt. The British media cares as much about our health as *Der Stürmer* cared about that of the Jews in the 1930s. This is especially wicked . . . as one friend of mine with Aids describes it, the emotional resources needed in trying to repair one's immune system are all too often used up in defensive measures against the surrounding incendiaries of hysteria. (1997: 4)

Wellings found that deaths of heterosexuals were reported in much greater individual detail than had been the deaths of homosexuals in the early stages of the disease. A distinction between innocent and guilty vic-tims of the disease was constructed. Thus a *Daily Express* story about a schoolchild with AIDS was headlined 'Why must the innocent suffer?'; a *Sunday Telegraph* journalist wrote revealingly: 'Of course people should not be persecuted or blamed for catching AIDS, because that is vindictive and uncharitable and anyway, it *can* be caught *innocently*' (quoted in Wellings, 1988: 87; emphasis added). The category of the 'innocent' was further emphasised by including only those who had contracted the dis-ease through non-sexual routes (for example, haemophilia). Where HIV was acquired through sexual contact, the moral reputation of the person was adjusted accordingly. Thus Wellings records that the death of a nun working with prostitutes in Haiti, who had a single sexual contact while there, was designated as that of a 'vice work nun' by one paper and 'red light nun' by another (1988: 89). Perhaps most telling was *The Times* headline, in which a sub-editor's Freudian slip resulted in calling the disease 'acquired *immoral* deficiency disease' (1988: 95).

Along with the usual exaggerations of the numbers involved or pre-dicted to be involved, British media outlets also enhanced scare stories by making the disease seem easy to catch from everyday objects and routines. The result, Wellings notes, was a public afraid of 'insect bites, shared cups and cutlery, swimming pools, kissing and shaking hands as possible sources of infection' (1988: 97). The finding, in laboratory conditions, that the virus could, with difficulty, be isolated in saliva led to headlines such as 'Kiss of Death' (*News of the World* quoted in Wellings, 1988: 97). Just as herpes had led to calls for schoolchildren with cold sores to be banned from school, so fears about HIV-positive people employed in food preparation, medicine and dentistry were fuelled by media reports.

In France, the media coverage was similar. Herzlich and Pierret (1989) analysed French press coverage between 1982 and 1986, identifying an early phase in which the cause of the disease was a mystery, at which time terms like 'homosexual pneumonia', 'homosexual syndrome' or 'gay cancer' emerged. AIDS came to be represented as the outcome of membership of high-risk groups and this easily translated into punitive attitudes towards homosexuals in some press reports, although others stood back from this and reflected on the topic of such stigmatisation itself, reporting the efforts of celebrities, for example, in campaigning for AIDS awareness and sympathy for its victims. Jones (1992) reports similar currents in German popular magazines during 1986–90, noting that prostitutes and drug addicts took over from gay men as hate figures from 1987 onwards. Such people, Jones found, were rarely quoted in press reports; interest in subjectivity instead focused on the fears of male clients of prostitutes, or on the parents of small children who found and played with discarded injecting equipment. German media also gave considerable space to discussion of hard-line policies of exclusion, quarantine, compulsory blood testing and the like. At the same time, some space was given to letters and views expressed by gay activists and reports of street protests aimed at countering stigmatisation.

The treatment of AIDS in the Australian media has been thoroughly documented by media analysts (Brown et al., 1996; Lupton, 1993a, 1994a; Tulloch & Lupton, 1997). Lupton (1993a, 1994a) notes a shift from anti-gay prejudice to a more generalised concern with the regulation of sexuality from the 1990s onwards. By the late 1980s, Lupton notes, the dramatic qualities of AIDS coverage had largely been lost as the story became routine. There was therefore a shift from 'gay plague' stories to more generalised warnings about the dangers of promiscuity, associated with moralistic overtones about the desirability of marriage and monogamy. Thus headlines included 'Matrimony is back in fashion', 'Promiscuity now a dirty word' and 'Back to old virtues' (1993a: 320). Lupton concludes:

> AIDS discourse in the Australian press has drawn upon . . . prevailing notions of blame and sin, of risk as a moral concept, casting those who became infected sexually or by injecting drugs as villains who are worthy of little sympathy because of their irresponsibility. (1993a: 325)

A case study of Australian media coverage of a doctor–patient contact, tracing investigation done in response to the discovery of a doctor as HIV positive, shows how themes of guilt and innocence are rapidly deployed to create stigmatised categories. Brown et al. (1996) examined all press and television coverage of this incident, which happened in 1994 when the patients of an HIV-positive hospital obstetrician were traced and tested. Although health officials stressed the smallness of the risk, media coverage sought to emphasise dangers and fuel anger. Thus a television presenter (Stan Grant) interviewed the husband of a woman who had tested negative, presenting leading questions to influence responses:

> *Grant*: What went through your mind then? It must have been a great sense of relief but [you were] also very angry I imagine?
> *Husband*: Yes, I was angry! Why [should] this sort of thing happen!
> *Grant*: But you must have obviously raised your concerns with them? You must have told them how angry you were?
> *Husband*: Yes . . . I will write to the hospital . . . about this.
> *Grant*: Just finally then, does it destroy your faith . . . in hospitals and the whole procedure, the whole checking procedure to ensure that no one is infected?
> (*husband agrees*)
>
> (Brown et al., 1996: 1692)

The story stressed the 'innocence' of the mothers and their babies, and then became associated with an underlying theme of hostility towards a health system 'accused of being captive to gay and civil libertarian politics' (1996: 1685) that allowed such 'guilty' doctors to continue to practise. The fact that a health service spokesman had revealed that the doctor had not contracted the virus from a needlestick injury was taken to mean that the doctor must be gay. This then led to references to 'the homosexual lobby group' and 'civil rights groups' exerting undue influence.

A particular theme of some analyses has been the claim that AIDS coverage, in the early years of the epidemic, really picked up only once news broke of a potential heterosexual spread. The implication is that mainstream media could ignore the problem if it was felt to be securely contained in an already stigmatised group, however deadly the disease might be. This argument has been made in relation to US media coverage by Check (1987). Klaidman (1991) takes the view that the initial reluctance to cover the story reflected general taboos about reporting gay lifestyles, only broken when news of Rock Hudson's HIV status awoke media interest. This argument, though, is countered by Baker (1986), who studied the *New York Times*, in which coverage in 1983 shot up to 128 articles, from only three per year in 1981 and 1982. Baker regards this as the response to a series of street demonstrations by gay organisations protesting at inadequate government responses to the disease. However, Baker herself notes that 1983 was also the year in which stories emerged about 'innocent' victims (haemophiliacs, female partners of HIV-positive men, and children of HIV-positive women), so it seems likely that a combination of factors led to the raised media interest.

In other respects, US media coverage of AIDS seems remarkably similar, in general terms, to the media in the other countries reviewed here, involving the construction of particular groups as guilty and others as innocent along the usual lines, with exaggeration, oversimplification and sensation being prominent features (Nelkin, 1995). Albert (1986) notes that in addition to the innocent (haemophiliacs, children, surgery patients) and the guilty (gays, drug users), a third category, the 'suspect', also emerged in US media. Haitian-Americans fulfilled this role, being regarded as 'closet homosexuals or drug abusers who conceal this fact from medical investigators' (1986: 174). Prisoners were another category of the 'suspect', their status being indicated in pictures from *Newsweek* and *US News and World Report* of prison staff 'wearing . . . protective gear . . . heavy gloves, what appear to be jump suits [and in one case] surgical gown, cap, mask and gloves . . . [There were also] police with special "resuscitation gear" to minimize the chance of contact with a possible at-risk patient' (1986: 174). This contrasted with the absence of protective gear worn by doctors and others pictured handling HIV-positive babies.

King (1990) analyses *New York Times* and *Washington Post* coverage of women prostitutes and HIV between 1985 and 1988, observing that concern about transmission to male clients dominated, with concern about the health of prostitutes being minimal. Coverage began when a medical journal published a report of infection of army personnel, several of whom traced their HIV status to contact with prostitutes. Out of 38 articles in the two papers, 28 were judged to be unsympathetic to prostitutes with AIDS. Such articles stressed the high risk of sex with a prostitute, implying or claiming that transmission from female to male was likely. One article, for example, was headlined 'Prostitutes transmitting AIDS to US soldiers' another reported calls for mandatory testing of prostitutes. Three articles were judged to have provided 'neutral' coverage and seven were judged to be 'sympathetic' towards prostitutes, as for example, they reported the views of city health officials that risks of transmission to men were negligible or portrayed prostitutes themselves as being at risk of infection. Clearly, then, the balance of coverage was unfavourable to the stigmatised group. Sacks (1996) notes that US media stories about AIDS have depicted prostitutes as indiscriminate, polluting and abnormal. Other women depicted in AIDS stories have generally been HIV-positive mothers, concern about them focusing on the effect on their babies rather than their own plight, since the women have been blamed for acquiring HIV.

Stigma champions

A less condemnatory view of media coverage of AIDS is contained in the argument that, however stigmatising it might be, the very fact that sexual practices had become a matter of public discussion was itself a move towards a more healthy, less inhibited acknowledgement of important facts of life. This in itself, this argument goes, is likely to produce a climate in which preventive measures, such as condom usage (Tulloch, 1995), gather public support. Ziporyn (1988), discussing the media treatment of syphilis in the early part of the twentieth century, notes a concerted effort from 1905 onwards by public health educators to break the public taboo on discussing syphilis, so that effective preventive and curative measures might be taken, as they had been for non-taboo diseases of the time such as typhoid fever and diphtheria. This campaign achieved only limited success in encouraging a more open public discussion.

It is arguable that even stigmatising coverage of AIDS by contemporary Western media is an improvement, in public health terms, on media silence about the subject. Criticisms of the early media treatment of AIDS in some African countries adds force to this view, suggesting that here there have been considerable problems in breaking public taboos concerning discussions of sexuality that have undermined public health efforts to control the spread of the disease, which has had devastating effects on mortality rates (Seale, 2000). Gibson (1994) attributes this to the closeness of ties between many African governments and their media when he argues that 'Years into the AIDS pandemic, most African governments and media continued to virtually ignore the crisis' (1994: 349). In part, this may be a legacy of oppression. South African reluctance to promote condom usage, Gibson suggests, may be due to suspicion of the policy, which many believe to have been used by the apartheid regime to try to restrict black population growth. People in other African countries may have been reluctant to admit to the problem because of resentment about accusations from Westerners that the disease was of African origin. The Kenyan government and media, Gibson claims, dragged its heels for fear of the impact on tourist revenues. Gibson notes, however, that these initial delays have for the most part been replaced by aggressive and high-profile media campaigns to encourage preventive behaviour. Such campaigns have been mounted even in countries, such as Zimbabwe, where a strong climate of homophobia is also promoted, as the disease in Africa is in practice largely one of heterosexual spread.

In addition to the view that any breaking of taboos of silence, whether or not this involves stigma, may be a good thing in terms of the effect of this on behaviour and the enhancement of public health, there is also a significant body of opinion suggesting that a simple story of stigmatisation by the media (for example, Watney, 1997) needs to be modified. Firstly, as we have seen, there is evidence that Western media covered sympathetically the viewpoint of HIV-positive people, to the extent that some sections of the media even refers to the media influence of a 'gay lobby'. Studies of the British media response have shown that even within the pages of a single newspaper, contradictory messages coincide; additionally, there is evidence to suggest major differences of emphasis between different sectors of the media, most notably between television and newspapers. Other evidence about the effects of media messages about AIDS on a variety of audiences also suggests a different direction of influence from that claimed by critics. I review much of this evidence below.

Berridge (1991) was one of the first analysts to mount a sustained argument against the view that media AIDS coverage was universally stigmatising in its effects. She, too, documents the shift from early coverage that focused on the 'gay plague' to a preoccupation with heterosexual spread, followed by a homophobic reaction in some sectors of the British press in the late 1980s against the view that AIDS was a major threat to heterosexuals. But she argues that these responses were 'virtually confined to the newspaper press' (1991: 181), with television coverage reflecting a more 'responsible' line, informed by the liberal line taken by government and public health officials. Stigmatising press coverage had no effect on government AIDS policy, Berridge notes, which resisted calls for punitive policies such as compulsory testing or quarantine in favour of health education for safer sex practices and harm minimisation. Even where the 'audience' of media messages is conceived as being the general public rather than elite policy makers, it may not be the case that stigmatising messages are easily absorbed. In a study of the effects of media AIDS stories amongst focus group members, Kitzinger and Miller (1992) report significant resistance to negative messages about Africa and AIDS, this being particularly marked in gay and black audience members.

Newspapers, though generally more negative than television, may nevertheless contain both positive and negative messages about AIDS. Beharrell (1993) notes that the British tabloid press was more irresponsible than the 'quality' broadsheets. The *Sun*, *Daily Mail* and *Daily Express*, for example, enthusiastically promoted the late 1980s backlash against government health education campaigns to alert the public about the risks of heterosexual spread, taking the line that this was 'homosexual propaganda' (1993: 217). Headlines included 'The Truth about AIDS' (*Daily Mail*), 'Normal Sex Is Safe Row' (*Daily Express*) and 'Straight Sex Cannot Give You AIDS – Official' (*Sun*) (1993: 218). Within tabloids, as well, contradictions existed. In spite of a generally homophobic line, the *Sun* could occasionally run stories that reported acts of discrimination against gays in negative terms. In part, such variation is due to differences between editorial, feature and news sections of the papers. The same papers that ran stories about heterosexual spread being a 'myth' could also, when it suited them, build up the 'scare' element of a story by stressing AIDS as a potential consequence of heterosexual promiscuity. Articles presenting 'sun and sex' stories, designed to titillate readers with accounts of sexual adventure in glamorous holiday locations, were opportunities to create such thrills, in spite of their contradiction of the paper's more 'serious' line of no such threat existing. Beharrell concludes that neither journalists nor readers of such newspapers are particularly concerned with consistency, a view that suggests audience interactions with media messages are considerably more complex than direct effect models allow.

The distinction between the press and television in British media coverage is also noted by Williams (1999), who took part in a major study of this area of media coverage (reported in Miller et al., 1998). Williams notes considerable co-operation between television producers and government agencies over this topic. Government sources, medical officials and public health doctors were frequently given air time for their views on British television, promoting a liberal, anti-stigma line. Many television reports concerned prejudice experienced by people with AIDS, provoking sympathy for their plight. The Terence Higgins Trust, an advocacy organisation formed on behalf of people with AIDS, frequently featured on television programmes, and was often asked for leads by television journalists wanting interviews with those with HIV infection or AIDS. In general, as a result of this, reactionary voices and punitive policies did not prevail. Miller (1995) goes so far as to claim that the anti-stigma messages that were developed in response to AIDS set up a template for later stories, including that in which researchers claimed to have found a gene for homosexuality. Clearly, a 'gay gene' story has the potential for an extremely stigmatising media treatment invoking eugenic ideas and so on, yet this did not emerge, the media instead running with the liberal line that the existence of a gene should not be taken as evidence of monocausality.

The AIDS story, then, appears at first to have been a paradigmatic case of negative stereotyping, reflecting both strong currents of hostility towards supposed carriers of infection, yet demonstrating that fixed categories of enemy are hard to sustain in societies where tolerance is promoted as an official virtue. Clearly, media audiences occupy a potentially contradictory position in relation to this, and it is important in this area, as in others, not to assume too much about audience responses in the absence of clear evidence. Media health contains a number of other such stereotyped categories, with associated counterblasts from stigma champions, several of which involve emphasis on deviation from normality. This can take the form of bodily blemishes, or mental disturbance, to which we can now turn.

FREAKS

A dictionary definition of 'freak' is helpful in pointing to both the mental and physical aspects of abnormality conveyed by the term. On the one hand, it seems, a freak can be defined as 'a sudden causeless change or turn of mind; a capricious humour, notion, whim or vagary'. On the other hand, the freak can be understood as 'a monstrosity of any species ... a living curiosity exhibited in a show.' At any rate, a freak denotes 'something abnormal or capriciously irregular' (*Shorter Oxford English Dictionary*, 1983). All of these things are conveyed in media images of mentally disordered and physically different people.

Mental disorder

Considerable evidence has been gathered from a variety of countries indicating that media depictions of mental illness present unrealistically negative stereotypes of people who are out of control and prone to violence. Unusually strong evidence exists to show that these images affect audiences, for the most part (though not exclusively) influencing them in the direction of the stereotypes. There is a consequent pressure on policy makers to exclude mentally ill people from participation in community life. Thus policies of psychiatric hospital closure and community care are significantly threatened by media depictions. Arguably policy makers have been less successful in resisting these pressures in this area than in AIDS-prevention policies.

The use of mentally ill characters in fictional genres, such as Hollywood movies and television dramas, has an obvious appeal for scriptwriters concerned to add excitement to a plot. A number of studies have documented the stereotyping that this involves. Winick (1978) reviewed 151 movies made during 1919–78. In early treatments, mental illness was a convenient way of marking a character as evil. An increase in the number of films dealing with the theme occurred in the 1960s and 1970s, reflecting social changes that saw the growth of 'counter-cultural' influence, encouraging people's interest in extremes of human behaviour and involving a growing interest in psychology in general. Winick's content analysis of movies reveals that these over-represented certain symptoms and conditions in relation to their epidemiological prevalence. 'Senile psychosis', for example, was never portrayed while schizophrenia and psychosis involving a proclivity to violence were common. Many plots involved the criminal activities of mentally ill people, but in the 1960s a somewhat less negative set of associations developed as the American public took an increasing interest in psychotherapy, and characters with neuroses and emotional difficulties were portrayed seeking such treatment. With movies like *One Flew Over the Cuckoo's Nest* a degree of glamorisation of mental illness occurred, as the idea that the world was an insane place grew in popularity. A degree of glamorisation is also seen in the film *Shine*, which showed the life of pianist David Helfgott in idealised terms, to the extent that it has attracted criticism for distorting the true facts of his life (Rosen & Walter, 2000). Films such as *Taxi Driver*, while sympathetic to the mentally disturbed chief character, nevertheless portray dangerousness and unpredictability. Unpredictability in movies depicting epileptic seizure is documented by Kerson et al. (2000), who note the use of this in 23 films to drive plots in more exciting directions through the depiction of 'unsympathetic, out-of-control and feared characters' (2000: 95).

Another comprehensive analysis of movie images (Hyler et al., 1991) describes a variety of stereotypes of mental disturbance that have occurred in these. The 'homicidal maniac' was classically portrayed in Hitchcock's *Psycho*, with films such as *Nightmare on Elm Street, The Exorcist* and *Friday the 13th* continuing this tradition. Other stereotypes of mental illness include the 'rebellious free spirit' (*Cuckoo's Nest*), the 'female patient as seductress' (Hitchcock's *Spellbound*), the 'enlightened' (following up ideas of the anti-psychiatry movement in which the person is seen as having unusual insight into matters of which 'normal' people are unaware), the 'narcissistic parasite' (Woody Allen's films) and the dehumanised 'zoo specimen', as in various historical depictions of asylums where mental inmates are shown raging in their chains. All of these may serve to designate such people as the Other, usually in a negative, threatening fashion. Hyler et al., in agreement with some other media analysts (for example, Byrne, 2000), do note occasional more realistic, less stigmatising movies, but in general conclude that significant change is required to change portrayals towards greater authenticity.

Studies of other media (for example, news and television soaps) show quite consistently across the media of various countries that violent behaviour in mentally ill people is considerably over-reported. This is understandable from the perspective of standard news values (Galtung & Ruge, 1973; see also Chapter 2) that recognise the attractions of sensational and negative stories. Allen and Nairn (1997), in a close reading of a sample of New Zealand print media, conclude that these provide 'repeated confirmations of the common-sense understanding that mental illnesses make people unpredictable and dangerous' (1997: 375). Wilson et al. (1999) present a similarly close reading, this time of a New Zealand television drama depicting mental illness. Particular techniques, including the use of music and sound effects, horror movie conventions, lighting, 'point of view' shots, characters' appearance and jump-cutting, were used to contribute to the impression of danger. Children's television in New Zealand has been studied by the same authors (Wilson et al., 2000), who analysed 128 episodes containing references to mental illness. Terms such as 'crazy', 'mad' and 'losing your mind' were commonly used to denote loss of control. Of the six characters depicted with mental illness as a fixed characteristic, 'admirable attributes' (2000: 440) were almost entirely absent. Nairn (1999) found that although psychiatrists in New Zealand media reports were shown giving out positive messages about mental illness, these depictions were undermined by other journalistic devices that emphasised sensationalised coverage.

In Germany, Angermeyer and Matschinger (1996) have shown that media coverage of violent attacks on prominent politicians by two individuals with schizophrenia led to significant changes in public attitudes towards mentally ill people, in the direction of desiring increased social distance. Holzinger et al. (1998) have demonstrated uptake by ordinary Germans of the media stereotype of schizophrenia involving a 'split personality'. Hoffmann-Richter et al. (1999) document German newspaper depictions of neuroleptic drugs, which are portrayed as 'close to violence and restriction, as punishment or even as torture, as paralyzing or even as "torturetherapy"' (1999: 175), thus reinforcing ideas of mental illness and its treatment as a harsh, abnormal and distinctly deviant experience.

US media depictions (outside the Hollywood movie genre) have been analysed in numerous studies. One of the earliest of these was reported by Nunnally (1961, reprinted 1973) in a comprehensive study of representative samples of a variety of US mass media from the years 1953–55. The US media at that time was found to portray mental health problems quite infrequently, but to present a 'distorted picture' (1973: 193) when this did occur:

> In particular, media presentations emphasize the bizarre symptoms of the mentally ill [frequently suggesting that] people with mental health problems 'look and act different' ... In television dramas, for example, the afflicted person often enters the scene staring glassy-eyed, with his mouth widely agape, mumbling incoherent phrases or laughing uncontrollably. (1973: 194–5)

Being ignorant, dangerous, dirty, unkind and unpredictable were all found to be associated with mental illness. However, in an associated investigation of the attitudes of mental health experts and the American general public, Nunnally found that media stereotypes were not shared by these potential audiences, suggesting that such messages were, in fact, largely discounted. As we shall see below, this finding has not been supported in later studies of media effects in this area.

In a study of prime-time US television drama between 1969 and 1985, Signorielli (1989) reports somewhat higher frequencies of portrayal of mental illness than did Nunnally; one-fifth of these programmes involved mental illness in some way, and 3 per cent of major characters were shown with such troubles. Her findings are worth quoting in detail:

> Although relatively small in numbers, the mentally ill make up the group most likely to commit violence and be victimized in the world of television. Out of all prime time dramatic characters, 41.6% are violent, but 72.1% of those characterized as mentally ill kill or hurt others ... Almost one in 10 characters (8.7%) are killers and 4.3% are killed; but 21.6% of those characterized as mentally ill are killers and 20.7% are killed ... overall, and especially in relation to women, being cast as mentally ill greatly increases a character's chance of being involved in hurting and even more so in killing. (1989: 327)

Mentally ill characters were also more likely than others to be portrayed in serious rather than comical roles, to be 'bad' rather than 'good', and to be failures rather than successful; for example, they were more likely to be shown as unemployed. Signorielli concludes that these images are 'likely to contribute to ... ignorance and neglect ... perpetuate unwarranted views about mental illness ... and frustrate efforts at health education and integration of those who have recovered from a mental illness' (1989: 330). A more recent study of US television (Diefenbach, 1997) suggests that little had changed in subsequent years: 'The mentally ill were found to be nearly 10 times more violent than the general population of television characters' (1997: 289). Wahl (1992), in a comprehensive view of the US literature on this subject, concluded that 'numerous studies' had shown 'inaccurate and unfavorable depictions to be prevalent', though studies of the effects of this had been relatively neglected (1992: 343). Nevertheless, Wahl (Wahl & Lefkowits, 1989) has himself reported a study in which groups of college students viewing a film about a mentally ill killer were shown to have acquired from it unfavourable and stigmatising attitudes towards mental illness.

The most comprehensive and revealing study of the effects of stigmatising portrayals of mental illness is reported by Philo (1996; Philo et al., 1994; Philo & Secker, 1999), in a UK study which is exemplary in including an analysis of the process that produces images, the messages of the images themselves and their effects on a variety of audiences. Covering a variety of media – print and broadcast, fictional, news and current affairs – in 1993, the analysis of media content demonstrated an overwhelming association of mental illness with violence, largely involving harm done to others (66 per cent of all 562 items), but also including depictions of self-harm (13 per cent of items), with 18 per cent of items being judged sympathetic to mentally ill people and 2 per cent involving parody of mental conditions (Philo et al., 1994). A selection of news headlines conveys the flavour of such reports: 'Bingo hall bloodbath' (*Mirror*); 'Maniac sets little boy's face on fire' (*Daily Sport*); 'Axe maniac in attack on pet pony' (*Sun*); 'Psycho fan stalks Cindy' (*Daily Sport*); and, in relation to a nurse convicted of killing small children, 'Hospital was warned nurse was mad but did nothing' (*Sun*) (Philo, 1996: 51–64). Fictional representations, women's magazines, children's fiction, and soap operas were all found to share such negative imagery. Thus, computer games magazines revealed considerable preoccupation with armed and dangerous 'nutters' who have to be defeated; and one game involving world mastery was called MEGA-LO-MANIA!

One of the research team (Henderson, 1996) reports on a study of the production values that lead to this coverage. In a case study of the popular soap *Coronation Street*, she traces the development of a new character, Carmel, a young woman employed to look after a child, who becomes obsessed with the father of the family. She is designated as suffering from 'erotomania', an extremely rare condition if it is one at all, made famous by a similar portrayal in the movie *Fatal Attraction*. The producers could then portray a disturbing, manipulative and potentially violent person presenting a threat to 'the security of a regular soap family' (1996: 23). One producer explained:

Carmel, the nanny from hell, and stories like that [are very strong]. Where you get someone new like Carmel who introduces a catalyst into a happy family and suddenly it all sort of festers and turns bad. I mean there's a really good story. (Quoted in Henderson, 1996: 23)

Henderson notes that in a competitive environment where audience rating figures are all, 'underlying assumptions about audience needs can subordinate other concerns and result in distorted and misleading images' (1996: 36).

The third aspect of this study examined audience responses to depictions of mental illness, involving innovatory qualitative methods for estimating this. Some focus group members, for example, were asked to write their own news stories in response to popular press headlines, or to make up sections of dialogue of the sort they associated with mentally ill characters on television whose pictures they were shown. These scripts contained marked similarities with those that had actually accompanied the headlines and characters, suggesting that audiences possessed a considerable ease of recall of the messages themselves. Unlike Morley (1986), who had found television audience members actively discussing the content of programmes with other family members, Philo (1996) found that there had been very little discussion of depictions of mental illness between members of the same family, who often exhibited widely divergent views. In one family, for example, the mother worked as a matron in a hospital and had experience of psychiatric patients, rejecting the view that they were violent. Her husband and three children, on the other hand, all did associate mental illness with violence. Thus one of her sons said:

I would say that people that have a mental illness would be violent. I have this idea as I have seen films about people with mental illnesses being murderers or violent. In newspapers it is always referred to as a 'psycho' killing someone. (1996: 102)

While there was some variation, with some people with experience of mental illness – either as users or providers of mental health services – rejecting stigmatising images as inaccurate, in general, negative views of people with mental illness were common in the focus groups assembled by the researchers, and these views were clearly derived from media sources. Two examples from people in the study give a flavour of the responses:

They [mentally ill people] could be all right one minute and then just snap – I'm kind of wary of them . . . [in] that *Fatal Attraction* she was as nice as nine pence and then . . . (1996: 96)

> Hungerford [scene of a public mass killing by a man with guns], that type
> of thing – anything you see on the news, it's likely to be violent when it is
> connected with mentally ill people. (1996: 96)

At times, audience members revealed violent feelings towards those with
mental illness. When asked, for example, how they would have reacted to
the 'erotomanic' Carmel had they been the woman whose marriage she
threatened, two-thirds gave responses that included violence. Examples
include 'killed her', 'hit her one', 'given her a belt in the mouth' and 'I'd
plant one on her chin'; the other one-third included nine replies that were
more sympathetic ('She was unstable and needed some kind of help') and
five that were non-committal (1996: 92–3).

Various suggestions are made by this research team to counter negative
stereotypes, including tightening up on censorship and regulation, and
involving users of mental health services in programming, something
which has been done in relation to physical disability in recent years but
rarely in relation to mental conditions. Philo and Secker (1999), as well as
Rose (1998), who reports a study of UK television's treatment of mental
illness and community care, argue that the fear of and hostility towards
mentally ill people that is fuelled by media imagery has a significant effect
on policies of community care. Rose, for example, provides numerous
examples of news reports that link a presumed 'failure' of community care
provision to individual acts of violence by mentally ill persons judged
to have been discharged 'too soon' from 'inadequately supported' institutional care. A variety of control and surveillance measures were passed
by successive British governments during the 1990s in response to such
public pressure.

At the same time, there are those who voice dissent from the media
analysis presented above. Torrey (1994), for example, reviews studies to
demonstrate that although the vast majority of people with serious mental
illness do not commit acts of violence, a significant sub-group do, and
Torrey argues that unless the problem posed by this group is acknowledged
and addressed, efforts to destigmatise mental illness through denying its
association with violence will fail. Morrall (2000) notes, in a UK context,
that media reporting of violent acts by mentally ill perpetrators causes
much anguish, reflecting a sensationalist agenda, and that this has led to
a variety of 'post-liberal' policies of surveillance and containment. But he
argues that this is not necessarily an irresponsible outcome; members of
the public, he says, do have the right to be protected; those few who perpe-
trate crimes out of their mental disorder themselves deserve the protection
and care that the new policies provide, and the press reporting of this
'social problem' has, in fact, led to more government funding for a

notoriously underfunded service. He concludes that concern about risk and opposition to violence reflects fundamental democratic rights. These dissenters may have a point about fear-provoking coverage having unrecognised benefits, but this does not detract from the overall message that media reports appear to be generally stigmatising in both their content and effects.

Distortions of the body

Unlike mental illness, and more like AIDS, negative stereotyping of disabled people (by which I mean, largely, physical disability) has been countered by an active political movement championing disabled people's perspectives and successfully gaining access to a variety of media in recent years. Images of disability are more polarised than those of AIDS and mental illness; 'supercrip' images that idealise disabled people as heroes (or others that show them to be the innocent victims of evil or misfortune) are as common as negative stereotypes. There is also some debate within the disabled rights movement as to what counts as a positive or negative image of disability, reflecting awareness of the instability of signs that may not in themselves carry fixed meanings. Disability theorists have thereby incorporated a degree of semiotic sophistication into political debates and are concerned to recognise the variable meanings that audiences may bestow upon particular images.

An intelligent discussion of the psychology of prejudice against disabled people is provided by Shakespeare (1994). He notes first that impairment – like mental illness – is widely used in fictional portrayals to indicate evil; it is also used to evoke pity for disability as a personal tragedy, an emotion which Shakespeare considers to be almost as negative as hostility. Like an old-fashioned circus freak show (as in the experience of the 'Elephant Man' portrayed in the film of that name), the Other becomes a spectacle, thus no longer threatening to the ontological security of the onlooker. Because disability is anomalous with regard to boundaries between life and death, humanity and animality, its bearers fulfil a liminal function in popular culture, potentially reminding people of the triumph of nature over culture. Disabled people, Shakespeare argues, are thus used to make able-bodied people feel good about themselves in a kind of pornography of the body, scapegoating the carriers of deformity. All of this, he argues, is rather similar to the psychology involved in oppressive images of women, as analysed in de Beauvoir's *Second Sex* (1949).

Shakespeare's (1999) analysis of the politics of representation, how-ever, suggests that it is not always easy to 'read off' a fixed message from a media product. Analysing two films involving portrayals of disabled people – *Breaking the Waves* and *Shine,* the first of which was condemned by disability activists, and the second of which was praised, both judgements supposedly emanating from a realist perspective – he argues that different readings are, in fact, appropriate. *Shine,* for example, praised by some for its portrayal of a musician's struggle to overcome the effects of mental disability, can be criticised, Shakespeare observes, for its sentimentalised approach that distorted the truth of the real-life character's experience. *Breaking the Waves,* on the other hand, condemned by some for portraying disability involving bitterness and self-hatred, Shakespeare argues should not be read as merely a literal depiction but can instead be understood as a complex symbolic meditation on religious themes. This anti-realist position allows Shakespeare to argue that 'it is dangerous to develop hard and fast rules of representation, against which the disability credentials of a particular film can be read off' (1999: 170). He agrees that there is a broad consensus about what counts as a stereotyped view, but argues that there is less agreement about what constitutes a 'positive image'. Clearly, qualitative audience studies would assist in understanding this variability more fully.

More crude stereotypes operate in products less complex than such art-house movies as *Breaking the Waves.* The film *The Elephant Man* is a case in point. Darke (1994) observes that although the film pretends a cri-tique of intolerance for the chief character's deformity, the film nevertheless perpetuates stereotypes. Finding a refuge in a medically con-trolled environment, the Elephant Man is deemed to have been rescued from a far worse fate as an exhibit in a circus freak show. Darke begs to differ with this reading, arguing that many of the participants in Victorian freak shows obtained a degree of agency and control over their lives and economic circumstances that was far in excess of the dependency and helpless gratitude depicted in the case of the Elephant Man in hospital, who was, in fact, experiencing a form of incarceration there. His exis-tence, Darke argues, is shown as a personal tragedy for which he is to be pitied, and his death (which was somewhat suicidal) is portrayed as preferable to continuing existence, suggesting that his life was not worth living and, for Darke, containing a eugenicist message. This is not a por-trayal that represents disability as 'human or valid in itself' (1994: 327).

Studies of routine television and print media output in a variety of countries have provided a considerable body of evidence for the exis-tence of stigmatising and patronising images. Barnes et al. (1999) provide a helpful review. An early study (Donaldson, 1981) of the visibility of

'handicapped' people on US prime-time television in 1979 is representative of such analyses: people appearing in major roles in dramas were
rarely disabled and almost no minor characters or crowd scenes included
people who were obviously disabled. Character associations, as for mentally ill characters, were largely bad or evil. Where disabled people played
'good' characters, their disability was shown as a central feature of their
existence rather than incidental, stories focusing on their struggle to overcome handicap. Such patterns have been found in several other studies.
Elliott and Byrd's (1982) review of some of these additionally points out
the demeaning imagery of 'telethon' fundraising activities, in which disabled people are portrayed as passive recipients of charity. The review by
Gerbner et al. (1981) of 10 years of US television noted the absence of disabled characters, as have studies of press and television since (Cooke et
al., 2000; Cumberbatch & Negrine, 1992; Makas, 1993). Cumberbatch
and Negrine's (1992) study of UK television found the wheelchair to
be the standard symbolic device used to indicate disability, meaning
that locomotor disabilities were shown to a disproportionate extent
(behavioural disabilities and those involving disfigurement were also
over-represented). Cumberbatch and Negrine also found that common
stereotypes included the disabled person as criminal, barely human, or
powerless and pathetic. Disabled people were less likely to be portrayed
as having jobs, being sexually attractive, or involved in relationships,
and more likely to be shown as loners, moody, violent or victims. They
were also three times more likely to die than non-disabled people on
television.

A particular feature of media portrayals of disability experience that is
rarely matched by characters in AIDS and mental illness stories is the
character of the 'supercrip' – the disabled person whose life project
becomes the heroic conquest of his or her disability. While superficially
this may seem like a positive portrayal, as the critique of *Shine* suggests
(where Helfgott was the supercrip character), it can contribute to the
portrayal of disability as abnormal and tragic, thus distancing 'normals'
almost as much as hostile stereotyping. Rolland (1997) has provided a critique:

> One insidious form of denial is our . . . tendency to create romantic, impres-
> sionistic stories about suffering, cleansing them of their more gritty side . . .
> Unfortunately, the media and popular literature are filled with the stories of
> 'superstar copers.' . . .[not recording] the . . . low points at which frustra-
> tion and demoralization [are] expressed and questions about giving up the
> fight [are] raised . . . Moreover, a positive attitude is important but often
> insufficient in managing the ongoing complexities of life with illness or
> disability. (1997: 438–9)

Rolland goes on to point out that not all people have the financial resources to make the kind of 'comeback' that has been shown in the case of Christopher Reeve, the *Superman* actor with a spinal cord injury. The promotion of heroic tales of ordinary people overcoming adversity is a key feature of media health and will be discussed in detail in Chapter 8. In relation to disability, though, it is worth staying with the topic a little longer in order to demonstrate the point that supercrip images are a mirror image, or flip side, to negative and hostile stereotyping. Wilkins (1996) has analysed blindness in movies and newspapers from this point of view, noting the juxtapositioning of opposing stereotypes: some blind people are treated as exceedingly dependent or evil; others are depicted as unusually talented, wise or musically gifted. In both versions the image can be read as oppressive. Dowson (1991) reports on media images of learning-disabled people, observing that these juxtapose stigmatising stereotypes (having an abnormal sexual appetite or lack of control) with idealised views of such people as angelic, blessed simpletons, leaving the people themselves with a very passive and dependent public image in which their voice is rarely heard. Schells's (1999) study of US television coverage of the Paralympics, on the other hand, argued that this was break-ing new ground in conveying more realistic images of the experience of disability, suggesting that the disability credentials of 'supercrip' images may be subject to varying interpretations.

A powerful example of media-fuelled idealisation is provided in the story of Terry Fox (Harrison, 1992), a Canadian who lost a leg to bone cancer at the age of 18, and who decided, according to the *Vancouver Sun*, that this constituted a 'challenge' and a 'fantastic stimulus for personal growth'. He took up long-distance running with an artificial leg and in 1980 began a run across Canada, 'one of the greatest examples of mind-over-body in history' (*Vancouver Sun*). A media circus began in which this freakish event was exploited to the full, Fox being described as a 'full-fledged Canadian summer hero' (*Globe and Mail*), encouraged by the 'cheers of thousands' (*Vancouver Sun*), as 'shoppers poured on to the street and ran to donation boxes' (*Halifax Chronicle Herald*) in an asso-ciated frenzy of fund-raising for the war on cancer. Although he failed to complete his run, since his cancer recurred fatally, the media eulogies continued. Harrison suggests that media coverage sent out a strong mes-sage of personal responsibility for illness and its mastery, as well as a view that the body can be treated as a machine, to the exclusion of a more social model of both illness causation and the experience of disability. For our present purposes, the Fox story demonstrates the capacity for negative stigma to flip into its diametric opposite: extreme idealisation.

These divergent readings of disability imagery suggest that audience research would be likely to uncover a rich variety of responses. The impact of media images of disability has not been as well studied as images of mental illness, but Ross (1997) presents the results of focus group research in which people with a wide range of disabilities expressed their views about media coverage. Many criticisms were expressed, these being rather similar to those of media analysts identifying stigmatising messages. Thus telethons were criticised and associations of disfigurement with evil rejected. Focus group members also said that they would like to see more disabled actors playing disabled people, and said that they liked it when disability is shown as a normal background feature of life, rather than a character's overriding focus.

Such media literacy in an audience sample reflects the fact that things are changing with regard to images of disability in Western media, in part due to the consistent lobbying efforts of disability activists. Gold and Auslander (1999; Auslander & Gold, 1999) review studies of media images over time in the US media, noting a gradual reduction in the incidence of negative stereotypes. These authors note a considerable difference in the media of Canada (where there is a strong disability rights movement) and Israel (where disability politics are more traditional). The language of Canadian newspapers was judged to be considerably less stigmatising, and Canadian papers were more likely to run stories about disabled rights issues, quote representatives of disability groups, discuss issues of government support and run stories of discrimination. Israeli papers, on the other hand, focused more on the functional limitations experienced by individual disabled persons, presenting a medical rather than social perspective on the alleviation of problems, and covering compensation claims rather than social services support.

We have progressed, then, from topics that have attracted considerable opprobrium and blame (AIDS), as well as fear (mental illness), to one where such negative stereotyping, while present, is mixed with quite powerful forces working in the opposite direction, towards idealisation. In all cases it is possible to see a degree of stigma championing going on, reinforcing the point that stigmatised categories are hard to maintain in a pluralist society where the values of tolerance are part of an official ideology. The requirements of media forms also involve twitches and reversals to established categorisations (see Chapter 2), contributing to the instability of fixed images of evil. The new shows put on by media-engaged disability activists – displays of disabled bodies, Paralympics and the like – may themselves be a continuation of an entertainment agenda that has roots in the freak shows of earlier times.

Yet another case of separation from the world of 'normals' is the media depiction of old age and associated health issues. Here, there are some similarities with the depiction of disability. People, on the whole, are not blamed for bringing old age upon themselves, as they sometimes are blamed for their condition in the case of AIDS, but instead are made to represent a liminal category that 'normals' find hard to contemplate, exhibiting, like disabled people, a degree of bodily deviation from ideals of youthful (able-bodied) beauty, and presenting media producers with unwelcome reminders of the end of pleasure and the body's death. However, the problem of old age is dealt with in media representations somewhat differently from the problem of disability, as will be shown.

SEQUESTRATION OF OLD AGE

While both negative stereotypes and idealisations of old age do occur in media depictions of elderly people, a more noticeable feature of coverage is simply the fact that their lives and health issues are rarely discussed in popular mass media. Additionally, some quite powerful gender stereotypes are involved in media depictions of old age. These things reflect broader issues concerning the lack of influential participation of older people in the mainstream social life of advanced industrialised countries, and of elderly women in particular. In short, media representations in this area reflect differing amounts of social power, in part arising from the fact that modern societies are organised to sequester death (Blauner, 1966). This involves the imposition of 'social death' on elderly people, so that their loss through biological death is minimally disruptive for the continuation of large institutions and the social order in general (the grief of bereavement then being experienced as a personal and private emotion, rather than something requiring community ritual repair). For this to happen, the lives of elderly people are designated, culturally, as largely uninteresting rather than bearing a threat in the way that, say, mentally ill people are constructed. Mass media coverage reflects these processes, although there are indications that recognition of the market power of growing numbers of 'grey consumers', able to use a lifetime of savings for a variety of consumption activities, will influence the media a little to redress this neglect.

Content analyses of a variety of media genres have consistently documented the under-representation of elderly people. Petersen (1973) reviewed studies from the 1950s onwards, recording under-representation in US media; her own study found a particularly marked under-representation of elderly women on US prime-time television in 1972, a pattern also found in Aronoff's (1974) study of the same genre during 1969–71. The review of 10 years of US prime-time television by Gerbner et al. (1981) found that although 11 per cent of the US population were over 65, only 2 per cent of television characters were in that age group. Cumberbatch et al. (1998), in a study of one week of UK television, found that 10 per cent of people shown were over 60, compared with 20 per cent in the UK population. Under-representation has been found in studies of US television advertisements (Roy & Harwood, 1997), magazine advertisements (Gantz et al., 1980), comic strips (Hanlon et al., 1997) and *Time* and *Newsweek* magazines (McConatha et al., 1999). A study of magazine advertisements by Miller et al. (1999) found a reduction in the percentage of portrayals of elderly people between 1956 and 1996.

Health issues relevant to elderly people are also less frequently discussed, in spite of the fact that most health problems increase with age. Thus Liebmann-Smith and Rosen (1978) analysed the popular US soap *Marcus Welby*, finding that very few of Welby's patients were elderly. Kristiansen and Harding (1984, 1988), in a review of UK newspapers, found 1,042 articles containing health information, of which only 8 were targetted on the health experience of elderly people. Amos (1986), reviewing UK women's magazines, found 'Practically no articles . . . devoted to the health problems of elderly women even in *Women's Weekly* where a quarter of its readership was over 65' (1986: 200). A variety of studies of breast cancer in the media (Clarke, 1999a; Lantz & Booth, 1998; Marino & Gerlach, 1999; Saywell et al., 2000) have found that there is a major focus on how this disease affects younger women, in spite of epidemiological prevalence being concentrated in older age groups. Studies of the media treatment of arthritis and other chronic conditions associated with ageing are themselves very rare, but those that exist suggest that these health issues are infrequently discussed. Thus Pichert and Hanson (1983), in a study of US television news during 1971–81, found only 23 items relating to arthritis during this period, compared with 215 about heart disease and 925 about cancer. Van der Wardt et al. (1999) report a study of Dutch newspapers, magazines and television over a 12-month period, in which 8 per cent of 1,384 items concerned rheumatic disease, compared with 37 per cent concerning heart disease and 43 per cent cancer. Mercado-Martinez et al. (2001) found that the Mexican press in the 1990s gave greater prominence to acute illnesses than chronic diseases. Death (perhaps the ultimate health problem!) receives media coverage if it affects the young rather than those whom it is most likely to affect. Thus Pickering et al. (1992), studying death in UK tabloid newspapers, found that only 3 deaths of elderly people were reported in a 3-month period, in spite of 41.5 per cent of all front pages containing news of one or more deaths. Moore and Mae's (1987) analysis of death in children's literature found that only 15 per cent of the 60 characters dying in 49 books were elderly.

Many of the studies I have mentioned have also examined gender and consistently find that elderly women are more rarely shown than elderly men. This and a number of other characteristics of media coverage of old age are best shown by reviewing the findings of a study of UK television (Cumberbatch et al., 1998), since this is representative of the findings of most other studies. In addition to the overall finding of under-representation, these analysts found that older men outnumbered older women (72 per cent male versus 28 per cent female), again reversing the true proportions in the population where women outnumber men due to their greater longevity. In factual programmes older people were less likely than younger people to be major or minor presenters and they were rarely quiz contestants. In fictional programmes sexuality in elderly people was rarely portrayed, compared with frequent portrayal of sex in younger characters' lives.

The findings about negative stereotyping were mixed, however. Depictions of elderly people as eccentric and the butt of humour occurred in some programmes, and in some there were expressions of negative prejudice (as where a character accused another of being a 'selfish, nasty minded, bigoted old git . . . you conniving, useless old fool' (1998: 86). Stereotypes also included living in the past, and being irritable, interfering, lonely and stubborn. Older people were more likely to be portrayed as crime victims (found also by Gerbner et al., 1980). Yet there were also occasional portrayals judged as challenging age-related stereotyping, as where women were shown talking openly about homosexuality or describing their own experience as lesbians. Older people in fictional programmes were more likely than were younger people to be shown courtesy and respect. Additionally, there was some evidence of idealisation, mirroring this phenomenon in depictions of disabled people, reflected in a higher frequency of stories involving bravery or achievement by elderly rather than younger people. (Idealisation of exceptional elderly individuals is also documented by Gibb and Holroyd (1996) for the Hong Kong print media.)

Variation between media genres in the degree of stereotyping is evident from a study by Cassata et al. (1983b) of daytime television in the US. Such programmes target a predominantly female and elderly audience, and health themes are very frequent. Cassata et al. found that equal proportions of elderly men and women were represented in daytime soaps, with women being on camera for longer. An 'almost unrealistically "good" image of the older person' (1983b: 43) was projected, older people being shown as influential in the community, upholding traditional morality, respected, involved, active and with a good self-image.

As with most other areas of media health, studies of production and reception are rarer than studies of media messages themselves. Explanations for under-representation centre around the relative youth of media producers themselves, operating in a cultural climate where elderly people are treated as irrelevant (Dant & Johnson, 1991). Smythe (1996) feels that this is particularly the case in advertising agencies, where values of youth and vitality are seen as selling a wide variety of products. Pacl (1998) presents a similar explanation for the neglect of elderly people in Czech mass media. Yet it seems likely, again, that there is variation here, and possibly this is a harbinger of future changes as the market power of elderly consumers is more appreciated by advertisers. Roy and Harwood (1997), for example, found that although elderly people were under-represented in US television advertisements overall, this was at its most extreme in advertisements for automobiles and travel, and least in advertisements for financial services and retail chains. As yet, however, empirical investigation of production processes that lead to the portrayals analysed here remains to be done.

Gerbner et al. (1980), whose study of US television during 1969–78 found a preponderance of stigmatising portrayals of elderly people, found that people who watched a lot of television, especially if they were young or had little personal contact with elderly people, held more negative attitudes towards elderly people. This included the idea that old age begins quite young, particularly where women are concerned. Ross (2000) reports a survey of 228 elderly people in the UK, in which they were asked their views about television coverage. Many criticisms of the under-representation and stereotyping of old age were made, particularly with regard to women, where media emphasis on youthful glamour was disliked. There were also criticisms of 'foul language' and expressions of embarrassment about portrayals of sexual activity, a particular issue for those watching with children present. Many believed, like some of the media analysts reviewed above, that broadcasters were basically not interested in the lives of older people. Nevertheless, some portrayals were commended, particularly where they showed older characters receiving respect, delivering wisdom and doing interesting things, including having a sex life. Like her earlier study of the views of disabled people about representations of disability (Ross, 1997), it seems that audiences share many of the concerns of critical media analysts about deficiencies in media messages.

CONCLUSION

In this chapter I have reviewed the media representation of four categories of person who, in various ways, have been represented as deviant, the Other and threatening to the population of 'normals' who are the implied mainstream mass-media audience. Stigmatisation and challenges to this have been a key theme. AIDS provided opportunities for certain sections of the media to engage in actively stoking the flames of fear and hatred of already vilified minorities. Yet this was not the whole story, as the intensity and public prominence of these feelings also attracted considerable criticism, itself covered in media outlets, and in most Western countries negative media coverage did not derail broadly liberal and tolerant social and health policies related to AIDS.

The stigmatising portrayal of mentally ill people as violent and unpredictable was shown to be quite marked, with largely negative effects on the attitudes of audiences. Stigma champions seem muted in this area, and there are even some media analysts who perceive hidden benefits to the barrage of negative imagery associated with mental illness, in terms of stimulating support for increased service funding, for example. Physical disability is markedly different from mental disability in this respect, as here there has been a successful and sophisticated movement to represent the interests of disabled people and to counter negative media images of disability, the interpretation of which is anyway subject to a certain amount of variability. Nevertheless, this group shares with elderly people a degree of invisibility, being somewhat under-represented in media stories. Elderly people, while probably less subject than any of the previous groups to active negative prejudice, are nevertheless treated unfavourably, in so far as they are relatively invisible – particularly where elderly women are concerned – and therefore perhaps suffer the ultimate indignity of being regarded as irrelevant.

There are other groups that could have been chosen as case studies for this chapter. In particular, there has been some study of media representations of illicit drug users (Winick & Winick, 1976; Gerbner, 1978; Shoemaker et al., 1989; Stepney, 1996), which demonstrates an overriding tendency to stigmatise, with occasional 'flips' in this picture, as where fictional portrayals glamorise drug experiences and drug culture as aspects of individual free expression. Images of illicit drug use, though, can usefully be understood in the context of a general discussion of the representation of chemical substances, and so receive further treatment in Chapter 7 where medicines are discussed. Additionally, media depictions of desirable body shape have attracted the attention of analysts interested in media health, particularly with regard to obesity, excessive thinness and eating disorders (for example, Kaufman, 1980; Bray, 1994; Botta, 1999; Owen & Laurel-Seller, 2000). These depictions contain considerable potential for stigmatisation, particularly with regard to obesity (Fouts & Burggraf, 2000) and are discussed further in Chapter 9, where gender issues in media health are analysed.

The media treatment of the four groups I have chosen for this chapter reflects a continuation of the scare stories reviewed in Chapter 4, where it was noted that stories involving the human agency behind scares tend to attract most media attention. The identification of villains and freaks who can be shown, either at the level of conscious risk (fear of infection) or subconscious threat (fear of death), to be dangerous is an important feature of media health portrayals, preparing the way for a variety of saviour figures to emerge (see Chapters 7 and 8). Where stigma champions arise to counter negative prejudice, the story can then become 'twitched' into one of support for the official morality of tolerance, while some other group is sought out to fill the vacuum. Stories of scares and evil influence are made all the more powerful when victims can be depicted as innocent, as Langer (1998) showed in his study of tabloid television. The ultimate symbol of innocent victimhood in contemporary society, it seems, is the child. Identification of dangers to children allows an irredeemably evil figure to emerge: the child abuser. The role of children in media health is discussed in the chapter that follows.

6   Innocent Victims

Media representations of children involve an intensification of scare-villain themes, juxtaposed with images of the innocence and vulnerability of children, and fuelled by a perception of their extreme social value. In part, the increase of interest in children's lives in advanced Western countries reflects demographic transitions, involving lower rates of infant mortality and lower birth rates generally. In these circumstances, each child is generally expected to survive into adulthood and each parent has fewer children amongst whom to spread emotional and financial investments. (The declining social value of older people in such societies is the concomitant trend, and is reflected in media coverage, as we saw in the last chapter.) Additionally, with declining faith in an afterlife, children's future lives can become vehicles for parental hopes for some form of immortality or memorial, generally understood to be both a genetic continuation and a psychological one in the form of continuing characterological influence. An increased surveillance of children's lives results from this, with associated anxieties about threats to children's health and safety. In this chapter I shall describe how this is reflected in media coverage of threats to children, focusing eventually on illness, but placing this in the context of media coverage of childhood in general.

I shall also draw, as in Chapter 8, more fully on my own data analysis of news stories of people with cancer than has been the case so far in this book. This work with regard to adults with cancer has been reported elsewhere (Seale, 2001a,b, 2002), but an associated analysis of newspaper stories of children with cancer has until now been unpublished. The study involved analysis of 358 newspaper articles published in the English language press worldwide during the first week of October 1999, where the experience of a person with cancer was reported. The sample included the stories of 42 children with cancer in 36 newspapers, this being 11 per cent of the total of 382 people with cancer in the sample. This is a higher proportion than is justified by epidemiological statistics, which show childhood cancer to be a relatively rare phenomenon. This reflects the social value of children and the news value of stories involving threats to them.

MEDIA CONSTRUCTIONS OF CHILDHOOD

We can begin our analysis of the role that the media plays in constructing childhood by considering commodification, before turning to depictions of childhood innocence.

Children as commodities

An increase of interest in childhood as a stage of life has led to a considerable amount of packaging, staging, surveillance and commodification, development in the early years of life being closely scrutinised for signs of deviation. This is a process in which media of various sorts play an important part, promoting knowledge of the 'stages' of childhood, advising on appropriate parenting and advertising the products necessary to become a healthy modern child or competent parent. Lieberman (1972) charted shifting fashions in toilet-training advice between 1927 and 1974 in a popular American magazine, *Parents*. These years were crucial for the emergence of the subjectivity of the child in popular discourse: from having been the passive objects of behaviourist regimes, children came to be seen as active agents in striving for developmental goals. Thus, in the 1920s and 1930s, advice in the magazine was in favour of an early start to a training regime emphasising strict regularity, everything to be done on time in order to build up regular habits of feeding, and bladder and bowel movements according to a system imagined to be scientific and efficient. By the mid-1930s, the start of a looser regime could be detected in some articles, with an increasingly co-operative relationship between mother and infant being recommended, so that the post-war years saw a greater concern with individual 'maturation' towards goals. Crucial to such a self-directed disciplinary regime is a notion of childhood as a (gender-segregated) progression through stages.

The architecture of ideas for the 'staging' of childhood is to be found in the many texts of developmental psychology that emerged as the century progressed. As Burman (1994) observes, 'change, growth and development has been fixed into taxonomies of ages and stages' (1994: 30). Concomitant with these are a host of graded products such as toys, games, food and clothing, organised to help structure experience. Luke (1994) has analysed how, as well as maturational stages, the toy industry marks gender differences, so that toys become an 'explicit pedagogy of gendered identity' (1994: 293). Thus, the toy retailer Toys 'R Us provides for boys' and girls' sections, colour-coding items according to assumed appropriateness for each gender, as well as other ways of marking sex difference:

> So, for instance, the recent best-selling toy 'Supersoaker' – a water gun shaped like a handgun – engenders different kinds of social and bodily behaviours than its equivalents for girls. 'Flirt Squirts' water guns for girls are shaped like compacts, lipsticks, and nail polish bottles, all in fashion colours. (1994: 293)

Turning to Australian, American and British parenting magazines, Luke also found that 'The construction of infancy and early childhood in the baby gadgets and world of instructional toys has produced ever-finer distinctions within childhood by the increased segmentation of mothering activities, developmental stages, and mother and baby needs that the infant commodity discourse claims to cater for' (1994: 295). In the almost exclusively white, heterosexual environment of parenting magazines, parenting is assumed to be carried out exclusively by mothers, producing intensively pampered and cosseted children. In this respect, Luke notes, parenting magazines convey more conservative messages than some other media, such as television dramas and movies, where 'new' visions of families (men as parents, post-feminist families) have emerged.

Children and teenagers themselves, as well as parents, are targetted by manufacturers selling the concept of 'stage of life'. Viser (1997), like Lieberman, notes the post-war shift that occurred in images of childhood, showing through a study of US magazine advertisements between 1940 and 1950 how newly discovered 'teenagers' were targetted as a potentially prosperous market. The age of children in advertisements rose during this period, and the level of happy excitement depicted in visual images of children increased. More space was given to images of products rather than text, and children were pictured facing and thus 'hailing' the reader, so that post-war youths were trained to 'see *themselves* – not just adults – as subjects of the ad image's discourse' (1997: 98). This increased targetting has now led to a very widespread commercialisation of adolescence as a time of life, separate from childhood and adulthood, and designated as needing a range of specialist products.

The commercial exploitation of childhood has, then, been associated with a set of ideas about what is normal at different stages of life, generating a widespread attachment amongst parents to these ideas in relation to their own children. Parental duty, these days, inevitably involves surveillance of children for signs of normality, and corrective action for any deviation. This culture of child surveillance has many institutional manifestations in schools, health centres and centres for psychological therapy

(Rose, 1989). It can be charted, too, in various scares about inappropriate behaviour, two of which I shall describe. These have received considerable media coverage: the social problem of hyperactive children and the phenomenon of the child beauty pageant.

Diller (1996) has estimated (from surveys of physicians and drug company figures) that 2.6 million Americans, mostly children aged 5–12, were taking Ritalin to control hyperactivity (known as attention deficit-hyperactivity disorder – ADHD). Production of the drug rose by 500 per cent between 1990 and 1995. In Britain there were similar rapid rises in the 1990s (Lloyd & Norris, 1999) and in both countries media coverage has fuelled the increase. Searight and McLaren (1998) note that the reasons for this lie in changes in diagnostic standards that mean that conditions previously categorised under different headings are now interpreted as ADHD. Additionally, 'social, cultural and economic factors may also contribute to increased diagnosis. ADHD has become a common topic in the lay media. Popular discussions of ADHD may serve as a metaphoric expression of social anxieties, particularly with respect to children' (1998: 467). In short, ADHD is a classic example of the medicalisation of a social problem, and the social problem is that of children who deviate from behavioural norms.

The media has played an important part in promoting the disease label and its drug treatment. Diller (1996) notes the prominence of ADHD stories in the US media, stressing the benefits of Ritalin, and contributing to a popular view of behavioural disorders as having a genetic-biological origin, and therefore a chemical rather than a social or even psychological solution. Diller also notes that this has occurred at a time of increased pressure to succeed in the economic climate of the 'lean and mean' 1990s, seen as a way in which parents can improve children's performance in an increasingly competitive society. Lloyd and Norris (1999) examine UK press articles over a period of five years, noting two major themes. On the one hand, much coverage features parents expressing concerns about difficult children, and complaining of delays in getting the 'right' diagnosis from professionals inadequately aware of the condition. When eventually forthcoming, the disease label absolves both the children from the moral charge of being 'bad' and the parents from the charge of inadequacy. The other major theme of press coverage features 'experts', usually psychiatrists, in favour of identifying the condition and speaking of its successful treatment by drugs, presented as forming an alliance with worried parents who have finally been rescued from the ministrations of professionals less committed to the diagnosis (or 'incompetent', as many press reports have it). The views of teachers or social workers, who might present a more social or behavioural view, are rarely featured. The authors of both studies observe that the profit motives of drug companies are served by the current situation.

The Ritalin story clearly reflects an intensification of child surveillance by an alliance of parents and professionals concerned to adjust behaviour towards acceptable childhood norms. Chemical methods for achieving this are attractive in reassuring parents anxious about their own role in generating children's behaviour disorders, as well as providing a cheap solution for professionals, who might otherwise be engaged in the difficult and uncertain business of modifying psychosocial environments. Thus children are returned to appropriate childhood behaviour by the magic of drug therapy.

The phenomenon of the child beauty pageant, on the other hand, has been portrayed in the media as a system for organising deviance from norms of childhood innocence, presided over by an apparently patholog-ical group of parents wanting to turn their children into sexualised commodities. Alongside condemnation, this also allows opportunities to titillate media audiences with clips from the pageants. Media critics denigrate the pageant counter-culture as sex stereotyped and abusive, marking the anxiety they arouse about the failure to preserve childhood innocence. Thus the JonBenet Ramsay case stimulated considerable media interest in the culture of pageants. The unsolved murder of this six-year-old beauty queen in 1996 led to saturation coverage, involving considerable focus on her family life: 'The Ramsays imposed their own strange fantasies on their daughter and in doing so denied her an identity suitable for a six-year-old. Instead, they positioned her within a child beauty pageant culture that stripped her of her innocence by blurring the boundaries between child and adult' (Giroux, 1998: 37). Pageant partic-ipants, it might be argued, are doing no more than taking the commodification of childhood to its logical conclusion, constructing chil-dren as miniature adults in a peculiarly extreme version of the general orientation towards seeing children as harbingers of their future selves. Indeed, there is an element of class conflict over the appropriate response to beauty pageants. Walkerdine (1997), for example, presents a revision-ist account in which success in such events is seen as a way out of working-class restrictions.

But pageant culture in fact suppresses important elements of the 'normal' construction of childhood, such as its sexual innocence, and its supposed freedom from the demands of adult competitive standards, and this is the source of the widespread public condemnation that pageants (as well as other expressions of pushy parenthood) have attracted. In this respect the beauty queen phenomenon differs from the Ritalin child, since ADHD is felt to stem from a fundamental disorder in the child, rather than a pathological parental culture. The response to both problems, though, demonstrates a commitment to keeping children in line with dominant cultural norms that are embedded in texts of child development and the age-graded entertainment industry products described earlier.

Innocence

The struggle to portray childhood as a time of innocence, involving freedom from adult worries and responsibilities, blamelessness and absence of sexual expression, is an important media theme. This, of course, influences the depiction of sickness in children, as we shall see, but is also evident in much other coverage. Burman (1994, 1996), for example, has analysed images of children in charity appeals to solve problems of poverty, warfare and famine in Third-World countries. Until recently, these frequently involved images of starving children, usually photographed from above and, classically, alone. This, Burman feels (as, eventually, did the charities, who now construct different images), draws on existing Northern stereotypes of children as passive recipients of adult initiatives to infantilise the populations of Southern countries, positioned as unable to help themselves because they are unable to help their children. Northern donors can thus indulge in comforting rescue fantasies, sometimes actually played out in dramatic air-lift stories in which individual children (sometimes without their parents) are magically transported to Northern countries' hospital facilities for life-saving therapy, Northern donors acting 'in loco parentis'. Linked to this is the notion of the (usually 'Southern') child whose childhood has been 'stolen', seen in reports of child soldiers or child 'slave' workers. Thus, the children in these stories are containers for (Northern) adult notions of what is, or ought to be, a child: a creature free of all responsibility and deserving of protection and assistance in reaching appropriate developmental goals.

Where actual children appear to deviate from norms of innocence, or reject an orderly progression through developmental stages, they can be subjected to extremes of stigmatisation. Both Burman (1999) and Kitzinger (1988) note that any sign of sexual awareness, interest or initiative by girls in media coverage of their sexual abuse is either censored or seen as a reason for a loss of sympathy for the child or teenager. Where children kill, as in the Bulger case where two older boys murdered a younger child, an active demonisation of the killers is implemented, so that these children are decisively expelled from childhood. As James and Jenks (1996) have noted, the killers in this case were portrayed in press coverage as fundamentally and essentially evil, the media playing a significant part in representing and orchestrating pressure from the local community for extreme punitive measures towards them. In another less well-known case, where teenagers stabbed to death their head teacher (Lumley, 1998), a surge of stories emphasising youth crime resulted, drawing similarly on ideas about evil residing within the perpetrators, rather than analysis of social conditions that gave rise to such crimes. Thus the actions of children that threaten dominant norms are the occasion for thoroughgoing media condemnation. If, as the case of JonBenet Ramsay shows, the deviant children cannot themselves be blamed, then local sources of corruption (such as beauty pageant culture) are identified so that childhood innocence can be defended.

The tension between innocence and evil can also be perceived in media images of learning-disabled children (once called 'mentally handicapped'). By definition, such children deviate from childhood norms, being deemed unable to reach particular developmental goals. They are therefore a potentially threatening category of person for dominant media discourse. Dowson's (1991) study of UK press coverage of learning disability revealed a tendency to treat all such people, whether chronologically adult or not, as if they were children. Yet, as children, they are inadequate and can be somewhat threatening: their sexual desires are problematic, leading to stories about inappropriate behaviour or the potential of sterilisation. One newspaper referred to 'mentally deficient children' as 'affectionate and outgoing, with the kind of warm instinctive sexual response of puppies' (1991: 167), and much coverage was about the desire of residents in various localities not to have facilities for learning-disabled people built near them. At the same time as being sources of such unease, learning-disabled people could also be portrayed as innocent to an angelic extent, 'God's creatures', 'poor souls' or 'a race apart' (1991: 167). Thus media coverage treads an uneasy line when faced with an anomalous category.

CHILDREN IN DANGER

In a climate of intensive surveillance of children, in order to monitor and preserve their innocent progression through developmental goals that are felt to end in a normally fulfilled, well-adjusted, successful adult life, threats to progression are particularly distressing. Such is the closeness of surveillance that threats, in fact, may be perceived before they occur, small events being amplified as warning signs. If, in spite of these defences, threats are realised and can be pinned on someone, anger is very extreme, and calls for harsh punishments are loud. Nowhere is this more evident than in the media coverage of child sexual abuse.

Abduction

We saw in Chapter 3 that media stories frequently take the form of a scare followed by a resolution, and in Chapter 4 it was shown that fear-provoking coverage is a major feature of media health stories. Altheide and Michalowski's (1999) study of the increasing news coverage of fear over time noted that a major focus for anxiety has been the safety of children since 'the symbolic value of children has risen dramatically in public life' (1999: 500). Best (1987, 1988) has documented the social construction of the 'missing children' problem in the US media in a case study that illustrates the power exerted by the theme of threatened children. In the 1980s, media coverage of this social problem, which emphasised that strangers abduct children for sexual abuse, had reached epidemic levels. As Best puts it:

> By the mid-1980s, the missing children problem had achieved extraordinary visibility. Americans saw photographs of missing children on milk cartons and grocery bags, billboards and televised public service messages. Toy stores and fast-food restaurants distributed abduction-prevention tips for both parents and children. Parents could have their children fingerprinted or videotaped to make identification easier; some dentists even proposed attaching identification disks to children's teeth. Commercial child identification kits were available, and at least one catalog offered a transmitter which could be attached to a child's clothing. (1987: 102)

Quite systematic distortions were involved in the media construction of the problem. Firstly, definitions of what counted as a missing child were kept fuzzy and as inclusive as possible, so that individuals in their twenties or 'runaways' who returned home after a day or two were included in the figures. Secondly, atrocity tales reporting particularly horrific cases were generally featured to grab readers' attention, so that stranger abduction, for example, became the imagined fate of all missing children when, in fact, this cause was statistically rare. Thirdly, very large figures were generated and talked up for an exaggerated effect, using the capacity to blur distinctions (between one-day runaways and others, for example) in order to present ever-increasing estimates. Numerical claims, where feasible, also attempted to paint a picture of the problem as 'growing' and 'indiscriminate' in terms of class, race or region, in spite of an actual absence of reliable statistics. We have seen these kinds of numerical distortions before, of course, in the coverage of health scares (Chapter 4).

Best analyses the 'warrants' that, in the social construction of such problems, are used to justify drawing conclusions from the 'grounds' listed above. These contain all of the matters concerning the general value of children that have been reviewed so far in this chapter, as well as some other factors thrown in, as it were, for good measure: the preciousness of children, Best claims, is an important 'warrant' for the construction of missing children as a social problem; others include their blamelessness and their inherent right to be free from harm. Additionally, associated evils such as drugs and child prostitution warrant concern about the problem; the police are criticised for not acting fast enough (as were doctors reluctant to prescribe Ritalin), so new legislation, measures and awareness are therefore required. The result is a raised media awareness and the campaigns (milk cartons etc.) that then emanate; advice on prevention and extensive measures for the social control and surveillance of both children and suspected child abductors are advocated. As a final irony, in view of voices making counter-claims about the inadequacy of the statistical base on which the whole edifice depends, there are then calls for more effort to be put into the gathering of accurate statistics, so that the extent of the 'problem' can be properly established.

The focus on 'stranger danger' in such stories clearly diverts attention away from sources of danger closer to home. Kitzinger (1999b; Kitzinger & Skidmore, 1995) notes that sexual abuse by male relatives, who are by far the most common sources of such abuse, is relatively underplayed in media reports. She argues that this is due to the discomfort that this creates in audiences, as well as news editors, whose conceptions of harmonious family life are threatened by such stories. Kitzinger (1999b) argues further that the sexual abuse of children within families is concomitant with current norms of appropriate male sexual behaviour, which involves the exploitation of power in sexual relations. It is much easier, she observes, to externalise the threat, so that hostility can be projected outwards onto supposed deviants, and media coverage is highly supportive of this. Thus the UK media in the late 1990s saw a great deal of coverage of the advisability of, and methods for, the containment and surveillance of 'paedophiles' released from prison. Local media played a part in orchestrating local campaigning groups' efforts to exclude such individuals from their territory, a vigilante and even 'lynch mob' mentality leading to the hounding of certain individuals so that, for one individual, the only place of refuge was eventually a police cell. Another man was said to have committed suicide partly in response to harrassment from vigilantes (Bell, 2002). The socially constructed nature of this phenomenon is revealed in a quotation from a local government official involved in finding housing for released offenders:

> I talked to the other senior managers who were in the same hot seat I was in. The general feeling was: this is difficult, this is *new*. I don't know why that is. I'm quite sure abusers were being released from prison ten years ago and going and living in places. But no one was taking any notice. This was something that happened new, different, over the last two years. (1999b: 208)

At the same time, the media commonly tires of stories and, as was noted in Chapter 2, 'twitches' may be invented so that the poles are reversed, or at least questioned, in order to stimulate jaded interest. In Chapter 2, this was shown to be the effect of the false memory syndrome story in relation to child abuse, whereby abusers became the abused. The 'twitch' on the missing children phenomenon came when the *Denver Post* ran a Pulitzer Prize-winning series in which the statistical evidence for the magnitude of the problem was quite effectively challenged, though, as we saw, this was countered by pressure groups arguing for better statistics-gathering facilities, so that the story continued to run. No 'twitch' has thus far appeared, however, for the framing of paedophiles as irreversibly evil, in spite of the availability of psychodynamic or even genetic explanations that might be incorporated in a construction of such individuals as being themselves victims. Attempts by abusers themselves to construct justifications for sexual contact between adults and children have rarely, if ever, been given media space. I would suggest that the power of this taboo rests in the overpowering influence of the childhood innocence theme, which is relatively intolerant of attempts at reversal.

Abuse

The media reporting of child abuse is highly sensationalistic, focusing in particular on abuse outside the home, with lurid tales of 'ritual' abuse or, as we have seen, abduction by strangers, attracting considerable attention. Most of us will be familiar with such material, and I have already referred to a number of studies, so rather than review studies (Gough, 1996, gives a good overview) I shall describe a single case study of media behaviour. This was originally reported by Berlin and Malin (1991), two psychiatrists caught up in media reporting of their treatment programme for

sexual offenders, whom they term 'paraphilic patients', who are 'at heightened risk of committing particular sorts of sexual offences . . . [including]
public exhibitionism, sex with children, voyeurism, frottage, and rape'
(1991: 1572). They argue that treatment failures rather than successes
tend to get reported in the media, leading to biased opinion against psychiatric care for such persons, and document their experience of this at the
Johns Hopkins Sexual Disorders Clinic in Baltimore.

In spite of the documented low rate of recidivism in people treated by
the clinic (3 per cent of paedophiles reoffend after five years, for example,
and the overall rate for 600 patients with a variety of sexual disorders
is 10 per cent), a television series about the clinic, stimulated by the
admission of a high-profile patient, emphasised failures rather than successes (claiming that 'The [clinic] has had many, many fail' [1991: 1573])
made lurid claims about the nature of these offences and interviewed
parents of victims to produce atrocity stories. The clinic staff had been
reluctant to give interviews to the journalists, fearing excessive focus on
the celebrity case, being portrayed as defensive (as most of the programme
had been made by the time the interview request was received) and being
reluctant to discuss details of individual cases out of concern for patient
confidentiality. In the event, their silence was used against them as evidence of an attempt to hide the clinic's alleged failings ('Dr Berlin [the
clinic director] would not talk to us for this series' [1991: 1573]).

Berlin and Malin complain that the television reports used the real
names of nine ex-patients, breaching their right to anonymity, and made
exaggerated claims that these nine had returned to offending after treatment at the clinic had failed. It turns out that one of these nine had not
been treated at the clinic. Another had been offered treatment but refused;
two others had refused to comply with treatment after starting it. Another
(himself a father of a young boy) had refused requests of boys to ride on
his motor scooter (his previous mode of enticement) and had otherwise
resisted situations conducive to his reoffending, yet had eventually been
convicted because of an incident in which he had 'put mulch down [the]
pants' of three boys, one of whom had done this to him. Police investigation of this incident was initiated at the request of a local parent–teacher
association where one parent had complained about having a sex offender
living in the local community. Another was also a sufferer from manic
depression; contrary to the television report, he had not been convicted of
a sexual offence but of manically spraying aerosol in a public place, causing no injury to anyone but a great deal of disturbance. Another had
'offended' in so far as he had not followed his treatment programme, a
condition of his probation, but had not been convicted of any new offence
against children at the time of the television broadcast.

Berlin and Malin do not claim universal success for their clinic, but complain bitterly about such media distortion of their work. They observe that treatment facilities are rare, and their availability is not well known to the general public because too few professionals advocate them. They note that 'strong emotions are often elicited when individuals suffer at the hands of an individual who has failed in treatment [but] the suffering and humanity of those afflicted with psychiatric disorders, and the suffering of their families, must also somehow be communicated to the public' (1991: 1576). In particular, the authors hope that stories of treatment success might help, although for this to happen the newsworthiness of reporting solely tragedies would need to be resisted.

The apparent hopelessness of finding stigma champions willing to face the media on this issue, or of media producers being willing to give space to such views, stands in marked contrast to the situation faced by other stigmatised groups. In the cases of disability and AIDS, grass-roots support and advocacy groups have become extremely high-profile media sources, routinely consulted by journalists when covering stories. No such group has emerged for child sex abusers, who remain figures that are safe to hate. This is a direct result of the extreme value that is placed on the preservation of childhood innocence

Bunglers

A further feature of child sex abuse stories is the identification in media reports of a variety of professional bunglers, who, through their incompetence or overzealous approach, end up either failing to protect children at risk or identifying the wrong perpetrators. This stems from the fact that such people – classically, social workers – are in general involved in identifying family members as perpetrators, rather than strangers. While the protection of children may be a universal commitment, the media and public opinion generally prefer to identify more external sources of threat, so that there are mixed feelings about publicly appointed guardians who do not share this view. Additionally, by doing this, journalists and other media producers can quite easily position themselves as the authentic representatives of their audience base. Thus, they curry favour with readers and viewers if they can place themselves in opposition to official opinion from time to time, or at least portray officialdom as divided. Media producers thereby artificially generate situations in which they emerge triumphant, causing endless annoyance to professionals caught up in these events. We shall see in Chapter 7 that this methodology is nowadays increasingly applied in media reporting of health-care professions.

British media interest in the social work profession began, as is pointed out by Franklin and Parton (1991), with the Maria Colwell case in 1973, where the social worker involved was vilified for failing to prevent Maria's death, to the extent that she had to be protected from an angry public when entering and leaving the public inquiry into the death, and eventually had to change her name to escape media attention. A series of such cases have created a climate of fear and defensive practice amongst social workers, with resources being disproportionately allocated to child protection work as a result. At the same time, cases in the 1980s, such as the Cleveland crisis in the UK, in which social workers and others were criticised for unnecessarily removing children from their homes, represent the opposite pole of media opinion. Franklin and Parton observe that the 'public drama of child abuse enacted on the media stage require[s], it seems, that social workers must be cast in the role of wimps or bullies, fools or villains' (1991: 14).

Franklin and Parton show that the 'fool' stereotype is supported by British press portrayals of social workers as rather witless individuals, lacking in intelligence or common sense, who have a theoretical view of the world and, as one newspaper put it, do not 'know what life is about' (*Daily Express*, quoted in Franklin & Parton, 1991: 16). Additionally, they may be characterised as too liberal or casual, with 'laid back attitudes' (*Mirror*, quoted in Franklin & Parton, 1991: 17). However, this incompetence in the case of a child death extends to wickedness by default. Thus the *Sun* newspaper pictured a social worker in such a case next to the headline, 'They Killed the Child I Adored'; and the *Mirror* reported that 'a bungling social worker was blamed yesterday for the death of four-year-old Kimberley Carlile' (1991: 17). Social workers are depicted as unrepentant for these lethal omissions: 'No-one even said sorry' (*Mirror*, quoted in Franklin & Parton, 1991: 18). Lack of readiness to remove children at risk from abusive families is the clear implication for newspapers in such cases.

However, it is precisely such removal that exposes social workers to an alternative set of charges when the circumstances are right. The Cleveland case (also discussed briefly in Chapter 2) exemplifies this, providing the template for a number of subsequent cases. Here, the stereotype applied is that of the social worker as insensitive bully. This case, in which numerous children were removed from their families following diagnoses of suspected sexual abuse by two doctors employing a controversial method of physical examination, also gave ample opportunity for the media to exploit professional difference. Indeed, the case can be best understood as a duel between opposing forces, social workers and the doctors on the one hand, and the local member of Parliament (Stuart Bell) and a police surgeon on the other. This is an example of the general media strategy of placing opposites in juxtaposition (see Chapter 2). The opposing forces in fact formed 'teams', recruiting other professionals as players to their side, following a convenient division of genders. The only player to cross the gender divide was a second diagnosing doctor (Wyatt), who was duly dropped by the press as a source of interest in favour of Marietta Higgs, the female lead, whose personality, family situation and attitudes were subjected to closely critical attention by the press. Nava (1988) points out that the Higgs team was characterised as foreign, middle-class, urban and feminist. The Bell team, by contrast, was depicted as local, with 'salt of the earth' and fatherly qualities, representing aggrieved parents falsely accused and unnaturally separated from their children. The eventual outcome of this unequal media contest was, predictably, critical of the decision to remove, and largely failing to report the findings of an independent panel that many of the initial diagnoses had been correct (Donaldson & O'Brien, 1995). A single television follow-up programme some years later, in which the 'twitch' story was that many of the allegations of abuse had reasonable grounds, had an unusually muted reception from other media (Kitzinger, 2000).

Franklin and Parton (1991), like Berlin and Malin (1991) in relation to the Johns Hopkins clinic story, feel critical of the misrepresentation involved in such coverage. Distortions in budgetary allocations result from it, they say, and a negative impact on morale is experienced by professionals. Kitzinger (1999a) reports audience research demonstrating further negative consequences: a parent who delayed seeking protection for her child out of fear that social workers would separate them, and a young girl who 'suffered sexual abuse in silence because "I used to think I'd get sent away if I told"' (Kitzinger, 1999a: 10). Kitzinger also found that media emphasis on 'stranger danger' added to parental fears about allowing their child outdoors, and contributed to the perception that sex abusers were easily recognisable as unkempt loners, rather than the male relatives and friends that they often are. Franklin and Parton (1991) advocate a variety of strategies for influencing media coverage towards more enlightened views. Yet the appeal of child abuse stories, and of the concomitant vilification of professionals involved, seems irresistible, its naked appeal being succinctly explained by a journalist:

> Child abuse makes good copy. Here is the trial that involves hundreds of column inches devoted to the details of the child's grisly end. This allows for both public conscience and appetite for horror to be satisfied at the same

time. Then there is the ritual purification: the inquiry into what went wrong and the public execution of the guilty parties – the social workers. (Hills, quoted in Franklin & Parton, 1991: 47).

SICK CHILDREN

Media images of sick children draw on many of the themes I have reviewed. The innocence of child victims is contrasted with the evil of disease, and children and their parents emerge as heroically struggling against this evil. Family and community life under these circumstances is portrayed in idealised terms. Although a significant body of professionals (largely doctors) is designated as participating in the rescue of such children, there are plentiful opportunities to stigmatise bunglers – largely the bureaucrats and politicians who run health services and set the limits for funding rescue efforts. These fairy-tale media presentations involve significant areas of repression and silence, in the depiction of family life, the suffering involved in illness, and the realities of clinical practice.

Rolland (1997) has argued that inspirational stories of sick and disabled children heroically overcoming obstacles too often represent adult fantasies that may be experienced as oppressive by disabled children and families who find themselves unable to cope in this way. Romanticised images of the family life of children with cancer, with parents positioned as endlessly self-sacrificing, children as invariably optimistic and brave, can involve serious distortions (Moller, 1996). In practice, family discipline can break down in the face of the immense pressure to treat one child as possessing special rights to parental attention; sibling rivalry may become intense under these conditions, especially if the painful procedure of bone-marrow donation becomes the sibling's obligation. The provision of 'special treats' by well-meaning adults hits reality rather harshly in a story told to me by a nurse working with terminally ill children. A child in her care, offered a trip to Disneyland, wondered whether this meant death was around the corner for her. In her experience, she said, all the other children she knew who had made this trip had then died.

My own analysis of news reports of 42 children with cancer (see earlier in this chapter for an account of this study) found plentiful evidence for the idealisation of sick children and their families. The stories follow a fairly well-established pattern, initially setting out the grounds for perceiving the children as childish. Childishness in the stories was signalled by the frequent demonstration of their entitlement to the category-bound activities (CBAs) of childhood. This is a concept taken from Sacks (Silverman, 1998), who uses it in his broader project of analysing membership categorisation devices in talk. CBAs are the activities taken to be appropriate, in a given society, for particular groupings of persons. Children are thus expected to enjoy childlike things, and if they do not, there may be a threat to established assumptions about normal behaviour. As we saw earlier, the activities and things of childhood are nowadays subject to quite careful age-gradations, which themselves have a scientific foundation in the disciplines of child development, and a commercial aspect in the provision of age-graded products such as toys. In the news reports the entitlement of children to childlike activities was used to produce the subjects of the reports as children, to show that illness threatened this production, and to engage in rescue dramas in which communal activity (of which the journalistic report is itself a part) repaired this damage.

Childhood was thus 'produced' in a variety of ways. Most commonly in the news articles that I studied, this was done by citing the sporting activities of children with cancer. Sixteen-year-old Michael Penon, for example, 'loved basketball' (*News Tribune*); eight-year-old Steven Newkirk 'liked sports so much that he began reading the newspaper when he was four, to learn about his favourite Chicago teams, the Cubs and the Bulls ... "he loved baseball and basketball" [said his father]' (*Chicago Tribune*). Otto Tang, who died aged 17, 'swam in the Class 4A state championships' (*Seattle Times*). Other sports activities of children with cancer included watching car racing and playing golf.

The possession, enjoyment and grateful receptions of toys and other kinds of presents was the next most common indicator of childish CBAs. At a charity event, three-year-old Hunter Elizabeth Jones was presented with 'a stuffed animal dog ... she gratefully named him "Atlas"' (*Press Journal*). The cancer clinic where 11-year-old David Stewart was treated contained 'Mickey Mouse toys and bright tropical fish stickers' and he spent much of his time there 'playing charades, exploring an aeronautics museum, and riding a toy bike around the pediatric ward' (*Boston Globe*). Eight-year-old Sarah Dowson 'can ride a bicycle and roller skate with help' in spite of her leg amputation (*Daily Press*). Ashley Suian's 'love of dogs keeps her in good spirits most of the time' (*Edmonton Sun*).

Another common device was to cite educational and other achievements as evidence of future potential, which is of course an entitlement of children in particular. '"He completed 2nd grade at Pritchett last year and would've entered 3rd grade this year" [said his mother]' (*Chicago Tribune*); Kelly Freeman, who died aged 17, was a 'school athlete and an author of children's books on "dogs, school and other subjects"' (*Cincinnati Inquirer*). In Michael Penon's case, educational achievements combined with his sporting interests: 'Michael Penon loved swimming and scuba diving, basketball and math. He was a junior historian and knew the Bible backward and forward' (*News Tribune*).

Appearance also indicated childishness: 'little Louis Dwyer, 5 . . . [is a] cute, blond-haired, chirpy rascal' (*The Mirror*); 'Zachary Collins's chubby 2-year-old face smiled' (*Providence Journal-Bulletin*); six-year-old Jason Stephenson was described as a 'bubbly youngster' (*Birmingham Evening Mail*). David Stewart's appeal for those who raised money for his experimental treatment lay in his appearance as well as his other CBAs:

> Hundreds of Massachusetts residents weren't about to extinguish hope. Not for an 11-year-old boy in cargo pants and basketball sneakers, who smiled and waved at the door of the plane taking him to his uncertain medical future . . . 'His father says, "Here's a boy out riding his bike and doing magic tricks, and I'm not ready to see this end."' (*Boston Globe*)

Additionally, childhood was depicted as a time of entitlement to parental love and support, friends and playmates. Michael Rutter's mother took leave of absence from her job to care for her son (*St Petersburg Times*); Ulises Magana's mother was pictured as she 'hugs her son', another picture showed 'hugs from his sister' and yet another posed Ulises with his father (*Ventura County Star*). Five-year-old Autumn Jensen, who was partially paralysed and unable to swallow because of radiation treatment, 'rested her head on her mother's shoulder' (*Milwaukee Journal Sentinel*). Eleven-year-old David Gaetke 'got a hug from his mother' (*San Diego Union-Tribune*). Louis Dwyer's adoption as a charitable cause for 'Superstar Daniel O'Donnell' involved the said superstar's being described as 'a new playmate' in a picture caption (*The Mirror*); David Stewart's 'playmates' were said to 'keep in touch' during his hospital treatment in another city (*Patriot Ledger*).

Thus childhood was routinely produced as a time of life in which certain stereotyped activities, entitlements and relationships are considered normal, healthy and desirable. Sickness could then be brought in as the destroyer of such innocently enjoyed entitlements and activities. Thus the mother of 14-year-old Bradley Rutter found that:

> It was a rare day this summer when Dora Rutter could keep 14-year-old Bradley inside. Her son's inline skates, dirt bike and fishing pole were his constant companions. But that changed in August when Bradley was diagnosed with Burkitt's lymphoma, a rare form of cancer. Since then, Bradley's

days have passed either in a hospital or at home in bed. 'Before all of this, he lived outside,' Rutter said. 'It's hard on a kid, especially in the summer.' (*St Petersburg Times*)

The effect of cancer in threatening normal childlike or teenage appearance was emphasised: 'chemotherapy has claimed his blond hair' (*St Petersburg Times*); Jason Stephenson's determination to 'live life to the full' is achieved 'despite losing his hair' (*Birmingham Evening Mail*). Natalie Willis, 14, underwent treatment 'which caused her long hair to fall out' (*Houston Chronicle*).

The tragedy of the death of Steven Newkirk was given emphasis by the stress on how this disrupted his future, whose especial brightness was emphasised by his teachers:

> 'He was a very bright child. He was one of those kids you could see a bright future for,' said Jane Kier, principal of Pritchett Elementary School in Buffalo Grove, which Steven attended. 'He was charismatic. He was interested in things.' Steven went through kindergarten, first grade and second grade at Pritchett. His illness prevented him from starting the third grade this year. 'Our whole staff, we've all known him. We're all grieving together,' Kier said. 'You hate to lose a kid, any kid, and Steven was a very special one.' (*Chicago Daily Herald*)

Similarly, the promising school careers of two teenagers, 'both from the school's gifted and talented classes . . . classmates who compete with each other for the highest grades at Westfield Middle School', were blighted by diagnoses of brain tumours (*Indianapolis News*). Due to his illness, Eric Gilliland had to take courses at home last year rather than attending junior high school: '"He was so sick at times, but he never really complained," [his mother] said. "He got four A's and two B's that year"' (*Ventura County Star*). David Stewart's ambition to be a pilot was produced poignantly by his father, who waited to see whether his son would respond to last-ditch experimental treatments after conventional therapy had failed (*Boston Globe*).

Contrast between the innocent enjoyment of childish activities and the looming threat of illness is clearly, then, a key device for journalists wishing to increase the human interest value of their stories. This contrast between innocence and evil was particularly marked in the *Toronto Sun* story of Tina Beauvais, who, having died from a malignant melanoma aged 13, was laid to rest next to the grave of Dennis Melvyn Howe, a suspected 'sex killer', 'career criminal and child killer', in whose apartment was found a bag containing 'a little girl's underwear . . . [perhaps] some kind of macabre trophy'. The reporting of his death from cancer made much of the fact that this man (who, we learn, smelled, abused alcohol, was covered with nicotine stains and had no friends) had not told anyone of the existence of his pet dog, so that it starved to death in his apartment as he lay dying a 'painful death' in hospital. The Tina Beauvais story focused on her mother's response to the news that her daughter's grave might be disturbed by plans to exhume Howe's body, but its chief appeal lies simply in the (literal) juxtaposition of the two bodies, representing opposite poles of good and evil: 'The suspected career criminal and child killer is surrounded by Christian crosses and headstones carefully tended by surviving loved ones.' In this story, then, we see a conflation of two threats to childhood innocence – cancer and sex abuse – providing a powerful journalistic opportunity.

More usually, cancer alone was used to represent evil, and the fact that much childhood cancer is now curable allowed journalists to engage readers in the kind of tense speculation about the outcome that is a familiar ploy in the reporting of sports events. As will be shown in Chapter 8, there is close connection between sports and cancer reporting, as established in other media analyses (Clarke & Robinson, 1999; Seale, 2001a), since both genres can be understood, either metaphorically or literally, to invoke a struggle for survival. The underlying drama in the childhood cancer stories was the issue of which force would win, the evil cancer or the innocent child, the more immediate news interest being the way the contest was fought. The drama of searches to find bone-marrow donors before a child died was a particularly exciting way to present this tension: '"We've been to hell and back countless times, hoping and praying the right donor would come along before it was too late," said grandmother Teresa Dwyer' (*Belfast Newsletter*). Seven-year-old Coby Howard failed to make it to the finishing line: 'Howard's family mounted a desperate fund-raising effort [to pay for a bone-marrow transplant] but could not raise the money in time to save Coby' (*Boston Globe*).

Parental love, community support and friendship were not shown as threatened, but instead as enhanced by the cancer experience. Indeed, much of the newsworthiness of the stories was derived from events that depicted almost superhuman efforts on the part of parents and others to protect and in some cases restore the threatened entitlements of childhood. In US news reports this could be made particularly poignant where parents were under-insured for the massive expenses of treatment, so that much of the immediate news interest sparking the stories were in charity fund-raising events for the treatment of particular children.

The contrast between the world of childhood and the world of sickness could be made especially poignant if the child could be designated as innocently unaware of a danger that only an adult mind could properly perceive:

> Even at the most difficult moments, his family says, David [Stewart's] mind lingers on typically boyish thoughts. [His mother] recalls seeing David look glum and introspective after a Friday bone marrow test. When she sat down to console the boy, David revealed his thoughts: he prefers Monopoly to war games. 'He's doing better than I expected,' [his father] said. (*Boston Globe*)

Here, the continuation of childish activity helps the journalist imaginatively 'rescue' David from the looming threat of illness by emphasising his immersion in the CBA of game playing. David's interest in a variety of childlike activities was, as has been shown earlier, repeatedly emphasised in the reports of his bike riding and museum visiting in Seattle. Rescue efforts were more usually reported as literal, concrete community activities, which often surrounded the children with (newsworthy) special events and ceremonies whose effects were predictably positive and resulted in the continuation or restoration of category entitlements threatened by illness.

The focus of a benefit for eight-year-old Jason Perch, for example, was on a drag race and car show, enabling the journalist to write about Jason's 'passion for cars' and to quote his father saying, '"Jason is a car buff"' (*Allentown Morning Call*). Teenager Eric Gilliland's passion for golf was such that it inspired the Orange County chapter of the Make-a-Wish foundation to get him a membership of a local golf club: 'The day got better when Gilliland was presented with bag after bag of golf shirts, balls, hats and tees. He even received a golf bag . . . "This is better than Christmas," said Gilliland' (*Ventura County Star*).

There was a distinct tendency in the reports towards idealisation of the child's character, perhaps made particularly so by the fact that five of these involved children who had died, thus introducing a eulogistic element to the report. Thus qualities of special insight, bravery, cheerfulness and altruism were commonly reported qualities of children with cancer. For example, Michael Penon's qualities were remembered by his parents, whose reminiscences are introduced sympathetically by the journalist:

> Throughout his illness, Penon never lost his propensity for caring. When interviewed on national television shows, he repeatedly called upon potential marrow donors to help the many people in need. 'He didn't just say "Help me,"' Angela Tucker said. 'He was looking out for other people. Most kids would say "Help me."' (*News Tribune*)

Children still living with cancer, however, could also attract such eulogising discourse. Nine-year-old Ulises Magana attracted a number of comments from members of the community engaged in supporting him and his family:

> 'He just draws you to him,' she said, choking back tears. 'Now you're going to make me cry. He's just very sweet and special and, what can I say, he's just a great kid.' Ulises is 'one of God's jewels,' said Martha Brunner, a school worker who is close with the Magana family. 'He's just a wonderful, wonderful person,' Vlahakis said. 'I don't know what it is.' (*Ventura County Star*)

Obstructive forces

As in all good fairy tales (Langer, 1998; Propp, 1968), heroes must overcome the obstacles put in their path by their opponents. Just as social workers are portrayed in a negative light in child abuse stories, so health-care administrators are stigmatised in child cancer stories. In fact, the view that health care ought to be an unlimited resource is promoted in a variety of media representations of health, illness and health care, as we shall see in Chapter 7. Television medical soaps, for example, consistently involve the stigmatisation of health-care administrators, who are shown variously obstructing, impeding or attempting to cut back on the health care that doctors (usually heroically) attempt to provide. Drs Kildare and Casey possessed apparently limitless resources for patient care. The harassed medics in later soaps, such as those working in *St Elsewhere*, were perhaps less heroic, but were nevertheless depicted as oppressed by a hospital bureaucracy that obstructed the implied ideal of endlessly available health care (Turow, 1989). The economic context of health care receives little serious attention in such fictional portrayals and probably contributes to a generally low level of public understanding of political debates about health care (Turow, 1996; Gerbner et al., 1981; Signorielli, 1993).

One study of the media reporting of childhood cancer, conducted by Entwistle et al. (1996), focused on coverage of a single case by British newspapers. The case of 'Child B' hit the headlines in March 1995, involving parents taking a Health Authority to court for refusing to fund experimental leukaemia treatment for their daughter. Coverage, Entwistle reports, underemphasised clinical considerations of the low likelihood of success and the potential for harmful side-effects, instead presenting it as a story about financial considerations denying a child a chance of life.

One other relevant study (Manning & Schneiderman, 1996), this time in a US context, reports an analysis of children's hospital promotional literature. The authors note that ethical committees in US children's hospitals spend half of their time debating cases where parents of terminally ill children object to a professional's wishes to cease expensive treatments that offer a hope of cure. They identify a cause of these unrealistic hopes as being an emphasis on medical miracles in the promotional literature of the hospitals themselves.

In the childhood cancer stories that I analysed, the villains were commonly obstructive health-care bureaucrats, denying children last-hope treatments for reasons kept deliberately obscure by journalists. Thus the David Stewart story hinged on the decision 'last month when the state Medicaid program refused to pay hospitalization costs associated with the disease and its treatment' (*Patriot Ledger*), prompting a surge of community fund-raising activity that resulted in David's being flown to Seattle for 'experimental' treatment. His parents 'remain angry at Massachusetts officials who they say cost David precious weeks in his fight for life . . . "They cost us some time," [his father] said of the state officials. He said David's condition had worsened considerably' (*Boston Globe*). In another report we learn that 'The Relland foundation is named for a cancer survivor whose parents had to raise money themselves after Alberta Health rejected their plea for coverage of his treatment in the US' (*Edmonton Sun*). A British report, by contrast, focuses on the bungling efforts of Derby City Council, who took two years to fit a specially adapted shower for 16-year-old Zoe Woods, whose operation for cancer had resulted in a leg 'so delicate they say that if I fall and damage it they will not be able to save it'. Once fitted, the shower seat fell off the wall: 'I couldn't believe it . . . [said her father] If that had been Zoe she would have been in serious trouble' (*Derby Evening Telegraph*). Health and social service bureaucrats, then, were aligned with the cancer itself in conspiring to destroy children's health.

In view of Manning and Schneiderman's (1996) analysis of the promotion of hopes for miracle cures in children's hospital promotional literature, it is of interest to note the reported words of David Stewart's doctor, who, while commenting on the slim chances the experimental treatment offered, was quoted as saying: 'I feel that this is valuable for the family because, obviously, if he has a successful response, that's wonderful . . . If he has not, that really clarifies for the family that they have not left a stone unturned.' (*Patriot Ledger*). These reports of children's cancer, then, appear to reinforce the tendency to regard medical care as an unlimited resource by generating a readiness to stigmatise bureaucrats. They also fail to dampen hopes for miracle cures, since, unlike bureaucrats, doctors (who provide these extremely expensive treatments) were nowhere criticised in the news reports, being aligned with the family and community in leading efforts to rescue children.

CONCLUSION

The analysis of childhood cancer news reports shows that these participated in the construction of childhood as a time of life where innocent children are entitled to childish activities. Cancer, in fact, is presented as an evil equal to other evils that threaten childhood identified by media sociologists, such as the spectre of child abuse, abduction or the more distant evils that seem to happen to children in poorer countries. The threatened disruption of childhood also provokes the identification of villains and helpers. I have argued in Chapter 2, following Langer (1998), that this rhetorical exploitation of characters standing in opposition to each other is a somewhat standardised feature of news reports designed to evoke sentiment and identification in human dramas. A ready supply of villains, who, at least in imagination, are conceived of as the allies of cancer itself, are the heartless and bungling bureaucrats who run health-care systems without prioritising the unique demands of sick children, who are deserving of limitless resources of care. While bureaucrats are stigmatised, placing them in the same camp as social workers, medical professionals, who of course benefit from this unquestioning valorisation of their expensive efforts, are conceived of as allies and helpers in the childhood cancer story. Primarily, though, help at the most heroic level emanates from 'the community', conceived of as gathering round equally heroic but nevertheless overwhelmed sets of parents, who are portrayed as confronting the limits of an almost endless supply of parental love. Thus parents both represent the best and most intensive aspects of community endeavour, and are at the same time in need of community support against the combined forces of disease and bureaucracy. Hence the opportunity for the journalistic report, which both records and orchestrates community effort.

Although doctors get off lightly in the reporting of childhood cancer, it will become clear in the chapters that follow that this is not always the case. To a significant extent, contemporary portrayals of health matters in the media have participated in challenging medical authority. In the two chapters that follow I shall show how this has occurred, and how media-sponsored, somewhat narcissistic consumer-heroes have emerged in recent years to take centre stage.

7 Professional Heroes

Scared by the dangers of modern life and its environmental threats, persecuted by wicked or freakish people, the innocent victim is now ready for rescue by a conquering hero. Two main sources of heroic rescue generally present themselves to the mass media audience: the medical profession and the special heroism that ordinary people themselves show when under threat. This chapter deals with the first of these, and the next chapter with the second. It will become clear that the doctor's status as hero has become particularly insecure in recent times as media producers have found that challenges to traditional sources of authority create an entertaining effect, allowing the pantomime-like opposition of good and evil in media health representations to be given a further twist. In addition, portrayals of conflict between experts throw individual members of the media audience back on themselves as the primary source of authority in health matters. This is in accord with Giddens's (1991) portrayal of self-identity in late modernity, in which he emphasises the obligation of modern individuals to treat the self as a project, involving information gathering, risk profiling and a chronic anxiety about which expert to trust (see Chapter 1). Media producers are primarily committed to the acquisition of larger audiences, and this is a powerful motive for constructing ordinary people as possessing exceptional qualities of character, an imagined community of everyday heroes. This is enhanced by an extreme valorisation of lay beliefs and a demotion of professional authority and knowledge. Thus the myth-making media health producer feeds the narcissism of mass audiences, a process made more effective if the trustworthiness of professionals can be held in a tantalising balance.

As we saw in Chapter 3, sociological commentators (for example, Bury & Gabe, 1994; Karpf, 1988) have been concerned to assess the degree to which medical prestige and cultural authority have come under threat in recent years. I think that there is no doubt that they have, although there seems little prospect that the medical profession will undergo the same level of unremitting vilification as social workers, whose therapeutic effectiveness is harder to assess (Franklin & Parton, 1991; see also

Chapter 6). Instead, medical people are portrayed as having considerable, even magical powers, which they can wield for good or evil, or sometimes be unqualified to hold by virtue of character. Thus images of medical heroes are juxtaposed with images of both medical villains and bunglers.

This chapter charts these oppositions in a series of case studies of medicine in the media, showing how media portrayals of doctors have changed over time. Soap operas, news stories about genetics, coverage of high-technology versus low-technology medicine, and alternative therapies are discussed in turn. I also discuss the powerful magical substances – drugs and medicines – that are wielded by doctors but also have an independent life of their own in the world of media health. Portrayals of other health-care professionals – particularly nurses – are an important area, as are the gender stereotypes that exist in media portrayals of doctors, but these topics will largely be discussed in Chapter 9, which focuses on gender issues in media health.

MEDICAL SOAPS

The television medical soap opera is a primary location for media portrayals of heroic doctors wielding magical powers and has been analysed by a number of commentators, most extensively in Joseph Turow's (1989) book, *Playing Doctor: Television, Storytelling and Medical Power*, on the history of medical soaps on US television. Turow interviewed many of the people involved in the production of the soaps, and so offers considerable insight into the influence of medical interests over time, describing the relationship between media producers and the medical profession as symbiotic and negotiated. Medical organisations in the early days showed a keen interest in promoting a positive image of the profession in the soaps, and television producers needed the stamp of approval that medical organisations could give, since this enhanced their claim to authenticity. The early *Dr Kildare* movies of the 1930s, which later became a popular radio and television series, were pleasing to the American Medical Association (AMA), as they showed doctors in heroically positive relations with patients. Dr Kildare's motives were always above reproach, showing a noble dedication to healing ideals rather than financial reward. On this and many subsequent series, the AMA and other medical organisations were therefore pleased to offer advice to scriptwriters on the accuracy of their accounts of medical procedures. Keen to resist socialised medicine and preserve private practice, the AMA supported such series as *Dr*

Kildare and *Ben Casey* in the 1950s as an ideal way to preserve the cultural authority of medicine, at a time when a general faith in scientific progress was anyway frequently attached to medicine. Stories showing doctors covering up for colleagues' mistakes, being rancorous, swearing, sitting on patients' beds and drinking alcohol on duty were all censored by an AMA advisory committee, whom television producers regularly consulted. Storylines commonly involved acute rather than chronic illness, so that a dramatic closure could be reached, typically involving a life/death situation with medical intervention causing eventual recovery.

Television doctors also displayed unusual levels of empathy and insight into their patients' emotional lives, being apparently willing to go to extraordinary lengths to solve patients' personal problems and thus demonstrate their superior human wisdom over a wide range of human affairs. Thus the time doctors had available for patients in these series was depicted as endless, and here Turow makes one of his main points about such soaps: they provided the public with a misleading impression of health-care policy and finance, contributing to a view that health care is a limitless resource. Yet attempts to deviate from the Kildare/Casey formula were dogged by low ratings. For example, series featuring the contribution of nurses, clinical psychologists and psychiatrists to health care were all run but were short-lived, since these professions were hard to portray as being routinely involved in taking life or death decisions, the main appeal of medical soaps for audiences. As Turow puts it, the core concern of successful medical soaps in the 1960s was to depict 'human emotions entangled in a male physician's technological struggle with death' (1989: 105).

The *Marcus Welby* show in the late 1960s and early 1970s showed some shifts in this genre, being about a family doctor rather than hospital practice, and incorporating some treatment of social problems such as sexually transmitted disease and child abuse. Pleased about the publicity the series gave to their members, the American Association of Family Physicians gave the series its support. However, the withdrawal of the AMA from direct involvement marked the beginning of a relative disengagement from the production of television soaps by medical organisations, whose enthusiasm for these had waned. Now, medical organisations expressed concern about the unrealistic demands placed on doctors by excessively idealistic portrayals, and the 'Marcus Welby syndrome' was coined to describe patients demanding miracle recoveries.

Attempts at shows that were critical of the integrity of medical practitioners were slow to emerge and largely unsuccessful when they did, even in a climate of general willingness to criticise traditional sources of authority in the social upheavals of the 1960s and 1970s. In academic and policy circles, and in news items from time to time, concern might have been rising about the costs of health care, the excessive remuneration of doctors, their paternalistic relations with patients or the rising medicalisation of social problems, but these criticisms were not evident in television soaps. Instead, doctors' personal problems in achieving their heroic goals were emphasised more, in an attempt to 'humanise' the god-like image previously portrayed, and innovations such as female or black doctors were tried. *MASH* was eventually to hit on a successful formula, showing harassed medics struggling to cope with unreasonable pressure, an image that was applauded by the AMA. Since then, there have been many soaps that chase the spirit of *MASH*, though not always seeking comedy status. *St Elsewhere*, for example, in the 1980s, focused on young medics working in a run-down environment, struggling against an exploitative hospital bureaucracy to deliver an adequate service nevertheless. Since Turow's book, series like *ER* and, in the UK, *Casualty* have emerged as recent popular versions of this theme, showing hospital bureaucrats in stigmatised roles enacting penny-pinching policies and struggling medics facing impossible odds, yet staying very human, in casualty scenarios that resemble a war zone. In fact, such drama series are close to the 'reality television' shows that reconstruct 'real-life' rescues (discussed in Chapter 1) and are similarly uncritical of the rescue personnel. There is very little to suggest any criticism of the fundamental ethical commitment to patient care exhibited by doctors in these soaps. As late as 1996, Turow was still able to take the view (in a *Lancet* article) that in soaps

> economic and health-policy issues [are] rarely discussed adequately . . .
> The position is that . . . empathetic physicians ought to keep controlling
> health care, and that all sorts of medical care, including the high-tech type,
> ought to be available quickly to all whenever needed. (1996: 1240, 1243)

The essential elements of Turow's analysis appear in a number of studies of medical soaps up to the mid-1980s (for example, Liebmann-Smith & Rosen, 1978; Gerbner et al., 1981; Kalisch et al., 1983; Lunin, 1987; McGlaughlin, 1975; Pearl et al., 1982). Evidently, though, the changes in the genre that have occurred since then, while largely positive towards the beneficence of the medical profession, open some chinks in the medical hero's armour. Lupton (1998a) notes the emergence in the 1990s of some shows (*Cardiac Arrest* in the UK; *GP* in Australia) that portrayed doctors as significantly more alienated and less caring about patients than previous soaps. Thus *GP* showed doctors displaying lapses of judgement and being criticised by patients on occasion. *Cardiac Arrest,* penned by a

British medical practitioner turned scriptwriter, disillusioned with the National Health Service, revelled in its depictions of medical cynicism in a show that mixed satire with black comedy.

These deviations may reflect different national television cultures, but some evidence suggests that even in American products the heroic image has been dented. Pfau et al. (1995) note that more recent US soaps (*Chicago Hope*, and *ER*, for example) depart from earlier depictions of 'front stage' behaviour. Instead they 'often expose back regions, revealing occasional uncertainties in diagnosis and mistakes in treatment, and exposing unflattering personal traits, including adultery, arrogance and avarice' (1995: 455). In their study of audiences these authors found that while perceptions of physicians as powerful and of high social status were still strong, people also saw them as 'lower in character . . . less moral, right, unselfish, good and honest' than did physicians themselves, and expressed concern over the 'erosion of public trust in physicians' that this represents (1995: 455). They also found that audience members were more likely to visualise doctors as young and female, a finding which highlights the shift that has occurred since the days of *Dr Kildare* and *Ben Casey*.

In view of this, it is of interest to note that there may also be movement in the medical profession towards a more ironic sensibility regarding fictional depictions. As we have seen in Turow's account, the history of medical involvement in soap production reflects an early intense preoccupation to hold on to a squeaky clean image through censorship, followed by a period of relative disengagement. A sign of change, perhaps, is the fact that John Collee (1999), a novelist and scriptwriter, was given space in the *British Medical Journal* to express dissident views. Collee argues against the view that medical people should concern themselves with inaccurate and unclear medical information in television soaps, or even positively health-damaging portrayals, such as a paracetamol overdose that might encourage copycat behaviour. Instead, it should be recognised that 'things are more interesting if they are not fully explained' (1999: 955), so that the mumbled technical instructions of *ER* staff are fascinating precisely because they are mysterious. The response to portrayals of dangerous behaviour should not be censorship, which results in bland drama, but acceptance that such fiction works at a deeper level if it is allowed to treat dangerous themes, leading to more 'profound meditations on the great imponderables of life' (1999: 955). This is a relatively sophisticated and permissive view of the relationship between audiences and texts, its appearance in a prominent medical journal suggesting some willingness to depart from a crude censorship-oriented model.

MAGICAL CURES AND DANGEROUS POTIONS

Medical soaps, in spite of the recent changes I have described, present more positive images of the medical profession than other media genres. In particular, news stories have been significantly more critical of the profession in recent years than have dramatic fictions. Before turning to this, though, I shall discuss some important components of medical power: the 'tools of the trade' employed by doctors. Medicines, drugs and other medical therapies are, in a sense, the 'spells' wielded by the magical doctor-hero, and it seems from media depictions that the power of these can be wielded for good or for evil. Sometimes the magicians themselves can use these for wicked ends; sometimes they fall into the 'wrong hands'. I shall begin by discussing medicines and drugs, and then turn to genetic therapies and other high-technology tools in order to demonstrate how these are employed in the media to generate entertaining oppositions that play with the theme of public trust in medical authority.

Medicines and drugs

The opposition of legal medicines and illegal drugs is a fundamental one for media producers, but within each of these there is room for further contrast: drug culture can be portrayed as negative, harmful and addictive, or it can be glamorised as an expression of freedom of spirit. Medicines can be presented as magical solutions to illness, or as having harmful side-effects that outweigh any benefits. Rarely do media presentations present a balanced picture of harm and benefit contained in a single substance, a point made, for example, by Entwistle and Sheldon (1999), who provide a collection of typically enthusiastic headlines accompanying reports of drug discoveries: 'Drug found to cut the risk of cancer by half . . . New drug to fight obesity "epidemic" . . . Cancer: is this finally a cure? New drug can destroy tumours' (1999: 130). The side-effects of such new treatments, argue Entwistle and Sheldon, are normally downplayed in favour of stress on the promise of cures – particularly where cancer is involved. On the other hand, once a medicine or drug acquires the status of a health scare story, it seems that it can have no benefits, reminding us that, as Sandman has put it, journalists are in 'the outrage business' (quoted in Nelkin, 1995: 63). Thus Norplant, a contraceptive implant, having been the subject of favourable publicity on its launch, was reported differently once the side-effect of heavy menstrual bleeding in some women became news: 'Media coverage . . . in 1995 and 1996 was almost entirely negative, focusing on the problems experienced by some users and losing sight of the usefulness and acceptability of the product to others' (Entwistle & Sheldon, 1999: 130).

A message underlying news about the benefits of medicines is that there are quick chemical solutions to complex life problems. This sentiment has been shown, in studies from the 1970s on, to be quite general in the mass media. We saw in Chapter 3 that Chapman's (1979) analysis of drug advertisements in medical magazines presented these as easily applied solutions to problems that could otherwise seem difficult to address. Gerbner (1978), in an amusing analysis of *Superman* and other superhero comics, points out that reliance on performance-enhancing substances is frequently presented as essential in the transformation from weakling to hero, contributing to a culture of drug dependence. This aspect of the culture is also revealed in Hanneman and McEwan's (1976) content analysis of US television, which indicated a high frequency of advertisements for headache pills and cold, stomach and allergy relief preparations, with few warnings about side-effects. Additionally, alcohol was commonly presented as benefiting the consumer by providing relaxation, enhanced sociability or sexual allure. Lowery's (1980) account of the portrayal of alcohol consumption in daytime soaps on US television similarly showed it being used for social facilitation, crisis management and an escape from an oppressive reality. This and other studies (see, for example, Signorielli's [1993] review) have shown that there is very little in media portrayals to indicate the harmful effects of alcohol consumption.

In a drug-oriented culture, then, it is hardly surprising that medicines themselves get a good press (although the activities of the drug companies that produce them are often subjected to criticism in the media). Van Trigt et al. (1994, 1995) have analysed coverage of medicines in newspapers and magazines in The Netherlands and concluded that these contain more good news about such drugs than bad, newspaper coverage being significantly less likely than professional journals to contain stories of side-effects. This, they claim, on the basis of their study of science writers and their sources, is because pharmacy professionals, who might provide a more balanced view, are rarely consulted by journalists. Further evidence of the positive press that medicines receive is the coverage of Prozac and Viagra, which have been presented as largely unproblematic solutions to the life problems that they target. Nelkin's (1995) analysis of the Prozac phenomenon charts the 'extraordinary media attention' (1995: 71) that this drug received in the 1990s, leading to the drug becoming a 'star, appearing on talk shows, magazines, and news reports, as the "feel good" drug' (1995: 71). Sales grew enormously, in spite of a brief episode of negative coverage when it was suggested that the drug encouraged violent behaviour, so that it became widely seen as a technological fix to life problems. Viagra, a few years later, was to receive similar 'rave reviews' in the media, overwhelming any suggestion of negative effects.

It might be imagined, at a time when 'natural' products are widely presented as desirable, that negative messages might be more prominent about the artificiality or non-naturalness of drug solutions, yet these are relatively rare. In fact, drugs can at times be promoted as 'natural' and even as alternatives to orthodox medicine if circumstances are right. The rows of pill bottles next to organic products in health-food shops are a testament to this. Uusitalo et al. (2000) have documented Finnish press coverage of anti-oxidant food supplement medications, designed to counteract the cancer-inducing prevalence of 'free radicals' in the body. These substances, criticised by many orthodox medical practitioners as ineffective and unnecessary, were presented by the press in largely positive terms, in language that stressed their impact on looking and feeling good. This resulted in the paradox of conventional medicine recommending a wholesome diet rather than medication, with pills being promoted by enthusiasts for alternative medicine. Miles (1998) presents a similar account of the commercialisation of natural remedies in Ecuador, in which radio stations influenced by local producers of the remedies presented them as containing concentrated doses of 'natural' substances. These were advocated for their effectiveness in combating the stresses of modern city living, a selling point for a population recently uprooted from living in rural areas. Thus medicines and pills of all sorts are widely regarded as containing sources of power. Perception that the medical profession controls access to many of these substances therefore inevitably enhances their status and prestige.

The magical powers of medicines and drugs, though, can also be presented as harmful if either doctors or lay people misuse them, and it is clear that media producers then take every opportunity to display outrage, condemning the products they may previously have supported. Taking doctors first, considerable work has been done on media coverage of tranquillisers and neuroleptic drugs, a fact which has important implications for the public image of the medical profession. Gabe and Bury (1988) report a study of British media coverage of the 'social problem' of benzodiazepine tranquilliser dependence. Consumer programmes on radio and television ran atrocity stories of dependence, criticising both drug companies for overselling these to doctors, and family doctors for being too ready to resort to them as well as negligent in subsequent monitoring of patients' use. The programmes conveyed a sense of alarm and panic about the supposed widespread nature of this dependency and, predictably, showed no positive images of these drugs, whose effectiveness in relieving distress was 'old' news and therefore not reportable. 'Doorstepping' of individual rogue doctors, deemed to have peddled tranquillisers irresponsibly, was a feature of one exposé programme. Finzen et al. (1999), in a study of German media coverage of minor tranquillisers, similarly found far more negative coverage than positive. (The study of Hoffmann-Richter et al. [1999], summarised in Chapter 5, which found atrocity stories being reported in the German media regarding neuroleptic drugs, is also relevant here.) Such negative media treatment of drugs, Bury and Gabe (1994; Gabe & Bury, 1996) argue, along with media coverage of other failings of doctors, provides powerful evidence that the public image of the profession is no longer secure, its heroic status being under threat.

Yet drugs, it seems, are not solely extensions of medical power in the popular imagination, having independent potency, which, when released into the wrong hands, has dangerous consequences. Coverage of the use of illegal drugs, many of which also have a medical or scientific use but have somehow 'escaped' these controls, generally emphasises harmful effects. Gerbner's (1978) study of the comic books used in anti-drug campaigns showed them to contain state-sponsored stigmatisation of drug users as hopelessly dependent creatures, swinging between pathetic cravings and violent and otherwise anti-social behaviour. Media-orchestrated moral panics about epidemics of drug use occur from time to time. Thus Kline (1996) charts the US media obsession in the late 1980s with the effects of crack cocaine usage by mothers on their unborn babies. Shoemaker et al. (1989) note that this was part of a general press feeding frenzy in covering a state-sponsored programme waging 'war on drugs' at the time, and involving significant distortions of the scale of drug problems. It is worth noting, however, that drug counter-culture may at times be glamorised in certain sections of the media – notably in films (Winick & Winick, 1976).

Recent developments that involve direct-to-consumer advertising of prescription drugs in the US suggest that pharmaceutical companies are exploiting the decoupling of medicines from medical control. Pinto's (2000) analysis of such advertisements in popular magazines suggests that these combine information about the drugs with powerful emotional appeals. Bell et al. (1999) surveyed a sample of Californians and found that just under half said that they would be disappointed if their physician were to refuse their request for such a drug, with sizeable minorities saying that they would seek the prescription elsewhere or terminate their relationship with the physician. Professional monopoly of medicines, it seems, may thus be undermined as consumerism advances.

It remains the case, however, that much of the power and authority of the medical profession stems from the public perception that effective cures are available for a variety of conditions through its services. Drug-based cures are generally presented as evidence of these professional powers, even though these substances may at times be presented in the media as possessing independent powers. The media treatment of medicines and drugs demonstrates a tendency to idealise or stigmatise, creating oppositional extremes. Clearly, there are opportunities for polarised accounts of the profession to be rehearsed under the cover of such stories, and some evidence (for example, regarding tranquilliser dependence) suggests that negative stories about medicines reflect an implied critique of the cultural authority of the medical profession. The ability of doctors to perform heroic rescues (or to misuse this responsibility) can also be demonstrated in media coverage of other kinds of medical technology, to which we can now turn.

Genetics

Genetic knowledge is usually covered as a science story with therapeutic spin-offs and is useful for demonstrating the hopes and fears that become attached to cutting-edge bio-scientific activity. Doctors are widely perceived to be the key personnel involved in turning such scientific discovery into therapeutic benefit, and the status of the profession rests in large part on its image as one that is deeply involved with science. The promise of new medical treatments is usually presented as the chief justification for this genetic research. Analyses of media coverage suggest that over time positive messages – at least in relation to medical therapies – have become more dominant than negative ones, with the views of scientists and other DNA research enthusiasts being given prominence over more critical views. Nevertheless, the media, as with the reporting of medicines, exercises its power to provide news of scares from time to time, teasingly building up and then questioning the level of public trust in medical science.

Coverage of the recombinant DNA industry in the 1970s in the US press has been analysed by Pfund and Hofstadter (1981), who note a switch from early stories about fears to later ones stressing benefits. Dissident scientists and environmentalists sparked a first wave of coverage of possible risks of the new technology, but this soon subsided, leaving biotechnology industry representatives free to stress benefits, resulting in headlines such as 'DNA's New Miracles' and 'Interferon: The IF Drug for

Cancer' (1981: 149). Singer and Endreny (1987), whose survey of US news and television in 1984 found coverage that was roughly equally balanced between risks and benefits, show how fears were downplayed in one *Wall Street Journal* report:

> 'Who knows whether those microbes are going to migrate and cause havoc? . . . Once these bacteria get out, you can't put them back in a drum' [said Jeremy Rifkin, an industry critic]. Scientists working with the ice-minus bug scoff at their fears . . . 'This whole controversy is bloody absurd' [said John Bedbrook, an industry spokesman]. (1987: 21)

Since then, of course, in the 1990s there has been a wave of negative coverage outside the US relating to genetically modified crops and foods, based on fear of environmental risk. Frankenstein-like fears have also been generated by stories of cloning, especially where larger animals (for example, Dolly the sheep) have been involved. But the application of human genetic research to medical therapies has received markedly positive coverage from the 1980s onwards, intensifying in recent years with news of the Human Genome Project. Nelkin (1995) has described this as the 'new frontier' (1995: 10) for science journalists after the decline in newsworthiness of space travel. She points out that news of discoveries of genes linked to common diseases, such as cancer, often promote unrealistically high expectations of cure, leading to a degree of disappointment when these are slow to emerge. Yet the appetite for such tales appears to be insatiable. Conrad (1997), surveying US news reports of genetics stories, charts the way in which genetic explanations for a variety of human behaviours – alcoholism, mental illness, homosexuality, violence and links between race and IQ – have been promoted. (See also Spanier [2000] for a feminist analysis of this phenomenon in relation to explaining homosexuality.) The rise of this 'genetic paradigm' (1997: 142) has, in Conrad's view, involved significant distortions: news that discoveries have been disproven has been suppressed, for example, and the paradigm underplays social and environmental causation of human behaviour, such genetic essentialism containing disturbing echoes of eugenic ideas. Press enthusiasm for genetic explanations and therapies is partly explained, Conrad (1999) feels, by the fact that journalists (whom he interviewed) rely largely on scientists and researchers for stories, rarely using dissident voices (except in the case of the 'gay gene' story, where gay activist organisations were used as sources).

Nevertheless, the potential exists, as in all media health coverage, for 'twitches' to the general story of benefits. Kitzinger and Reilly's (1997) study of UK media coverage in 1995–96 of human genetics research found, like Petersen, largely favourable accounts of the promise of such science (for example, 'Breakthrough in the search for cystic fibrosis cure' [1997: 322]), but some indications that news of the risks of human genetics research was about to gather pace as the Dolly story broke towards the end of the period they covered. Petersen's (2001) study of Australian news media during 1996–99 also revealed an overwhelmingly positive treatment of gene research, but he stresses that this was most secure when it could be framed as contributing to medical therapy. Fears about the implications of cloning were also evident, and had to be dealt with by drawing a boundary between 'good' medical uses and 'bad' uses of cloning for reproductive purposes. Like Conrad (1999), Petersen found dominance of scientific sources in media reports, emphasising the unlocking of 'nature's secrets'. Thus, typical headlines included 'Gene find may lead to vaccine for malaria'; 'Cancer gene identified'; Discovery of mutant gene offers HIV hope'; 'Discovery of bowel cancer gene gives hope of prevention' (2001: 1261). But, although rare by comparison, there were deviations from this optimistic coverage, stressing fears of cloning gone out of control, as in 'Maverick will clone his wife' and 'Organ-farming' (2001: 1266). In an interesting further development of these 'twitches' and reversals, Nelkin (2001, personal communication) notes that recent press coverage of the death of an American teenager undergoing gene therapy received massive US media coverage, to the extent that it can be compared with the effect of the *Challenger* shuttle disaster on support for the space programme. If confidence in the medical application of gene therapy can be so significantly dented by a single story, it seems clear that a more wide-ranging questioning of trust in this weapon of medical heroism may emerge in the future. A cycle of 'boosterism' followed by disappointment and vilification is, of course, a general feature of media health coverage (see Chapter 2).

High technology/low technology

Genetic therapy is an example of the application of cutting-edge high technology to medicine. Historically, it is the latest in a long line of high-technology medical developments that usually attract a great deal of media interest. Heroic images of modern medicine are partially built from the perception that doctors have a variety of instruments containing concentrations of power at their disposal. A number of critical media analysts have concluded that there is a distorted focus on high-technology medicine, diverting attention away from low-technology health care, issues of public health, preventive medicine and therapies that are alternatives to orthodox biomedicine. By contrast, I believe that, while it is true that high technology receives a great deal of media attention, this is not always supportive. There are significant developments to suggest that media championing of consumer power increasingly involves criticism of older images of the high-technology medical warrior-hero.

We have seen that the tendency to present health care as an unlimited resource, stigmatising health-care managers and politicians who attempt to impose rationing, is an important theme in media health representations. Much of this involves demand for expensive new medical technology, to be used by hospital-based doctors. Garland (1984) presents a content analysis of British BBC television programmes in the early 1980s, finding that 'hospital-based, technological and expert-dependent issues' rather than 'primary care and community health' were predominant (1984: 316). Doctors were the most frequently interviewed professional group when health-care matters were considered and, of the 70 doctors interviewed on television during the three-month period, 74 per cent were hospital doctors. General practitioners and nurses were significantly under-represented.

Johnson and Johnson (1993) found the same things in a study of British television in 1988–89, additionally noting that the emphasis on high-technology hospital medicine was facilitated by focusing on unusual and more serious diseases, and by rarely covering alternative medicine. Karpf's (1988) account of British television up to the mid-1980s expands on these studies by providing qualitative details of the coverage of heart transplantation, arguing that such stories followed a template:

> Journalists regularly clone the heart transplant story, producing perfect replicas of previous reports. They stress the desperation of those waiting for a heart, and the fear that time will run out. The fatal alternative is made plain. The operation is depicted as offering the chance of a new life or future, an opportunity to vanquish death. Grief and joy are voiced, and the press conference following the operation is an aria of hope . . . Cameras follow the patient's first post-operation cup of tea, the first meal, and their first faltering steps . . . viewers are enlisted as partisans in their dramatic 'battle against rejection'. Human interest doesn't come in larger size. (1988: 149)

The death in 1991 in a bungled street robbery of Australia's most prominent heart surgeon, Dr Victor Chang, prompted Lupton and Chapman (1991) to further analysis of the extreme value placed by the media on heart transplantation technology at this time. Chang's work with transplantation and artificial hearts was described in superlative terms, portraying him as a 'secular saint . . . a hero, saviour and life-saver, able to bring people back to life' (1991: 1583–4). An extract from one of many articles eulogising Chang and his work conveys a flavour of the coverage:

> In the early days of the heart transplant team there was always a kind of electricity at the weekly meetings whenever the surgeons had come straight from an operation. It came from Victor Chang. The charge he felt after a transplant would excite the room of 30 or more people. Victor Chang endured 12 hour shifts with enthusiasm and tireless energy . . . the mission at the core of Victor Chang's life [was to] use his skills to restore as many people as possible to health. He said its job satisfaction was unbeatable. (*Sydney Sunday Telegraph*, quoted in Lupton & Chapman, 1991: 1584).

As heart transplants have become more routine, their news value has lessened. They are covered now only if an extra twist can be produced, as in reports in June 2001 of the donation, to an Israeli, of a heart by the family of a Palestinian shot by Israeli soldiers. Here, the interest is no longer in the wonder of the operation, but on the political element of the story. This should not detract, however, from the point that there is considerable media interest in medical applications of the latest technical advances, this interest finding new objects (such as genetic therapy) as new technological developments emerge.

A number of media analysts have therefore focused on what the high-technology story misses out. Kristiansen and Harding (1984, 1988) note that press emphasis on the rare and the dramatic, with medical technology coming in to rescue the afflicted, suggests that illness is a matter of fate or chance, rather than healthy behaviour. These authors note that socio-economic causes of ill health are missed out in such media portrayals. Signorielli (1993) also notes the lack of focus on preventive medicine and environmental causes of illness, observing, too, that coverage of occupational health issues is almost non-existent in the US media. Raymond's (1985) analysis of occupational health coverage in the US media notes a difference between mainstream media and the more radical 'advocacy press', whose coverage is far more critical of political power structures as they impinge on occupational health, stressing the exploitation of workers impelled to take health risks in order to find work or keep their jobs. Westwood and Westwood (1999), in their study of Australian news media, complain that public health and health promotion news was presented less often than what they call 'medical model' news (1999: 53) of things like treatment, technology and research.

As well as occupational, public and preventive medicine, some media analysts (for example, Karpf, 1988) have claimed that alternative therapy is undervalued because of the dominant media emphasis on high-technology medicine. Yet Karpf recognised that coverage of this topic has become notably more sympathetic than it once was. In fact, media promotion of the benefits of alternative therapy is often associated with attempts to construct media producers as representing the 'voice of the people' against an oppressive medical establishment. In a fascinating case study, Smith (1992) makes it clear that media interest in alternative therapies can, in fact, quite easily switch between positive and negative coverage. During the 1980s in certain sections of the Canadian media, Dr Stanislaw Burzynski, inventor and purveyor of an alternative treatment for cancer, was vilified as a charlatan and swindler, Canadian media representatives mounting a strong case against paying for Burzynski's therapies from national health service funds. At the same time, Burzynski was treated far more sympathetically in the US media, where a view was taken of him as an individual persecuted by pharmaceutical companies wishing to sell conventional cancer medicines. Thus the media of both countries used Burzynski as a tool to create an 'exposé' story, on the one hand the malpractice of a quack, and on the other the excessive greed of big business. This is a rather neat illustration of the ambivalent view that media producers may take when covering expertise, concerned to champion the consumer, but choosing from a range of oppressors as targets, including medical therapists themselves should this suit the circumstances.

OVERTHROW BY CONSUMERS

Views that oppose organised medical interests are not as weakly represented in the media as is suggested by some 'critical' media analysts. This was demonstrated by Leask and Chapman's (1998) study of Australian print media reporting of anti-immunisation campaigning (summarised in Chapter 4). These authors argue that the appeal of this media-reported campaign is to a sense of individualism, enhanced by the portrayal of individual struggle against the forces of commerce and bureaucracy – a 'deservedly newsworthy' story for media producers since this enables the campaigners to 'locate their cause under a canopy of similar newsworthy discourses that centre on the moral authority of the individual' (1998: 23).

In fact, we are now in a position to argue that the dominance of high-technology treatments in the media is by no means as complete as some analysts have suggested. As seen in the case studies of medicines and genetic therapies, as well as the relatively low-technology issue of vaccination, oppositional voices (such as those advocating alternative therapies) are also championed in the media, and chief amongst these is that of the health-care 'consumer', who, I shall argue in the chapter that follows this one, is nowadays constituted as an alternative hero to professionals in media health representations. Reverence for the consumer-hero, and a concomitant decline in respect for high-technology medicine have been highlighted in several studies of media health, although their significance has not always been appreciated. Karpf (1988), for example, although largely stuck with a view that medical dominance of the media is here to stay, nevertheless provides early evidence for the oppositional rise of consumer power in her account of media reporting of childbirth issues. During the 1970s and 1980s a critique of high-technology medical dominance of childbirth was successful in capturing the media agenda, and in forcing obstetricians to rethink the humanity of routine procedures that medicalised the experience. Karpf, however, regards this episode, as she does other emanations of consumer power, as little more than a readjustment of the nature of medical dominance, so that doctors learned new holistic, patient-centred methods of control.

Yet it is clear, from a later perspective, that the old-style medical heroism involved in technological rescue motifs is now increasingly questioned by media producers concerned to work up stories of the heroism of ordinary people. This is by no means as superficial as Karpf suggests. Bunton's (1997) study of changes in health reporting over four decades of the American magazine *Good Housekeeping* is revealing in this respect, finding a decline in articles revering medical authority in favour of articles criticising orthodox biomedical approaches to health problems and giving positive coverage to alternative therapies. Advice columns written by doctors disappeared from the magazine during the 1980s, so that the magazine now directly invites its readers in a joint enterprise of consumption of healthy lifestyles. A much more narcissistic, pleasure-seeking image of the medical consumer was presented in the 1990s, compared with the 1950s, when a more docile submission to medical expertise had been depicted. The new consumer, in fact, is shown choosing from a collage of potential healthy selves and health-enhancing products, which have themselves proliferated, so that now a range of things not previously associated with health considerations – margarine and Volvo cars, for example – are now seen to be health matters. In this new scenario, the doctor-hero is very much in the background, and if present at all, is not so much demoted as irrelevant. Bunton presents this within a Foucauldian analysis of the exercise of power under advanced liberalism, yet it is clear that this form of 'power' is very far removed from notions of dominance by the cultural authority of any one group, such as the medical profession.

Perhaps recognising this shift towards consumer 'power', Lupton (1998b) has modified her earlier, rather more trenchantly critical, views of oppression by medicine via media representations (for example, Lupton 1994b) to make the valuable point that the emergence of the consumer depends on a willingness to question medical expertise, and that this critical line has been an important feature of media coverage in recent years. Her review notes that many media stories nowadays toy with issues of trust, holding out the possibility that previously revered medical figures may not be so perfect after all.

Livingstone and Lunt's (1994) study of television talk shows demonstrates rather precisely the ways in which these achieve the effect of placing experts on the defensive when confronted with the life experiences of ordinary people. In these participatory discussion programmes (such as *Kilroy* or the *Oprah Winfrey Show*), 'expertise is undermined and lay discourse is elevated' (1994: 97) in an exercise that intensifies distrust of established power. Experts are required by the hosts of these programmes to speak in lay terms and to be accountable to a lay audience whose credibility is enhanced because they speak 'from experience' rather than from the more abstract knowledge traditionally relied upon by experts. This can lead to episodes of almost ritual humiliation for the experts who take part, with the show's 'host' acting to protect or speak for the lay participant. In one episode from *Kilroy* about the adequacy of doctors' consulting styles the host said, after a lay member of the audience had recounted a horror story about insensitive communication by her doctor:

> Do you doctors recognize yourselves? All the doctors are sitting very quiet aren't they, but I know where you all are (laughter) . . . all very . . . no doctors want to respond to all this? Doctor, do you recognize yourself, looking at your watch when they walk in, giving prescriptions without listening? (1994: 103)

A viewer summarises the effect of this:

> On the television, the doctor is on an equal footing with any of his patients, just as the Archbishop of Canterbury is with a pop star and yet in real life that is not so. People are not equal in society . . . and yet on the box, everyone is the same, and maybe it is good that this should be so. The telly is a great equalizer, a leveller if you like. (1994: 101)

In fact, knocking the image of the traditional medical hero in order to make way for the media-sponsored consumer voice is a major theme of contemporary media health coverage, and it is to this that we can now turn in the final section of this chapter.

FLAWED HEROES

Critical media coverage of doctors does not usually approach the level of vilification experienced by social workers. But the Cleveland child abuse scandal (reviewed in Chapter 6) gave the media an unusual opportunity to include a doctor in the same frame as social workers. It will be recalled that this scandal involved a local politician and his allies opposing the decision of local social services to remove children from families suspected of abusing them. A doctor, Marietta Higgs, was singled out for particular criticism by media producers, since she (along with another, male doctor, whose reputation was largely left intact by the press) was responsible for the application of a controversial physical examination technique to children. This technique, of 'reflex anal dilation', proving positive in numerous cases, sparked off social work inquiries, leading to the removal of many children. Higgs was depicted as a zealous feminist crusader, and her status as 'foreign' and a picture of herself as perhaps psychologically disturbed were built up by reports of her German mother and Yugoslav father, who separated when she was two. Her unconventional domestic arrangements, whereby her husband stayed at home to look after their five children, was produced as further evidence of unusual proclivities. Through a process of association, she was implied to have sullied the objectivity of her medical practice with feminist ideology. Even when colleagues testified to her exemplary commitment to her professional role, this was used against her, as her very correctness in carrying out her responsibilities was portrayed as obsessional and therefore typical of an ideologue (Nava 1988).

Here, then, we see a thoroughgoing character assassination of a particular doctor. There were, though, notably gender-biased elements to this story that meant Higgs was made to stand for feminism rather than the medical profession in general. Her male colleague in diagnosing abuse, and the male police surgeon associated with the anti-Higgs camp, were not subjected to such media treatment. Arguably, then, we could see this as an exception to the rule of general media adulation of (male) medical authority. Other evidence, though, shows that there has been an accumulation in recent years of media criticisms of doctors who have fallen from grace, suggesting a readiness to generate more widespread concerns about the trustworthiness of the profession.

Bradby et al. (1995) report a study of UK tabloid media coverage of professional misconduct cases brought before the General Medical Council (GMC) during 1990–91. The vast majority of cases reported in the press turned out to involve accusations of sexual exploitation of patients by male doctors. Ten out of 15 'sex' cases that came before the GMC during the period were reported in the press, compared with only 7 of the remaining 41 cases. Predictably, the chief aim of the stories was to titillate readers with detailed accounts of 'romps' or 'sex sessions', with the doctors in such cases treated fairly sympathetically. Gender-biased values imbued the reports, with patients depicted quite frequently as siren-like, tempting doctors who perhaps lacked comfort and affection in their marriages. Thus the female patients involved in such cases were very frequently described as 'blonde' (even when photographs showed them to have brown hair!), 'busty' or 'pretty'. Doctor's wives, on the other hand, attracted such adjectives as 'devoted', 'prim and proper' or 'smartly dressed'. Doctors were depicted as understandably succumbing to temptation and attracted headlines such as 'Dirty Doc' and 'Doctor Grope'. While this hardly amounts to a thoroughgoing condemnation of the abuse of medical power, press interest in such stories seems unlikely to enhance the reputation of the profession. The authors disagree with Karpf's (1988) view that the media remains dominated by medical interests, and suggest that the overall effect of such stories may be 'to make doctors "fair game" for public opprobrium where they were once a "protected species"' (1995: 473)

The Australian media has also been shown to combine reporting of medical miracles with tales about doctors' falls from grace. Lupton and McLean (1998) surveyed newspapers and magazines in 1994–95, finding that 'cases of medical negligence, sexual assault and avarice on the part of doctors were often reported' (1998: 947), alongside positive images of medical authority. Chapman and Lupton (1994b) present an analysis of health coverage on Australian television during one week of 1993. Amongst the tales of life-saving technological rescues and other positive coverage were a minority of negative stories (3 out of the 21 stories involving doctors). One involved accusations of a medical cover-up of the fact that a doctor was practising when HIV positive: 'Doctors were represented as endangering their patients' lives and refusing to acknowledge it, casting into doubt their status as altruistic carers' (1994b: 99). Another story concerned doctors facing litigation for negligence and mistakes regarding childbirth; another concerned failures to detect HIV, for which a doctor was being sued. Lupton (1993b) has also documented Australian media coverage of a psychiatric hospital scandal in which doctors were deemed to have misbehaved, leading to calls for greater regulation of psychiatrists by the state.

In their review of recent British media reporting, Entwistle and Sheldon (1999) take the view that 'The authority and power of medical doctors has been substantially challenged and their mystique has to some extent been deconstructed' (1999: 127). This has been associated with a variety of government moves to increase lines of accountability for the profession, as well as inspecting and regulating standards of clinical practice. Increased attention to the views of patients and the public has meant that a 'rise of consumerism' (1999: 129) has accompanied medical decline. A number of headlines help show the tenor of recent coverage: 'Patients claim they woke during surgery'; 'Therapy error in cancer cases'; 'Surgeon is suspended over breast operations'; and 'Disease could be spread by surgical tools' (1999: 128–9).

A significant event in the media deconstruction of professional mystique was coverage of a scandal in Bristol, where surgeons with a very high mortality rate for operations on children for heart problems went on operating in spite of concerns expressed by a 'whistle-blowing' anaesthetist colleague. This led to an eventual inquiry by the General Medical Council, and many opportunities for press and television to report criticisms of medical paternalism, arrogance, lack of regulation and the like. An official report on the scandal prompted the *Independent* newspaper to run an editorial advocating 'the end of doctors' lack of accountability' (19 July 2001); the *Sun* on the same day ran a piece headlined 'The baby killers club'; the *Daily Mail* ran a front-page headline, 'End of doctor knows best'. The original story led to further media exploitation of the theme, media producers being quick to relay other stories about medical mistakes. Thus a series of television programmes called 'Why doctors make mistakes' was screened on British television in 2000. Martyn (2000), in a *British Medical Journal* review of the series, summarises their message:

> Screw ups, slip ups and cock ups; miscalculations, misjudgements and misdiagnoses. That, I'm sorry to have to tell you, is this four part series' appraisal of our professional performance. (2000: 904)

Since 1999 there have been two more major medical care scandals that have hit the British media headlines: the case of Harold Shipman, a general practitioner who lethally injected numerous elderly patients, and the case of organ storage at Alder Hey hospital. Much media coverage of the Shipman case focused on the abuse of trust involved, Shipman's actions contrasting with his personal appearance, which was the epitome of a warm and friendly family doctor. One could argue, though, that it was possible to portray his behaviour as so deeply pathological that it hardly reflected on the reputation of the medical profession as a whole. The Alder Hey scandal, however, was different. The organs of people who have died in British hospitals have, for many decades, been removed and stored in hospitals for scientific and teaching purposes, usually without the knowledge and consent of relatives. While the enthusiasm of a particular doctor for such organ collection was undoubtedly excessive, leading to the breaking of the story, this is not sufficient to explain why subsequent coverage focused on patient groups throughout the country, who besieged numerous hospitals demanding the restoration of missing body parts so that their loved ones might be finally laid to rest intact. The case could only have acquired this status as a widespread scandal because public opinion had already reached the point of intolerance for certain kinds of paternalistic medical behaviour previously considered acceptable under a regime of respect for medical authority. Indeed, the story reflects a direct challenge by consumers of medical power, orchestrated by an actively campaigning media.

In response to mounting media criticisms of professional standards, British doctors have been taking unusual levels of defensive action, reflecting the seriousness with which they take the damage such stories have done to their previously respected public image. Ferriman (2001) triumphantly reports in the *British Medical Journal* the decision of the Broadcasting Standards Commission to uphold two complaints against television programme makers for treating doctors unfairly. The chief executive of a children's hospital involved explained that '[We have] never complained . . . about a programme before. However, we felt this programme so misrepresented the work of the hospital that we had to complain' (2001: 438). The case involved accusations in a television documentary that doctors in the hospital had unreasonably failed to agree with parents that children with chronic fatigue syndrome were suffering from a physical disorder, and that in some cases they had wrongly accused parents of inducing the children's symptoms. In another case, a doctor had been criticised for harming a child patient with an experimental treatment. In both cases the broadcasters were forced to retract these charges.

It is now common to see doctors complaining of media coverage of medical errors. Thus Goodman (2001), in the pages of the *British Medical Journal*, decries news coverage of errors in interpreting cervical screening tests, pointing out that a certain number false negatives are inevitable in such screening programmes. Jackson (2001), in the same journal, complains that focusing on individual errors (such as the death of a child because the wrong gas was delivered to her during an operation) distracts attention from solving system-level flaws in safety procedures. Particularly galling for doctors' representatives, then, and reflecting the general disillusion with the profession generated by several years of such negative reporting, was press coverage of a one-day strike by British general practitioners in November 2001, which was universally critical of the strikers on the grounds that 'Doctors may protest, but they've never had it so good' (headline in the *Guardian* newspaper, quoted in Gulland, 2001). Doctors' representatives took the view that since the strike was designed to draw attention to the underfunding of the health service, rather than doctors' pay and conditions, this was unfair.

CONCLUSION

Clearly, then, media sponsorship of consumer power against medical authority has intensified in recent years. American soap operas have perhaps been a primary site for uncritical, adulatory accounts of medical heroism. The image of doctors in successful soaps has changed over the years, featuring increased emphasis on the vulnerability, stress levels and personal lives of doctors, as well as occasional moments of cynicism about ethical goals. Yet, even in the most recent soaps, the image of heroic rescue figure remains largely intact, albeit contained within a less supportive financial and organisational system than the dreamland of limitless health-care resource inhabited by *Dr Kildare* and *Marcus Welby*. Coverage of the magical tools wielded by medical staff – drugs, medicines, genetic therapies, and high-technology medicine generally – juxtaposes positive and hopeful coverage with stories of misuse and the danger involved in these powers. Medicines, for example, are frequently portrayed as quickly solving complex problems, but also as harming people if they fall into the wrong hands, or are applied by negligent or incompetent doctors. Some evidence, too, suggests that drug companies nowadays seek to exploit divisions between doctors and patients concerning control over drugs through the phenomenon of direct-to-consumer advertising.

Genetic therapy has largely received positive media coverage, being the latest in a long line of 'cutting-edge' or 'new frontier', scientifically derived medical technologies to attract public attention. Yet the potential is there for negative coverage to emerge in stronger form as the tendency of the media to 'twitch' a story by reversing good/bad polarities becomes irresistible. Historically, media emphasis on the wonders of high-technology medicine has been criticised by many analysts for underemphasising the contribution of low-technology public health measures, alternative medicine, and social and environmental determinants of disease. Yet there is considerable evidence that, in fact, the citadel of medical prestige, based on possession of technological resources for patient care, is under assault from a media-orchestrated consumerism. The value placed in media reports on the rights, wisdom and heroic endeavours of the ordinary people who suffer illness and use medical services is the subject of the chapter that follows.

8 Ordinary Heroes

With trust in traditional forms of authority under question, hopes of rescue from illness by medical heroes are diminished and modern individuals may therefore look anxiously around their environment for help. Chronic anxiety about risk, and intensive gathering of information (often from media sources) for risk profiling, within the context of reflexively aware self-identity was described in Chapter 1, drawing on the work of Giddens (1991). Incorporating a more emotionally laden view of human subjectivity is the analysis of the cycle of spectacle and narcissism that, for Abercrombie and Longhurst (1998), characterises media–audience relations. The focus on emotions is also characteristic of Craib's (1994) views, expressed from a psychoanalytic point of view, in his thesis on the meaning of disappointment in current social conditions.

My argument in this chapter is that popular mass media encourages an avoidance of disappointment by overloading media health representations with the spectacle of ordinary people displaying exceptional powers when threatened by illness. The commercial advantages of flattering readers and viewers in this way are obvious, and the 'tabloidisation', which many commentators believe increasingly characterises contemporary media products, is a phenomenon involving the extreme valorisation of individual experience, in part by adopting an intensely personal mode of address. The appetite for stories of lay heroism is sharpened by a constant supply of health scare stories (for which see Chapters 4 and 5) and tales that place in doubt the reliability of rescue from other quarters (Chapter 7). Thus media health representations first throw individuals back upon themselves and then, to give a soft landing and ensure the continued attention of media consumers, produce overblown evaluations of the exceptional powers of ordinary people to deal with adversity. A by-product of this is the growing interest in certain 'alternative' or 'complementary' therapies, whose practitioners frequently appeal to the imagined power of mind over body, thus placing themselves in the role of facilitators of heroic powers, inevitably somewhat in opposition to orthodox biomedicine. Indeed, discussion of the supposedly negative effects of mind–body dualism in orthodox biomedicine is now routinely produced in popular sociological commentary and appears to be in close alliance with the media discourse on lay heroism.

In this chapter, then, I firstly review the ideas of Craib (1994) about the avoidance of disappointment, as well as those of some other writers concerned with such matters as the elevation of consumer sovereignty and the promotion of a culture of narcissism. I relate this to a number of examples of heroism in the field of media health, pointing out the extreme contrast of these with the 'villains' of Chapter 5, continuing the classic media form whereby juxtapositions of opposites create an entertaining effect. The chapter then moves into a detailed case study of media representations of cancer experiences, drawing on the study of newspapers that was used in Chapter 6 on child victims. This analysis is important in demonstrating the uses of metaphor in the media construction of lay heroism, and it leads into the final chapter of this book that describes gender in media health reporting, since gender stereotypes are very prominent in stories about cancer experiences.

THE AVOIDANCE OF DISAPPOINTMENT

Craib (1994) argues for the importance, in creating a healthy self-identity that is free from psychically damaging illusions, of accepting disappointment as an inevitable part of life experience. Not all losses can be repaired and, as a corollary to this, not all desires can be realised. In arguing for this he draws on the ideas of psychoanalysts such as Freud and Melanie Klein, approving the dictum that psychotherapy may be unable to make people happy, but may nevertheless help people live with, and understand better, their despair and inevitable inner conflicts. For Craib the chief culprits in generating a disappointment-avoiding culture are poorly informed therapists who offer clients the promise of self-actualisation and seemingly endless opportunities for personal fulfilment or growth, in a melange of 'psychobabble' treatments. People then come to hope for too much and look for someone to blame when they cannot realise these hopes. Thus there is a growing culture of litigation to remedy medical errors, previously accepted as an inevitable part of life. Craib does not spend a lot of time analysing popular representations of these optimistic ideas about the possibilities of the self, but no doubt would endorse the view that the mass popularity of superficially appealing psychobabble is assisted by saturation coverage in the media.

In a case study of mourning, Craib expands his ideas, arguing that contemporary psychiatric accounts of the 'stages' or 'tasks' of grieving (for example, Parkes, 1986) are unrealistic in presenting mourning as an opportunity for personal growth. In fact, Craib argues, pain (and guilt) are inevitable in such losses, and the attempt to move the mourner through 'stages' of grief towards a final resolution may have more to do with providing comfort for bereavement counsellors than providing realistic help for clients. Additionally, Craib argues that talking about emotions has increasingly come to be seen as desirable: women are seen as particularly good at this: 'emotionality and the ability to talk about feelings . . . often regarded as a feminine quality . . . now is often claimed to be [a mark] of superiority' (1994: 88). For women, Craib says in an amusing passage, anger is 'in'; for men, fear and vulnerability are promoted as desirable. Thus Gulf War pilots are shown on television describing their fears about being shot down, a far cry from the war heroes of 50 years ago for whom such admissions would have signified a damaged reputation. Moves to rehabilitate soldiers shot for 'cowardice' in the First World War involve expressions of similar sentiments. The increased visibility of emotions is accompanied by an unhealthy promotion of superficial 'expert' views about how to manage them, so that the public sphere unhelpfully invades the private sphere, encouraging illusions of self-mastery.

Craib explains these phenomena in terms that are very similar to Giddens's (1991) explanations for the extreme individualism involved in late modern projects of self-identity (see Chapter 1), although on some other points he disagrees with Giddens's views, particularly concerning the rationality with which Giddens's subjects appear to guide themselves, and Giddens's optimism about the freedom experienced by people in contemporary conditions. Because allegiance to traditional forms of authority has declined, and religious views of the self no longer capture the imaginations of the majority of people, people's problems no longer appear to be moral choices in the context of community norms of duty and obligation, nor are they seen as struggles with impersonal forces of destiny. Instead, mental health is all, and the self must be found through introspection. There is a neurotic obsession with trying to become our own therapists, and expectations of continual emotional satisfaction drive many people into mistaken courses of action. Instead, argues Craib, we ought to learn to embrace things that are not perfect, risk the loss of these, and understand that choosing some things means relinquishing others.

Of course, this somewhat gloomy vision of mature human development sits uncomfortably with the pleasurable fantasies provided by media stories. In Chapters 1 and 2 of this book, Langer's (1998) account of 'tabloid television' was reviewed, making it clear that stories of ordinary people heroically overcoming great odds are very common. Indeed, the threat of some dangerous force juxtaposed (and usually overcome) with the will-power and courage of ordinary people is an example of the general media format that involves a series of oppositions, often personalised by stock characters (villains, fools, helpers, victims, heroes and so on). We saw in Chapter 1 that such devices can be understood as substituting for religiously inspired mythologies, charting the progress of an 'Everyman' figure through various trials and tribulations, and creating also a sense of belonging in an imagined community of fellow adventurers through the consumption of a jointly shared media product. Thus confessional tales have ritual qualities that generate a sense of awe, encourage idealisation and result in viewers and readers realigning their own projects of self-identity. Sontag (1991) has a rather insightful view of the way in which popularly promoted psychological notions of the self in illness create a promise of eventual triumph:

> There is a peculiarly modern predilection for psychological explanations of disease, as of everything else. Psychologizing seems to provide control over the experiences and events (like grave illnesses) over which people have in fact little or no control. Psychological understanding undermines the 'reality' of a disease ... A large part of the popularity and persuasiveness of psychology comes from its being a sublimated spiritualism: a secular, ostensibly scientific way of affirming the primacy of 'spirit' over matter ... people are encouraged to believe that ... they can cure themselves by the mobilization of will; that they can choose not to die of the disease. (1991: 56–8)

Alternative or – as the medical establishment has gradually adopted a more tolerant approach – 'complementary' therapies have become in recent years increasingly prominent in the orchestration of such super-power fantasies of cure through an effort of will. In fact, the source of tension between orthodox and alternative medicine largely hinges on the truth or falsity of curative claims: 'complementary' therapies are usually designated as such when their practitioners agree to relinquish their claims to cure disease, and instead accept designation as palliative or comfort care. Nevertheless, many of these therapies rest on their promises to help people avoid reversals, the acceptance of which Craib considers to be the mark of a more mature approach to life's disappointments.

Coward's (1989) Foucauldian analysis of 'holistic' claims made by alternative health practitioners is revealing in this respect. In line with Sontag's views, she notes that this is a quasi-religious discourse that promises people a sense of control over their personal well-being, often proposed as being in stark contrast to the passive, objectified patient identity said to be offered to clients of orthodox biomedicine. Encouraged in lengthy consultations to link episodes of illness with biographical events, in a context of ideas about intricate links between mind and body through such mechanisms as 'stress', in Coward's view patients are encouraged to take personal responsibility for disease causation and recovery. Orthodox medicine, modern industrial society, pollution and other negative aspects of modern social organisation are contrasted with the 'natural' way of life, to which a patient – cast as a victim struggling against the effects of this conspiracy of forces – may hope to be returned through therapy and a therapist-supervised change of lifestyle. Like Karpf (1988), she points out that this constitutes a highly individualistic approach to matters that might be better addressed through political endeavour to change the social circumstances that create stress. On the whole, though, Coward eschews any Marxist analysis for one that suggests holism is an exercise in self-surveillance, realising a pervasive disciplinary power that contains profoundly moralistic and indeed punitive messages, leading to a rather neurotic, self-obsessed and guilt-ridden approach to illness that bears striking resemblance to the profile of the sinner, under a religious regime, seeking to find the way to salvation. All of this is based on a social construction of 'nature', 'stress' and mind–body relationships, which therefore, for Coward, could (and perhaps should) be otherwise. Like Craib, Coward points out that the utopian myth of the harmonious 'whole' person is an illusion, contrasting this with Freud's vision of the self as always and inevitably in a state of conflict, for ever split in fact, a condition which it is our life's task to understand and accommodate. We shall see that media production of lay heroism in the health field frequently draws on holistic discourse of one sort or another.

LAY HEROES IN THE MEDIA

We have already met some of the ordinary heroes achieving prominence in media health representations. In Chapter 5, in which the 'villains and freaks' portrayed in media health stories were reviewed, we saw that 'twitches' to stigmatising coverage could sometimes produce idealised images. Disability activists, having a sophisticated understanding of these matters, were shown to be as critical of such excessive idealisation as they were of negative prejudice. Images of one-legged men walking across Canada to raise money for charity (Harrison, 1992), 'telethon' events, and 'supercrip' characters, such as David Helfgott and Christopher Reeve, were all identified as examples. In the case of old age we saw that Cumberbatch et al. (1998) found a high frequency of stories of exceptional achievements by elderly people, co-existing with negative stereotypes. In Chapter 6 it was shown that idealised portrayal of children as innocent victims also involved considerable emphasis on the remarkable inner resources that all sick children, it would seem from media reports, draw upon in battling life-threatening illness.

While media images of mental illness were in general very negative, some heroic stories are also told on occasion. Thus, amongst the negative stereotypes found by Hyler et al. (1991) in their study of American movies and television, there was the relatively positive one of the 'rebellious free spirit', often portraying people struggling against an oppressive psychiatric regime to assert their individuality, albeit expressed through behaviour labelled as 'madness'. This stereotype was particularly popular in the 1970s, at a time when the ideas of 'anti-psychiatrists' were popular and perhaps the best known of these ordinary heroes is the character played by Jack Nicholson in *One Flew over the Cuckoo's Nest*. More recent versions of this tale include *An Angel at My Table*, in which the autobiography of writer and poet Janet Frame was used for the story of one mistreated by the psychiatric system who emerged eventually to achieve greatness.

The AIDS story, a fertile source of extremely hostile coverage of 'carriers' deemed responsible for spreading the disease, like most of the other stigmatised categories, can on occasion provoke accounts of personal heroism. The case of Oscar Moore, a journalist with HIV/AIDS who wrote a column in a national UK newspaper about his experience of the disease up to the point of his death in 1996 (later collected as a book called *PWA: Looking AIDS in the Face*: Moore, 1998), introduces a type of media health hero that has so far not been discussed in this book. The phenomenon of the columnist with terminal illness, promoted to celebrity status from a previously humdrum journalistic career through the device of a personal column recording the experience, became increasingly popular in British media in the 1990s, with a number of examples surfacing. In general, this is not a 'tabloid' phenomenon, being featured in 'quality' or broadsheet papers, and the kind of heroism displayed in these accounts is of a wry, somewhat self-mocking kind that at times contains a critique of more simple-minded popular images of what it is to face death heroically. All of this was present in Oscar Moore's column, the effect of which can be gauged by an extract from an obituary:

But it was, poignantly, his own ill-health that drove Moore to create his best work: a column for the *Guardian* entitled 'PWA (Person With Aids)', which he wrote for the last three years of his life. In it, with unflinching honesty and a wry, black humour, he charted his physical descent . . . What is perhaps most remarkable about this short, brave life is that he had HIV for more than a third of it; 13 years – his entire working career – spent writing despite (and also partly because of) ill-health and anguish. Oscar Moore had a fierce will to live – which surely kept him alive long after many of his peers had died of Aids – but he never avoided contemplating his death. (Justine Picardie, the *Independent* [*Gazette*]; p. 16, 18 September 1996)

Such 'progressive' illness narratives as those of Oscar Moore have been detected in the stories told to research interviewers in a number of qualitative studies of illness experience (see Seale, 1998: 24–9, for a review), suggesting that stories of the self struggling against illness and successfully finding exceptional strength of character are widely acclaimed in contemporary society.

CANCER HEROICS

Cancer stories provide a further demonstration of the concordance between media accounts of lay heroism and the actual understandings of people facing illness in contemporary society. In the rest of this chapter I shall demonstrate this by juxtaposing my own research work on the way people interpret the experience of terminal illness with my analysis of media representations of cancer experience. That concordance, rather than conflict, between the two is the norm will be a controversial claim for some media analysts who prefer to see media representations in this area opposing or even oppressing ordinary people. The oppression argument is often found in studies of media representations of breast cancer, and it is worth reviewing this argument here before turning to the research evidence that refutes it.

The oppression argument

This view – that cancer media representations are out of tune with or oppressive towards 'real' experiences of cancer – is expressed most powerfully by Lupton (1994b) and Clarke (1999a), who studied media representations of breast cancer in the Australian (Lupton) and North

American (Clarke) print media. Both analysts are influenced by Sontag's (1991) account of military metaphors in cancer language, in which a powerful case is made for the harm that these do to people experiencing disease. Sontag says, for example, that the effect of the dominant war metaphor means that cancer, for many people, is 'experienced as a ruthless, secret invasion' (1991: 5), in which cancer cells 'colonize' a body whose 'defenses' are then invoked; treatment involves metaphors from chemical and aerial warfare, and 'the disease itself is conceived as the enemy on which society wages war' (1991: 67). The effect of thus portraying cancer as 'an evil, invincible predator, not just a disease' is that 'most people with cancer will indeed be demoralized by learning what disease they have' (1991: 7). People with cancer are, as a result, likely to experience the illness as 'not just a lethal disease but a shameful one' (1991: 59), and 'brutal notions of treatment' are too often justified as 'counter-attack' (1991: 65). The solution to this damage is to 'rectify the conception of the disease, to de-mythicize it' (1991: 7). In particular, she points to the importance of publicising successful cures, as this may generate a sense of being able to live with the disease on less antagonistic terms. Sontag's analysis, while insightful in many respects, does not draw on research evidence about personal experiences of cancer, or on any data about responses of cancer sufferers to the representations she criticises.

Lupton and Clarke expand Sontag's views to argue that the prevalence of military metaphors in media representations of cancer reflects patriarchal social control. In the newspapers she analysed, Lupton (1994b) found numerous stories of celebrities who had 'fought' or 'battled' to overcome their cancer, extolling the virtues of life-saving medical treatments. Interpreting these as 'living examples of the victory of medical intervention' (1994b: 84), Lupton says that they also involve a 'victim blaming' (1994b: 85) press discourse, leading to a 'valorization of medical technology . . . to the exclusion of the needs, wants, and feelings of women in the general population' (1994b: 83). Clarke (1999a) continues this theme in her study of breast cancer stories in North American magazines, where she pays particular attention to the portrayal of women as fearful and emotionally volatile, whereas doctors are described as objective and rational, 'as if they are above feelings and bodies' (1999a: 123). This, for Clarke, denotes injustice and harm to the interests of those experiencing cancer. Like Sontag, neither analyst presents research evidence about audience readings to support these estimates of damage.

Cancer pathographies

Sontag's (1991) account of cancer representations draws largely on literary sources, and at various points she compares cancer with tuberculosis (TB). TB, in romantic art and literature of the nineteenth century, was often portrayed as a rather glamorous way to die, especially if the sufferer was upper class with literary or artistic leanings. Cancer, Sontag argues, contrasts with this greatly: 'Nobody conceives of cancer the way TB was thought of – as a decorative, often lyrical death. Cancer is a rare and still scandalous subject for poetry; and it seems unimaginable to aestheticize the disease' (1991: 20). Developments in popular (and indeed 'upmarket') mass media since Sontag's work, however, suggest that this judgement is no longer correct. The phenomenon of the cancer 'pathography' (an example of which is the celebrity newspaper columnist writing about his or her cancer experiences in a manner similar to Oscar Moore's PWA column) represents an idealisation of illness experience that contains many parallels with Victorian accounts of TB. Here, too, is to be found evidence that contrasts with the judgements of Lupton and Clarke about the supposed effects of media on cancer sufferers.

McKay and Bonner (1999) provide an analysis of three Australian women's magazines, identifying every item that appeared over a three-year period in which a story about a person with breast cancer was told. Forty-two examples were found, this high frequency reflecting, in the authors' opinion, a general growth in interest in personal stories about illness experience, itself the result of a general shift 'away from reliance on medical institutions and towards personal responsibility for health and well-being' (1999: 564). The stories followed a set pattern:

> The stories we found were heavily mediated by the magazines, initially through the provision of an attention-grabbing statement followed by the same basic structure: the discovery of a lump, tests, treatment, and recovery interspersed with details about coping with the associated anxiety (recurrently this was described as being through inner strength or the support of family and friends, rather than pharmaceutically). In almost every instance, the woman involved expressed a desire that her experience should not be in vain and that by reading her story, other women would be able to comprehend the implications of the experience of breast cancer. (1999: 565)

Particularly in stories focusing on ordinary people rather than celebrities, the authors found a tendency to 'conclude if at all possible with positive statements about triumphing over adversity' (1999: 569). McKay and Bonner end by recommending these tales for 'helping women deal with the experience of illness' (1999: 570). Here, they draw justification for this view from the work of Kleinman (1988), who, along with other analysts of illness narratives (for example, Frank, 1995), has argued for the therapeutic value of sharing accounts. Clearly, this is a far cry from the view of Sontag, Lupton and Clarke that cancer stories in the media are likely to be oppressive to their audience.

Nevertheless, there are clearly degrees of sophistication in the pathography genre and some, paradoxically, show signs of influence by the very points made by analysts critical of popular depictions of illness experience. Some of the more extended cancer pathographies, particularly those appearing in regular newspaper columns or in books, contain an implied critique of more downmarket versions of the genre on these grounds. Thus the book compilation of columnist John Diamond's (1998) accounts in *The Times* of his experience of cancer of the tongue (of which he was eventually to die) was entitled: *C: Because Cowards Get Cancer Too* – embracing the anti-military identity of the 'coward' in order to distance the author from crude claims of personal heroism. Yet the reception of his account by other media writers revealed that an heroic effect was generated nevertheless, indeed was achieved by Diamond's very rejection of illusions of personal strength in the face of his cancer. Thus a newspaper commentator on Diamond's story effectively reasserts the military metaphor, writing under the headline 'Nicholas Mosley celebrates the indomitable spirit of those confronting mortality':

> Books about battles against illness seem to have taken the place of contemporary stories about war. Histories of war are as popular as ever, but modern war has become unfashionable; we are supposed to have moved beyond a cavalier attitude towards killing. But terrible and heroic tales can still be told of people's struggles against death; and, through these, readers can experience enthralment and edification. Cancer sufferers are in the front line of such battles, and they produce some of the most affecting books . . . there has recently been John Diamond's harrowing and bold *C: Because Cowards Get Cancer Too* . . . and he continues to send front-line dispatches in his weekly column in *The Times*. He says that he is not brave, because courage is only relevant if you have a choice. But there is always a choice of attitude towards suffering; and John Diamond's humour and self-deprecation as he endures more and more of his tongue being cut out is of the calibre of a fighter pilot in the Battle of Britain. (Nicholas Mosley in the *Daily Telegraph*, 21 November 1998)

Another such columnist was Ruth Picardie, who died of breast cancer in 1997, aged 33, after writing several instalments of a column about her experience for the *Observer* newspaper, later collected in a book called *Before I Say Goodbye* (Picardie, 1998). Some extracts from media responses to her account demonstrate similarities with responses to the John Diamond story:

> Ruth Picardie's brave and moving *Before I Say Goodbye*. (Julian Critchley, the *Independent*, 11 October 1998)

> Ruth Picardie was a brave and original soul. Her voice rings out through her columns and e-mails. 'Shop yourself out of cancer,' she proclaims as yet another diagnostic nail is hammered into the coffin. Repudiating pity, she slavers over the latest limited edition mint KitKat, finds a skirt from Whistles with 'clever bias cutting' to disguise her liver tumour and mocks her 'complementary medicine panic'. (Lucy Maycock, *Observer Review* 19 July 1998)

This last reference to Picardie's rejection of complementary therapies is something shared by John Diamond, who is scathing about the illusions of recovery that these encourage. A rather British disdain for self-pity also runs through both accounts. Through such means, and through the rejection of conventional notions of bravery, these celebrity columnists, writing for upmarket newspapers that appeal to a highly educated audience, construct their distinction from more popular forms of heroism. The responses of others to their examples, however, reveal that this very distinctiveness occasions admiration and a degree of idealisation of the authors' characters.

Certain other cancer pathographies have claimed distinction by virtue of a counter-cultural critique, associated with anti-establishment views, and these have typically been celebrated by sociological writers who share this general commitment. Potts (2000) has reviewed pathographies that describe breast cancer experiences. She notes the frequency with which these involve criticism of medical treatments and (unlike the upper-class 'establishment' versions of Diamond and Picardie) demonstrate interest in the potential of alternative approaches – either in complementary therapy or in inner resources and self-reconstruction. Acker, for example, in one such account, writes that

> conventional medicine was reducing me, quickly, to a body that was only material, to a body without hope and so without will, to a puppet . . . Did I have anything in myself . . . that could help me know and so deal with cancer? My answer was; it takes strength to know. Where then is my strength? Answer: in my work, in my writing. (Acker, quoted in Potts, 2000: 120)

Saywell et al. (2000), in another analysis of 'alternative' pathographies, note that Acker opted for a double mastectomy, ostensibly on the grounds of its being cheaper than breast reconstruction on a single breast, but also implying a political critique of the importance of breasts in images of the feminine. Acker also abandoned conventional medicine in favour of alternative therapy. Rejection of both medical and patriarchal dominance is also shown by the decision by one pathography author (Lorde, 1980) not to wear a breast prosthesis. Both Potts and Saywell display considerable admiration for these flag-bearers of counter-cultural critique, taking the view that their stories are likely to enhance solidarity amongst an oppressed group:

> From the process of transformation ... through the act of speaking or writing out, emerges a revolutionary new figure, in collective solidarity with ... other 'women with breast cancer': the 'warriors' in Lorde's phrase. (Potts, 2000: 124)

Thus, heroic narratives of the self are promulgated in cancer pathographies even as the highbrow authors of these may claim distinction from cruder forms of the genre. Clearly, these are not the women with cancer referred to by Lupton and Clarke, oppressed and made passive by popular media representations. Instead, these are examples of women (and men) speaking out about their individuality, setting themselves against illusions and oppression wherever it is perceived to come from. Sontag's (1991) judgement that cancer cannot be subject to the kind of idealisation projected on tuberculosis in nineteenth-century romantic literature seems to be overturned by these examples. It might be argued, though, that these defiant narratives penned largely by and for an educated section of the population are different from the popular forms from which they claim distinction. To examine this, we can now turn to an account of everyday media practices in constructing images of ordinary heroes.

Cancer stories in the news

For this section I draw on the same study of news reports used in Chapter 6, where news stories of children with cancer were analysed. To recap the account given there, this was an analysis of the stories of 382 people with cancer in 358 newspaper articles published in the English language press worldwide during the first week of October 1999; it is also reported in Seale (2001a,b, 2002). Perhaps the best way to present this material, given that fuller details are available elsewhere, is through commentary on a single case that represents many of the themes identified in the sample of articles as a whole. This is the story of Toben Anderson, which appeared on 4 October 1999 in the *Vancouver Sun*. Extracts are reproduced here with numbered paragraphs for reference purposes:

HEADLINE: **Long road back ends on a peak: Breast cancer survivor Toben Anderson capped her three-year recovery by conquering her first mountain.**

1 When Toben Anderson, fashion designer and self-described slug, finally rested her ice axe on the summit of Antarctica's highest mountain, it was a double victory.

2 It had taken three years and a bilateral mastectomy that removed both her breasts, but at that moment, the Calgary woman not only conquered her first mountain, she symbolically conquered her breast cancer.

3 'When I was told I was fighting for my life and my chances didn't look great, I flat out refused to die,' Anderson said. After exploring every conventional and alternative therapy, she took the best medical science could offer and set to work visualizing the cancer away and working to improve all her personal relationships.

4 The combination worked.

5 'Suddenly a year that everybody thought would be hellish turned out to be an amazing year,' said Anderson, who is convinced her non-medical activity played a huge role in her recovery.

6 Although climbing a single flight of stairs left her breathless, she decided to climb Antarctica's highest peak to raise awareness for breast cancer. She trained for a full year, met her goal in January 1997, and returned, serendipitously, with a man who would become her husband – as well as to a new career as a motivational speaker.

7 Then her cancer came back.

8 'I was devastated,' said Anderson, now 41.

9 'Here I was as a newly-wed and I needed chemotherapy and that guaranteed I would go through menopause and we had wanted to start a family.'

10 Chemotherapy and a stem cell transplant wore her down.

11 'I was so weak and ill. I laid around just feeling despair and it was a long, long hole to crawl back out of.'

12 But she rallied and fought the battle again.

13 Many people with cancer are advised to 'just take it easy and be kind to yourself,' and women, in particular, tend to take that kind of advice, Anderson said.

14 Don't do it, Anderson urges. She advises people to get involved in their illness, get into support groups, get educated and take responsibility

for their lives. Active people may or may not live longer, but medical professionals believe active people do better during the course of their illness, Anderson said.

15 'I've had women say to me, "What if I decide to cure myself and I don't?" My response is if you try and don't succeed, you'll be dead, so who cares? At least you will have found some meaning in the journey. We all have things we need to address in order to be truly happy. Address them, face them, resolve them.'

16 'You've got nothing to lose by trying.'

17 'Live your life. It doesn't matter what the mountain is, illness, marital problems. We don't get through life unscathed.'

18 'We can put our heads in the sand and say poor me, or we can fight and we'll enjoy the journey much more.'

Clearly, this is designed as an inspirational story or, in Robinson's (1990) terms, a 'progressive narrative'. The movement from 'self-described slug' (paragraph 1) to 'motivational speaker' (6) is represented as a victorious transformation of the self that also, through drawing on inner resources and an active use of both conventional and alternative therapeutic methods (3), involved – at least for a while – a conquest of the cancer itself. Linked with this imagery of cancer-beating empowerment is a hint of feminist analysis (13), aligning her with Lupton's (1994b) critique of the oppression of women with cancer. Journey (15, 18) and battle (12) metaphors are linked with the overarching mountain-climbing metaphor, in which the sporting achievement is likened to the achievement of her cancer struggle (2). Importantly, too, there is an emphasis on finding and gaining support from others, attested by her efforts to improve her personal relationships (3) and her observations on the value of support groups (14). At the same time, Anderson's fear and despair at her illness are given space (8–11), a platform for her rallying response to this (12).

This story was chosen because it contains in concentrated form most of the themes made available in other cancer stories in the sample, in particular where women's cancer experiences are concerned. Let us focus first on the use of metaphor, as this leads to some interesting variations from the influential account given by Sontag (1991), in which she stresses that metaphors are essentially military where cancer is concerned. In a sense, my findings (see Seale, 2001a) do not differ from this, since words like 'victory', 'conquer', 'rallied' and 'battle' are clearly derived from the imagery of warfare. We saw earlier, in Mosley's *Daily Telegraph* account of the John Diamond story, that the opinion is that stories of illness may inhabit the space once occupied by stories of warfare, the key link being the struggle with death. In my analysis of cancer stories, however, I was increasingly struck by the connotations in such struggle language of sporting endeavour. Toben Anderson's headlined activity, after all, is not participation in warfare (here I concur with Mosley's view that 'modern war is unfashionable') but in the sporting activity of mountain climbing.

In the sample of articles as a whole there was considerable evidence of the sporting connotations of struggle language. Words like 'fight', 'battle', 'winning', 'losing', 'survivor', 'brave', 'courage', 'competition' and 'victory' were commonly used to describe the cancer experience. While none of the stories involved depiction of participation in warfare, many showed people with cancers participating in sporting events. This is evident, firstly, from consideration of the stories about celebrities with cancer. Twenty-two were celebrities through sporting activity, or through association with a celebrated sportsperson (35 per cent of all the celebrity characters). In other (non-celebrity) stories, sporting activity by people with cancer was often mentioned. Thus people were depicted engaged in athletics, badminton, baseball, cycle riding, fencing, American football, golf, karate, marathon running, mountain climbing, road racing or running, rowing, rugby, skating, soccer, walking for fitness, swimming, tennis and triathlons.

As in the Toben Anderson story, there was often an explicit awareness that sporting activity stood metaphorically for the experience of cancer. Thus, a participant in a 'Race for the Cure' breast cancer awareness-raising event spoke as follows about her experience of triathlons:

> 'The triathlon is the hugest thing I went through in my life . . . It was a huge day that I finally "got it" that I had breast cancer' . . . The triathlon was a catharsis that allowed her to work through what she had gone through emotionally two years before. 'The shock of the cold water (in the swimming event) was the shock of the diagnosis, it was swimming through the waves of pathology reports, pedaling through treatment and running to recovery,' she said. (*Denver Post*)

The theme of overcoming odds in a life-or-death struggle is thus shared between sporting and illness stories: more of the stories appeared in the sports section of newspapers than in the health section (12 per cent versus 5 per cent). This use of sporting metaphor, then, is consistent with the analysis presented in Chapter 1, where it was argued that health stories, like crime coverage, enable the creation of ritualised dramas addressing readers' basic existential concerns, supplying a quasi-religious experience. Such spectacles are also achieved in great sporting contests, which supply daily portrayals of heroic struggle with which to identify. Metaphoric interchange between these spheres seems therefore quite natural, as once was the case with stories of warfare in the mythologies of traditional societies.

Overt use of religious themes, as with direct comparisons with military adventures, was rare in the cancer stories that I analysed (Seale, 2001b). Nevertheless, the stories depicted people with cancer as being preoccupied with the same issues of responsibility and moral character that have traditionally been addressed in religious discourse. Toben Anderson's story, for example, contains powerful messages about the responsible way to behave in the face of adversity, by depicting cancer as a psychological journey towards eventual salvation.

At the same time, the stories about these lay cancer heroes contained powerful messages about the behaviour appropriate to each gender (Seale, 2002). For Clarke (1999a), the portrayal of women with cancer as suffering from intense and overwhelming fears, when contrasted with the detached attitude of doctors, is part of a conspiracy to portray women as unable to manage themselves rationally, and in need of rescue by cold, unemotional (male) medical authority. My reading of this phenomenon (for I also found that women's fear of cancer was stressed more than men's) is different. Women in the cancer stories that I analysed were, in fact, portrayed as particularly skilful and empowered, the initial stress on fears serving to highlight the subsequent skills with which women then transformed themselves. This contrasted with the unskilled performances of men with cancer. Toben Anderson's story of self-transformation is a case in point; there were many others.

As an example of the intensity with which women's fears could be depicted, a story in the *Knoxville News Sentinel* is illustrative:

> When a visit to Dr Caryn Wunderlich at Knoxville Comprehensive Breast Center confirmed Swaney's fears about the lump she'd found, her thoughts turned to her daughter, and she began to pray . . . 'I asked God to please let me live – for my little girl,' Swaney said tearfully. 'I kept thinking, "I just can't leave her now." . . . I was scared I was going to die. . . . It's scary to think about dying. It makes me nauseous to even think about the fear.'

By contrast, men's fears were more rarely dealt with and were milder:

> 'The first question (after being diagnosed with cancer) was, "When am I going to die?"' recalled Porter. . . . But, after talking to people at the Tom Baker Centre, he decided that prostate cancer wasn't such a big hurdle after all. 'I put it down as just another disease like the measles,' said Porter. (*Calgary Herald*)

Men, then, had less to overcome than women, and this was reflected in the relative frequency of journey metaphors. These included, for example, 'going through' the cancer experience, having it described as a 'journey', a 'road', a 'saga', a 'tunnel' or 'travel'. Such metaphors occurred 42 times in the stories of women with cancer, but only 15 times in the stories of men. Women's capacity to gather support from family and friends and, in many cases, cancer support groups was stressed, whereas men were portrayed as more isolated. Qualities of character were more often mentioned in relation to men (50 per cent of all stories about men) than women (17.5 per cent), suggesting that men's response to cancer highlighted unchanging, underlying personal strengths, such as altruism, determination, commitment to hard work, enthusiasm, cheerfulness, stoicism, strength and realism. Getting back to normal was shown as an overriding goal for many men. Thus *USA Today* described the experience of the manager of a car racing team: 'Healthy outlook: With his leukemia in remission and . . . making long-term plans with his racing team, Rick Hendrick is feeling better these days.'

Women, by contrast, engaged in heroic, skilful efforts of emotional labour in order to transform themselves – indeed, to become new women – as a result of their cancer experience. Frequently, as in the case of Toben Anderson, this resulted in a sense of mission to teach others how to manage cancer through their own example, reflected in the fact that in the single week's worth of news reports chosen for analysis in this study (Seale, 2002) there were accounts of 13 books about cancer experiences, of which 11 were by women concerning their breast cancer experiences. A typical account of two such self-transformations is contained in this story from the *Tennessean* newspaper:

> **Survivors of cancer teach us courage, not fear**
> In the past three years she has traveled a long road full of surgery, post-op pain, the illness and weakness brought on by chemo drugs, the loss of her hair, reconstructive surgery and repeated tests and checkups. Somehow, she has emerged from all this a gentler, funnier and stronger woman with a sure sense of herself and her priorities . . . The success of her journey came home to me again a few days later when I ran into another friend, also a breast cancer survivor, at a school open house. Vivacious, radiant, handing out fund-raising materials, she shared the good results of her own three-year checkup. 'I'm fine, fine,' she smiled. 'Did I tell you about the book I'm working on?' . . . In fighting breast cancer, in winning, they have given the rest of us good news indeed: while breast cancer may be life-changing, it is not a death sentence.

These gender differences, then, portray women in a favourable light as particularly skilful in their capacity to transform themselves through emotional labour, contrasting with the rather unskilled performances of men, whose approach appears old-fashioned and backward by contrast. As well as being in tune with Craib's (1994) analysis of gendered fashions in emotions (see earlier), this is in line with Giddens's (1992) analysis, in which he suggests that women have pioneered the transformation of intimacy that self-identity now involves, largely through the appropriation of emotional skills, so that women are 'the emotional revolutionaries of modernity' while men experience a 'lapsed emotional narrative of self' (1992: 130). Clearly, this directly contrasts with the oppression narrative told by Lupton (1994b) and Clarke (1999a). At the same time, media accounts of men's and women's cancer experiences share a common stress on psychological aspects, with the capacity of individuals to overcome cancer through exceptional efforts of will, or of character strength, being emphasised. How does this compare, we might ask, with the way in which ordinary people face life-threatening illness in contemporary society?

HEROIC DEATH

In another study I have investigated heroic themes in lay accounts of illness, and can summarise this here in order to show that these themes predominate and are in tune with the popular media representations analysed in this chapter. This is not to say that this is a study of 'audience effects', but it is indicative of a shared cultural orientation in which media representations are in a symbiotic relationship with everyday life experience. The material here comes from interviews with 250 people in Britain who knew people who had died and where death had been predictable (meaning that there was a high proportion of deaths from cancer). In the report of the study I concluded that:

> Scripts for proclaiming heroic self-identity in the face of death are promoted by cultural experts and appropriated by many lay individuals. This involves a struggle against external and internal enemies to gain knowledge, the opportunity to demonstrate courage and a beatific state of emotional accompaniment in which 'carers' and dying people participate. Unlike more traditional forms of heroism, this script deviates from celebrating solely masculine qualities and includes a female heroics of care, concern and emotional expression. (Seale, 1995a: 597)

As is common in the mythological depiction of heroic journeys, the initial steps of the journey were blocked by guardian figures, in this case in the form of doctors delivering a diagnosis of fatal illness. Unlike the classic myths, however, where the beginning hero is often given some trial of character or endurance by these guardians before being allowed entry, in these stories the character of the guardians themselves came under scrutiny and the issue of whether doctors' demeanour was caring when breaking bad news was of considerable concern. Once through this door, the dying persons entered a new territory where their own character was tried and tested by the strain of knowing. Responses to this contained many similarities with the media accounts described earlier.

As in the story of Ann Swaney ('nauseous with fear'), emotions at the point of telling included tears and a sense of fear, shock, anger or unfairness – 'She cried, she looked to me to help her, but I was more shocked than she was' – as well as some rather stereotyped gender differences:

> [He was] angry more than anything . . . [He was] so fit, [and] used to tire everyone. I was angry about it too. He was like John Wayne, boisterous. He swore a bit [saying] 'why the bloody hell does it have to happen to us when we've worked so hard all our lives?'

Yet, in line with Kubler-Ross (1969), whose stage theory of dying has attained mythical status, this stage of initial shock could be construed as the beginning of a journey. This script was apparently adhered to by most speakers at this point, as none of those who were told claimed that the painful emotions involved might have been better avoided by not telling. As one person stated: 'It was hard, and traumatic, but best.' Attempts to 'fight' the disease were described, following the usage of struggle or 'military' language in news texts. Speakers' evaluations of this were ambiguous. On the one hand, the 'determination', 'will-power', 'brave face,' and being 'a fighter' involved were admired: 'She was always going to fight and win for the boys' [her sons'] sake.' Some joined the fight: 'I said we can fight it together, but he just went down.' On the other hand, fighting could be associated with less admirable qualities, as where a woman was described as having shown 'sheer obstinacy', or a man was described that 'drove himself all the more, trying to prove he wasn't really ill'. A woman 'tried to fight it' but 'did not accept it to the very end'. Acceptance represented for many the goal of the struggle to know, marking a successful passage through the strains of knowing and the temptation to deny. Since these were stories where death had been the outcome (rather than recovery, as in the case of most of the stories in the study of news reports), the final 'victory' lay paradoxically in acceptance of 'defeat' by the illness, rather than a triumphant conquest of its effects.

The ultimate acceptance of death was expressed in beatific accounts. For example, a mother described her daughter's death:

> When I sat in with her on the Thursday afternoon – the nurses had made

her comfortable – I went in and sat with her, holding her hand and she had
a beautiful smile on her face as if she knew something. She just faded
away . . . I think she felt she'd lived long enough.

Telling, denying, fighting and finally accepting, then, were depicted as particular moments in the dying person's journey, enacting a classic stage
theory of emotional progress that is very much in tune with the accounts
given by the (female) emotional experts in news reports of cancer experiences. Many speakers sought to locate the person who died at particular
points on this journey, searching for signs of progress, explaining sources
of danger and identifying moments of defeat and victory. Some saw themselves as jointly engaged with the dying person on this enterprise ('we
both squeezed each other's hands') in a drama of accompaniment.

Thus talk could involve the negotiation of intimacy, commitment and
mutual trust, affirming and sometimes re-establishing a shared history,
often through confessional disclosures in which carers and dying people
jointly wrote and rewrote a shared narrative. 'We could face it together'
is a typical expression. In these deaths, as well as in the imagined lives of
cancer sufferers and survivors in news reports, we can see an alignment
with 'revivalist' discourse on the benefits of an open acknowledgement of
illness and death (Walter, 1994), imbuing illness with meaning and offering a secure sense of membership even up to the point of death.

CONCLUSION

This chapter has presented the argument that media health representations have increasingly come to construct the responses of ordinary people
towards illness as authoritative and admirable. In doing so, media producers have exploited the 'fall' of the professional hero that has become
a growing feature of modern life. We saw in Chapter 7 that media images
of doctors and of high-technology medicine have become increasingly
critical in recent years, accompanied by a decline in the level of trust in
expert authority generally. Media producers in the health sphere have
been quick to flatter their audiences with tales of the extraordinary
powers of laypersons, assertions of the 'rights' of consumers of health
care, and implicit theories of the power of mind over body.
Accompanying this, at times, has been a valorisation of alternative, 'holistic' or 'complementary' approaches to medical therapy that assist in the
task of breaking up the authority of orthodox medical expertise.

Additionally, evidence is beginning to emerge that commercial interests have detected this shift in power towards the consumer in recent years, and are beginning to exploit it. Yamey (2001) reports on 'direct to consumer' advertising by drug companies in California, promoting HIV drugs to the gay community. These have been criticised, Yamey reports, for unrealistic portrayals of HIV-positive men on the drugs engaging in impossibly heroic endeavours, and such advertisement is felt by public health officials to run the risk that people will imagine that HIV infection is not worth avoiding:

> In the ad that has caused the greatest outrage ... four attractive men in hiking gear are shown on top of a rocky mountaintop, gazing into space. The headline reads, 'Going the distance.' (2001: 804)

This elevation of the average person, here exploited by drug manufacturers, involves, for some commentators (such as Craib), an unhealthy and immature attempt to avoid the necessary disappointments of life. For others (such as Giddens), the opportunities offered by liberation from the obligation to follow the requirements imposed by traditional sources of expert authority are welcome. At any rate, the studies reviewed here of cancer heroes in the news, and of the heroism exhibited in everyday life by people facing serious illness, suggest that there is a congruence between most people's preferences for active management of their projects of self-identity, and media representations of the same. This stands in contrast with the oppression narratives told by some media analysts, who like to think that media organisations are primarily out to harm the interests of (particularly their female) readers. Gender differences are, indeed, very powerful in media health representations, and will be the subject of the chapter that follows. A simple story of oppression of one sex by the other, however, is insufficient to appreciate what is going on.

9 Real Men, Real Women

At various points in this book we have seen that gender stereotypes are a common feature of media health portrayals. Thus we saw in the last chapter that men's and women's experiences of cancer were portrayed in significantly different ways, with women depicted as skilful emotional labourers, in contrast with men, who occupied static and rather dated character parts. It was noted in Chapter 3 that breast cancer is featured in media reports more frequently than its epidemiological prevalence because of the presumed appeal of such 'soft' news to a female readership, as well as because it provides male readers and news editors with the opportunity to contemplate breasts. In that chapter it was also shown that media coverage of the side-effects of failed breast implants reflected significant biases towards the values of male-dominated newsrooms; the reporting of child sex abuse and false memory syndrome was shown to reflect similarly patriarchal values. At various other points in this book the existence of gender stereotypes has been noted but not yet been subject to sustained analysis.

Just as in fairy stories, which depend on extreme contrasts between characters (hero/villain, rich/poor), media health portrayals make use of contrasts and oppositions to create an emotionally engaging effect (see Chapter 2). The gender stereotypes in media health stories are at times as extreme as those in fairy stories or pantomimes. The vast majority of studies that focus on this have analysed the depiction of women rather than men, and analysts have largely been critical of the state of affairs revealed, suggesting that the interests of women are harmed by these images. We saw in the account of cancer stories in the previous chapter, though, that an overriding focus on the discovery of oppressive messages can at times obscure more subtle features of gendered media representations, which may nevertheless be highly stereotyped. To a significant extent, the lament about sex stereotypes is linked to more general charges of inaccuracy; if only media health stories were truer to 'reality', so this argument goes, less damage would be done. This is a persuasive case, but, as argued in Chapter 1, it underestimates other audience responses to media portrayals. In the present chapter I will assess feminist perspectives reflecting a growing awareness of the limitations of simple oppression narratives. First, though, I review a variety of studies of gendered messages in media health portrayals.

GENDER STEREOTYPES

The discovery of gender stereotypes in mass media is not difficult. A variety of published studies attest to the widespread nature of this phenomenon, which is by no means confined to health stories. Sport, for example, which we saw in the last chapter is often linked metaphorically with illness experience, provides plentiful data on gender stereotypes. Duncan and Messner's (1998) study of US television coverage of sport showed this to be a primary arena for the assertion of masculine dominance. Men's sporting events are covered much more frequently than women's, and significantly greater resources are devoted to them, both in terms of the technical features of coverage (for example, computer graphics budgets and ongoing statistics of a match), and in terms of the 'build-up' to events, where the sense of excitement about men's events is considerably greater than for women's. Thus a men's event may be described as 'the national championship', a women's as 'the women's national championship'. Women are 'girls' but men are 'men' rather than 'boys'. Portrayals of male sportsmen emphasise size and strength; portrayals of women their sexual appeal. In a detailed analysis of sports commentaries, these authors show that male success in sports is more frequently shown as a result of wilful effort, whereas women's success is more often portrayed as the outcome of luck. In basketball commentaries, the failure of men to score is described as the outcome of trying too hard; that of women is just a 'miss'. Discussion of women's feelings and their reliance on others for support is emphasised more, in an interesting parallel with cancer stories (see Chapter 8). Sport, being derived from male activities in hunting and warfare, is a central site for celebration of masculine heroism (van de Berg, 1998).

Fowler (1991) presents a critical analysis of the gendered use of language in newspaper texts, arguing that

> women are constituted in discourse as a special group with its own peculiar characteristics, set out from the population as a whole for exceptional evaluation. Irrationality, familial dependence, powerlessness and sexual

and physical excess are some of the attributes predicated of women.
(1991: 95)

Fowler notes that the family status of women is more frequently given
than their professional identities, a picture that is reversed when men are
mentioned. Women are also 'over-lexicalised' compared to men, indicating their 'abnormal' status – that is, there are numerous different terms
that refer to women, fewer being reserved for men. Such terms include
many that are sexually abusive ('whore'), dehumanising ('skirt'), trivial-
ising ('chick') or signifying possession by a male ('mistress'). Where a
sexual angle is stressed, the lexicon of terms expands. Thus, the attributes
of an actress in one story were variously listed: 'high heels, exquisite
figure, hair falling around her shoulders, prettiest little face and laughing
eyes, dainty feet, golden tresses, pretty [but not] dumb' (1991: 102–3).

In a study of the 'mythic elements' in US television news, Rutherford-
Smith (1979) found that males were more often depicted deciding and
acting, whereas women 'neither act nor are acted upon. They are part of
the chorus' (1979: 80). A more recent study (Signorielli & Bacue, 1999)
that charted prime-time dramatic programmes on US television between
1967 and 1998 found that, although in the 1990s more women appeared
in such programmes, they remained under-represented compared with
their numbers in the US population. Women at all times were categorised
as younger than their male counterparts. However, some changes that
reflected greater workplace equality had occurred, with the number of
women being portrayed as employed and in gender-neutral or professional
jobs having increased.

Age stereotypes commonly intersect with gender stereotypes. A number
of studies have documented the under-representation and relative degree
of stigmatisation of elderly women compared to elderly men in a variety of
media genres. Thus Signorielli (1993) and Gerbner et al. (1980) report
that elderly women are the most likely to be portrayed as fatal victims
in US television drama. Roy and Harwood (1997) found that the under-
representation of elderly women in US television advertisements was
particularly extreme in advertisements for cars and travel, and least in
advertisements for financial services and retail. Cumberbatch et al. (1998)
report that elderly women are under-represented when compared with elderly men on British television. Gantz et al. (1980) found that more elderly
men than women were shown in US magazine advertisements; Hanlon et al.
(1997) found the same in US comic strips; and McConatha et al. (1999)
had similar findings in a study of *Time* and *Newsweek* magazines, in which
elderly women were also shown in more passive and dependent roles.

Studies of sexual activity on US prime-time television in the 1980s and

1990s support Rutherford-Smith's (1979) account of active roles for men and 'chorus' roles for women. Sapolsky and Tabarlet (1991) found that the initiation of sexual acts was typically done by male characters, with little change in this over a ten-year period. Ward (1995) analysed the sexual content of programmes targetted at children and adolescents, finding that 'The most frequently occurring types of messages were those in which sexual relations were depicted as a competition, in which men commented on women's bodies and physical appearance, and masculinity was equated with being sexual' (1995: 595). Teenage magazines, too, have been found to contain profoundly gendered messages about sexual behaviour. Garner et al. (1998) analysed a sample of these, aimed at a female teenage audience, over a 20-year time span, finding that advice columns

> [serve] the rhetorical function of field guides and training manuals ... limit women's sociality and sexuality within narrowly defined heterosexual norms and practices. The rhetoric of sexual etiquette encourages young women to be sex objects and teachers of interpersonal communication rather than lovers, friends, and partners. Young women are being taught to subordinate self for others and to be contained. (1998: 59)

Teenage males are subject to similarly sex-stereotyped advice, as has been shown by Jewitt (1997) in an analysis of English health education leaflets and posters that appeared between 1986 and 1996. Women were represented in these materials as less active than men in the context of sex and in other respects were portrayed as passive and non-competitive (for example, women were shown taking 'exercise', whereas men were shown taking part in sports competitions). In both images and words, women were portrayed as risk reducers, men as risk takers. Male sexuality (usually white and heterosexual) was portrayed as more predatory and promiscuous, a physical rather than an emotional matter, although given the health promotion context it is unsurprising to see that a minority of the leaflets exhorted men to take greater responsibility for sexual health (for example, the use of contraception). In general, though, the irresponsibility and dangerousness of male sexuality was signified. Women, on the other hand, were depicted as guardians of sexual morality and safety, assessing, vetoing or acquiescing to sex and having a central role in enforcing protection against disease or unwanted pregnancy. A study of contraceptive advice in the US media (Watson et al., 1996) had similar results, coverage providing a bewildering variety of advice – particularly since fears about AIDS made explicit discussions of the topic more acceptable in the mainstream press – but almost all coverage targetted women rather than men, suggesting that contraception is largely portrayed as a female responsibility.

An analysis focusing more closely on gender in health portrayals, and which attempts an overview of a variety of health issues at the same time, was done by Weston and Ruggiero (1986) on selected US women's magazines over a 10-year period. A third of the health-related items in these magazines focused on diet, exercise and nutrition. Mental health issues, including stress, anxiety and depression, as well as reproductive health matters (childbirth features and contraception) accounted for a further third. Rarely covered, by comparison with their prevalence amongst women in the population, were topics related to cancer, alcohol and drug abuse, rape, eating disorders, accidents, diabetes and occupational health issues. Clearly, the focus on diet and exercise to improve appearance, and on emotions and childbirth, reflected dominant stereotypes of female preoccupations. Gender stereotypes, then, are very widespread in the media, and health coverage is no exception.

BODY SHAPE AND EATING

A variety of studies have demonstrated that media messages about eating (and drinking alcohol) portray high levels of consumption, and of consumption of fatty foods, without much stress on the health-damaging effects of this in terms of obesity and alcoholism. At the same time, media images have in recent years increasingly stressed the desirability of a thin body image for women. Numerous attempts have been made by researchers to link these contradictory messages to a rising prevalence in eating disorders generally and amongst women in particular.

The review by Gerbner et al. (1981) of ten years of US television found that in dramatic programmes grabbing a snack was portrayed about as frequently as eating a meal, snacks exceeding meals in children's programmes. Sweets and junk food were commonly advertised, and consumption of fruit and vegetables was rarely portrayed or advertised. Few characters were obese, and obese characters were never leading characters in dramas. Kaufman (1980) produced similar findings in his study of top-rated US television shows; sugary foods and drinks, desserts and sweets were frequently eaten by characters and eating on the move was common, as well as portrayals of eating things as a reward or a punishment. Images of overweight people were uncommon, in spite of these portrayals of obesity-inducing eating behaviour. Significantly, both of these studies showed that being overweight was least often portrayed for women's characters. Way's (1983) study a few years later found similar patterns, with the additional finding that characters were shown buying more healthy food than they were shown eating. The field is helpfully summarised by Signorielli (1993), who notes some other studies but no findings that significantly add to the picture described here.

Given these 'unhealthy' portrayals, it is relevant to ask whether they affect viewers. Dietz and Gortmaker (1985) found a significant association between the amount of time a large sample of American children spent watching television, and obesity. They suggest this is a causal influence, arguing that the activity of watching television itself reduces energy expenditure (many of these children watched for five or more hours per day), encourages snacking between meals, and is associated with increased consumption of the types of food advertised on children's television. Dietz (1990) found the same for adolescents in another study. Brown and Walsh-Childers, reviewing these and other such studies in 1994, concluded that television messages exert a significant influence towards consumption of unhealthy foods and obesity in children. Since then, the evidence has continued to mount: Signorielli and Staples (1997), for example, found a strong association between television watching and unhealthy perceptions of nutrition in children.

Several studies have tracked changes over time in media portrayals of female body weight. Silverstein et al. (1986) analysed television shows, monthly magazines, films and fashion photographs from 1901 to 1980, finding a shift towards a slimmer ideal for women across these genres. Wiseman et al. (1992) found the same over several decades when they tracked changes in the shapes of women submitting themselves for the 'Miss America' beauty pageant. Katzmaryk and Davis (2001) analysed *Playboy* centrefold models between 1978 and 1998, concluding that 70 per cent were underweight by current medical recommendations. Owen and Laurel-Seller (2000) also analysed these centrefolds, concluding that thinness was increasing over time so that 'many ... meet weight criteria for anorexia' (2000: 979), and finding also that an extremely thin body ideal prevailed amongst models advertising on the Internet. In a content analysis of US situation comedies, Fouts and Burggraf (2000) found a predominance of thin female characters. Negative comments (usually from males) directed at female characters increased in proportion to their body weight, with audience laughter following so that the comment was reinforced.

The stigmatisation of obesity, Coulter (1996) has pointed out, involves the association of fatness with other undesirable qualities, such as being from a lower socio-economic group or being black, and comedy roles are often assigned to fat women (for example, *Roseanne*). Considerable media coverage of the weight problems of celebrity women (Oprah

Winfrey and Liz Taylor) is accompanied by a plethora of media products devoted to diet regimes. Diet books, as a genre, became particularly popular in the 1950s and 1960s, best-sellers having titles like *Calories Don't Count, The Quick Weight Loss Diet* and *Dr. Atkins' Diet Revolution*, all of which sold millions of copies, making their (male) authors celebrities in their own right through promising readers a way to lose weight quickly and easily. Newspaper and magazine coverage of ways of losing weight increased from around the same time (Leonhard-Spark, 1978), with advice aimed at the more affluent stressing the benefits of exercise, sports activities and health spas. By contrast, advice aimed at the poorer classes promoted appetite-suppressing sweets and home exercise equipment. Moyer et al. (2001) note that there is excessive emphasis on dieting in American women's magazines, at the expense of more important health concerns. Nowadays, celebrity exercise and diet videos, and computer software add to the range of media products devoted to extolling the virtues of slimness, stigmatising obesity, and showing their audiences methods of achieving weight loss and bodily perfection.

With few positive role models for fat people, and stress on an increasingly thin ideal female body shape, it is understandable that a number of researchers have been concerned to establish links between media portrayals and eating disorders. Like attempts to prove the damaging effects of media portrayals of violence or sexually explicit behaviour, such studies can run into methodological difficulties in proving causal influence beyond reasonable doubt. Nevertheless, the results suggest that such influence exists, or is at least symbiotically related to body shape ideals that circulate in the culture (as would be suggested by the narcissism-spectacle cycle outlined by Abercrombie and Longhurst [1998]). Harrison and Cantor (1997) report a study in which levels of media use amongst US college students were found to be related to dissatisfaction with body shape, including a drive towards thinness and symptoms of disordered eating patterns amongst women. In men, a high level of media use was associated with attitudes in favour of thinness and dieting for women. A later study of adolescents (Harrison, 2000) replicated the finding that media exposure was related to eating disorder symptomatology amongst females. In a study of adolescent girls, Borzekowski et al. (2000) found a correlation between frequent viewing of music videos and weight concerns. Botta (1999), in another study of adolescent girls, found significant associations between media viewing and a drive for thinness, dissatisfaction with body shape, bulimic behaviours and endorsement of thin ideals. Murray (1999) compared the views of patients in an Australian eating-disorder clinic with those of non-patients, finding that men were generally less critical than females of the prevalent cultural emphasis on the desirability of thinness, and that this lack of a critical attitude was also more common in women with eating disorders, there being a significant relationship between the capacity for criticism and shorter duration of eating disorder.

In recent years, with the publicity accorded to high-profile cases such as that of Princess Diana, media interest in eating disorders has increased. This coverage has acquired the status of a freak show according to one critic (Bray, 1994), who studied popular Australian women's magazines. These pieces commonly featured confessional accounts by individual women, in which their experience of 'catching' the disease from exposure to the media was stressed, so that these women confessed to both an eating and a 'reading disorder' (1994: 8). Coverage also featured horror pictures of anorexic bodies, with a 1993 *Cosmopolitan* piece announcing such pictures with the headline, 'Anorexia: one woman's story plus the scariest pictures you'll *ever* see!', and another in *Woman's Day* that featured pictures of anorexic twins, announcing: 'Dying Twins *Horror*: Anorexia did *this*!' (1994: 8). Bray is concerned about these messages, feeling that they potentially pathologise all women as potential victims of the disease. Clearly, at this level, anorexia serves as a health 'scare' story (see Chapter 4) directed at women in particular.

In the light of such evidence, many media analysts have expressed highly critical views about media-promoted ideals of female body shape. A variety of counter-cultural social movements to resist dominant messages and develop alternative ideals have grown in strength as a result, including a body modification subculture (Pitts, 1999). This can involve piercing, branding or scarring the body to create a spectacular body style that may also involve participation in performance art. The growth in popularity of body-piercing ornaments, evident to anyone who surveys contemporary Western youth fashion, originated in this subculture. Pitts's (1999) study of coverage of these practices in the mainstream US and UK press suggests that, like the anorexic body, newspapers use images to promote a 'freak show' entertainment effect. More overt messages in newspapers, though, are condemnatory, often involving interviews with mental health practitioners who depict body modification practices as the outcome of individual psychopathology. According to a *Guardian* article quoted:

> Two psychologists who have worked with anorectics readily see the connections between all these forms of body modification. For Susie Orbach, 'there is a projecting onto your body of absolute hatred' . . . To psychologist Corinne Sweet, it's all just self-mutilation. 'From my experience as a counselor, what we do on the surface nearly always has some deep structure behind it. The expression of anger may be impossible, so we turn it in on ourselves.' (*Guardian*, 1995, quoted in Pitts, 1999: 294–5)

A *Chicago Tribune* piece in the same year featured a clinical psychologist likening body modifiers to the women she works with in a psychiatric facility who 'habitually slice their arms with razor blades as a means of alleviating overwhelming anxiety' (Pitts, 1999: 295). Pitts objects to this demeaning medicalisation of the subculture. Where body modifiers are themselves quoted in media accounts, justifying and explaining their practices, these are commonly juxtaposed with 'expert' psychiatric commentary so that 'dominant discourses' (1999: 300) prevail. Nevertheless, the fact that such practices are featured at all, and that the issue of their acceptability is sometimes framed as a debate rather than a foregone conclusion, is a sign that conventional media images of ideal feminine (and masculine) appearance are not unassailable.

WOMEN'S HEALTH

At various points in this book media representations of matters specific to women's health have been discussed. Thus media coverage of cancers, particularly breast cancer, has been shown to involve the construction of a breast cancer 'epidemic' (Lantz & Booth, 1998: 907) serving as a significant 'scare' story (Chapter 4), with personal accounts of this cancer being an important site for reporting the achievements of heroic women (Chapter 8). Media scares about the contraceptive pill and tampon-induced toxic shock syndrome have also been discussed (Chapters 1 and 4). Earlier in this chapter it was shown that media messages about sexuality and contraception contain sex-stereotyped messages. There is considerable mass-media interest in reproductive health issues in women. In part, this reflects medical priorities, which, as Gannon et al. (1997) showed in their study of the content of obstetrics and gynaecology journals, are heavily oriented towards issues of conception, pregnancy and childbirth. Far less attention is paid to other health issues faced by women, such as problems of menstruation, the menopause, women's cancers, sexually transmitted disease or birth control. The media coverage of abortion, technologically assisted conception, pregnancy, childbirth and aspects of child care, as well as menstruation and the menopause has been analysed with regard to messages about gender, and so these topics are reviewed here.

Abortion

Miller's (1996) analysis of US media coverage of abortion suggests that its primary focus has been on legal, moral and religious aspects of the issue, to the neglect of the women's health issues that are involved. Thus, in a computerised search of one index of news media between 1989 and 1992, Miller found 699 articles listed under 'political aspects' of abortion, 797 under 'laws, regulations, etc.' and only eight under 'health aspects'. Where health aspects were discussed, these tended to be used as ammunition in the fierce debate about legalisation. Thus pro-life activists promoted the idea of 'post-abortion syndrome', publicising testimonials from women deemed to be affected by this adverse psychological response, and giving the impression that such women had been forced into having abortions, their objections silenced by a pro-abortion medical establishment. The pro-choice lobby, on the other hand, in Miller's view, underemphasises the negative psychological consequences of abortion, out of a concern not to give ground to the pro-life lobby, this being reflected in media coverage. Miller concludes that this polarisation makes women's concerns 'subservient to political concerns' (1996: 45), and fails to represent the experience of abortion in balanced terms.

Assisted conception

Media coverage of technologically assisted conception, such as *in vitro* fertilisation (IVF), has been found both to reflect existing gender stereo-types and to contribute to a popular validation of parenthood as an overwhelmingly desirable experience, women being portrayed as naturally and inevitably wanting children. Noble and Bell (1992) analysed Australian press items on IVF from 1988, finding that the most frequently quoted sources in articles were from IVF proponents. Very few critics were given voice, and feminist criticisms of the technology were virtually absent from media coverage. Photographs of parents were generally of mothers for whom IVF had worked, and there was very little coverage of IVF failures, so that the technology was portrayed as delivering medical miracles. Typical headlines included 'Sally's $40,000 miracle', 'A ray of hope in desperate bid for baby' and 'IVF process gives hope to thousands of infertile couples' (1992: 25).

In a similar study of US newspapers and magazines during 1986–91, Condit (1996) found equally positive overall coverage, noting that 'mass media accounts have featured a bias that hides the risks of the procedures behind glamorized success stories' (1996: 341). The very high failure rate and expense of the procedure and its health risks were rarely reported, 'role model' stories of success and satisfaction with the procedure being more frequently shown. Underlying this positive portrayal of IVF was an extreme emphasis on the benefits of biological parenthood, with infertility, by contrast, being portrayed as devastating. Commonly, individual women were quoted on the overriding imperative to become mothers: 'Pamela says she'll never quit trying. Having a baby is the most important goal of her life'; 'I wanted [children] more than anything' (1996: 344). In contrast to psychological studies which, Condit observes, show that infertility is not a predictor of clinically significant psychological difficulties, media reports portrayed infertility as a 'catastrophic psychological disease worse than divorce or the loss of a family member by death' (1996: 344). Historically, the media and medical construction of 'infertility' as a medical condition (implying the possibility of reversal) occurred after the introduction of new reproductive technologies, before which words like 'sterility' or 'barren' were used, signifying a dead end. Defining infertility as present after one year of trying, Condit notes, is a generous definition which allows the market of potential consumers to be portrayed as large (many couples in fact conceive naturally during IVF treatment). The focus of media reports on the problems of 'the couple', Condit feels, is part of an agenda to persuade women to accept treatments that may not involve their own eggs, thus aligning ideal reproductive patterns with available technology.

In a rare treatment of masculinity in media health portrayals, Dwight (1997) has analysed 'sperm stories' relating to male infertility in the UK press. Accounts of conception in both press reports and medical text-books (Dwight draws on Martin's [1989] study of these here), portray sperm and egg in anthropomorphic terms, with the sperm adopting the 'masculine' qualities of competitiveness and activity (sporting metaphors are often used here), and the egg being appropriately 'passive' in its feminine wait for fertilisation. Because sperm and egg are imagined to be like people, descriptions of assisted conception can be portrayed as furthering the 'rights' of these 'people' to a natural union. Economic metaphors depict parenthood as an 'investment', albeit an 'emotional' one; sperm are equated with money and semen is portrayed as a 'liquid asset', or they are imagined as vehicles, technical things in themselves, whose journey is simply 'assisted' by the available procedures. Dwight feels that anxieties about paternity are expressed in stories about falling sperm counts amongst modern men subject to the 'stress' of modern life, so that the solution to this – IVF – plays on male fears at a time when masculinity is under threat from a variety of sources.

Pregnancy and childbirth

Analysis of media representations of pregnancy has found that it is generally portrayed as a time of considerable risk, in which the health interests of the foetus figure as large, if not larger, than those of women. Thus Beaulieu and Lippman (1995), in a study of North American women's magazines, found considerable concern expressed about the safety of older pregnant women and their unborn children. Such women were constructed as career women who had 'chosen' late motherhood, rather than having been constrained in their choices by a lack of childcare facilities or by male expectations of parenting roles. Late motherhood was then portrayed as a risky experience, in which women are obliged to make use of antenatal testing to minimise the chances of harm befalling themselves or, more often, the foetus.

Irresponsibility towards the health of unborn children can provoke media condemnation, as was seen in the US media in the mid-1980s when there was a media-fuelled moral panic about the dangers of illicit drug use by pregnant mothers. As with other media panics there was considerable distortion of the numbers involved in order to talk up the magnitude of the scare. An original report, in which an investigator suggested that there might be as many as 375,000 babies born each year who had been exposed to illicit drugs in the womb, was distorted so that this was translated first into the number of babies born affected by such use, and then into a likely estimate of pregnant mothers taking crack cocaine. The fact that many of the women involved will have been occasional users of marijuana, and that their babies will have been born unaffected by this, was then forgotten. Media coverage proceeded in classic 'scare' fashion by telling individual horror stories, the main emphasis of which was the plight of the child rather than the suffering of the woman involved. A discussion of options for punishment then became possible, with the arguments for and against imprisoning such women being publicly debated in the media.

At the same time, as Karpf (1988) has noted, media presentations of matters concerning childbirth have shifted somewhat from early images of mothers passively accepting medical advice. Feminist consumerism resulted in grass-roots movements to reform childbirth procedures in the 1960s and 1970s towards a less medicalised experience, with some media portrayals reflecting this switch of emphasis. At the same time, Karpf argues, coverage of newer approaches to childbirth has been somewhat androcentric, often featuring the efforts of charismatic male doctors who have instituted innovatory programmes, and rarely turning to women's organisations as sources. Nevertheless, significant movement has occurred. Accompanying this shift towards a more consumerist vision has been a corresponding de-emphasis of medical authority, following the general trend for the media validation of the views of ordinary people (see Chapter 8). (Martinez et al. [2000], though, complain of excessive medicalisation in American magazine depictions of post-natal depression).

A study by Dingwall et al. (1991), in which Japanese parentcraft literature was compared with British equivalents, is revealing in showing the shifts that have occurred in Western media. UK manuals stress parenthood as a responsibility shared by 'choice-making adults', whereas the Japanese literature 'marginalize[s] women and emphasise[s] their subordination to medical authority' (1991: 423), a characteristic once shared by British advice manuals but nowadays shaken off. In the Japanese literature, fathers rarely appeared and ideological statements about the importance of fathers were not accompanied by practical illustrations of what Japanese fathers might do to fulfil these ideals. In particular, involvement at childbirth was not shown for Japanese fathers, this event taking place in a highly medicalised, technological space. Photographs censored anything that might remind readers of animal-like aspects, such as the appearance of blood. The British literature, by contrast, combined greater emphasis on consumerism with an idealisation of childbirth as a natural process.

Infant feeding

Breastfeeding is widely acknowledged in medical and health-care circles to be beneficial to both babies and mothers, so the fact that it is rarer than bottle-feeding with artificial milk formulae in Western countries has been a cause for concern for many health educationists. Arora et al. (2000), documenting a low rate of successful persistence with initial breastfeeding decisions in a sample of American women, found that women identified a lack of information in mass media as a significant source of discouragement to their efforts. Analyses of media content have shown considerable bias towards the advantages of bottle-feeding and the difficulties of breastfeeding. Thus A. Henderson (1999) found that Australian press and popular magazines showed breastfeeding to be natural and best, but problematic in practice, with predominantly negative messages about breastfeeding being dominant. Wolf (2000) traces the history of medical and popular prejudice against breastfeeding from reports in the

1880s in which the stress of urban life began to be blamed for producing 'bad' and 'dirty' mothers' milk. 'Scientifically' prepared infant food appeared to give the best chance of avoiding germs, which were just then coming to popular consciousness as responsible for the spread of infectious disease. Human lactation as an 'unreliable body function' (2000: 93) thus became a truth that persists to this day in media accounts.

Perhaps the most thorough survey of media representations of infant feeding has been done by L. Henderson et al. (2000), in a study of UK television and newspaper output during 1999. These authors found that bottle-feeding was more frequently portrayed, and was presented as less of a problem, the health risks of formula milk and the health benefits of breast milk being rarely presented. For example, 27 references to problems of breastfeeding were contained in the sample, including mastitis, engorged breasts, sore nipples and practical and emotional difficulties. Bottle-feeding difficulties were mentioned only once, where the troublesome business of sterilising bottles was shown. Breastfeeding, in fact, was associated with middle-class or celebrity women. Thus a *Guardian* article on designer gear for babies said that 'if they throw up down the front of their Agnes B babygro, it's only handmashed organic vegetables or breast milk as gilt-edged as their parent's credit rating' (2000: 1197). Bottle-feeding, on the other hand, was shown to be the province of the 'ordinary' majority. In many respects the bottle, for scriptwriters, is an easy symbol for 'baby' (just as the wheelchair is for 'disabled'), and the portrayal of a baby being bottle-fed in a scene does not distract attention away from foregrounded events in the way that breastfeeding might; it also means that portrayals of 'new man' fatherly involvement can be depicted. At the same time, the commercial interests of formula manufacturers are clearly enhanced by the depiction of formula as the natural choice, so the interests of health educators (and, arguably, women) are opposed to this.

Menstruation and the menopause

A survey of US newspapers, magazines and broadcast media in the early 1990s (Kalbfleisch et al., 1996) revealed a large volume of coverage and media information about menstruation and the menopause, with the exception that there was little coverage of the onset of menstruation. In general, media coverage dwelt on the bad news rather than the good, with reporting of premenstrual syndrome (PMS) and endometriosis figuring large, the latter condition often being unhelpfully linked to being a 'career' or 'professional' woman due to the popular promotion of the view that childbirth protects against endometriosis. For these authors, there was insufficient attention paid in media portrayals to the psychological and emotional aspects of coping with menstruation, the portrayals focusing instead on physical aspects and, in particular, contributing to a medicalisation of menstruation by describing drug and other medical remedies for problems. Advertisements for tampons emphasised their effectiveness in making a secret of menstruation, contributing to a climate of embarrassment about its physical manifestations. The authors note, though, the possible beginnings of a shift, signalled by rumours in marketing magazines of a planned Tampax campaign to present the product as assisting a natural process using ecologically friendly products, thus bringing the company into line with contemporary environmental sensibilities.

Chrisler and Levy's (1990) account of US magazine coverage of PMS revealed 'a strong bias in favor of reporting negative menstrual cycle changes ... [supporting] the stereotype of the maladjusted woman' (1990: 89). Such negative coverage reflects well-known preferences for negative rather than positive stories in news organisations (Galtung & Ruge, 1973), but in this area the additional influence of gender stereotypes creates a veritable 'menstrual monster' (1990: 89). Content analysis discovered 131 different descriptive terms for women experiencing PMS, with a huge variety of symptoms, including many that had not been described in any scientific literature on PMS, such as cold sores, bruising easily or conjunctivitis. Water retention, a variety of negative feelings ranging from sadness and irritability to hostility and suicidal ideation, pain, changes in eating habits, impaired concentration, anti-social or violent behaviour, allergies, and constipation were just a few of the conditions associated with PMS. Typical headlines include: 'Premenstrual Frenzy'; Dr Jekyll and Mrs Hyde'; 'The Taming of the Shrew Inside of You', the phrase 'raging hormones' occurring frequently in articles (1990: 97–9). As is usual in scare stories, numbers were used to exaggerate prevalence, with most writers of articles suggesting that between 30 and 60 per cent of women experience PMS, a figure which Chrisler and Levy view as unsupported in the scientific literature. A great variety of treatments were recommended, often contradicting each other (for example, some said eat fruit, and others said eat no fruit). Biological rather than socio-psychological causation was emphasised. Positive coverage of women experiencing welcome changes, or coping well with menstruation, was rare.

The 1990s saw a growing media interest in the menopause, explained by Kalbfleisch et al. (1996) as the result of the ageing of the 'baby boom' generation, whose informational needs are supposedly served by this. For these authors, media coverage reflected conflict between a medical view of the menopause that emphasised symptoms and the applicability of drug and hormone treatments, and an oppositional view that sought to treat the menopause as 'natural', criticising its medicalisation. This conflict, of course, repeats the familiar opposition between professional and consumer power that runs through many other media health stories (see Chapters 7 and 8). Other studies of the menopause in the media reflect tensions between negative and positive imagery. There may also be national differences here. Shoebridge and Steed (1999), in a study of Australian newspapers and women's magazines, found that coverage predominantly 'drew on and reinforced schemata of ill-health, psychological disturbance, vulnerability, decrepitude' (1999: 475), with a concomitant emphasis on medical management, so that the menopause was portrayed as the cause of dysfunction and loss of competence. On the other hand, Kaufert and Lock's (1997) study of Canadian pharmaceutical literature and mass media found that a shift in imagery had occurred. In the 1970s, menopausal women were depicted as 'depressed and sickly', but in the 1990s exceedingly positive images were to be found: 'the menopausal woman is shown glowing with fitness, with well-maintained teeth, hair and skin, far too fit to break a hip' (1997: 81). A message in tune with popular feminist sensibilities, that menopausal women needed to take charge and shoulder responsibility for their health and happiness, had emerged to replace the pharmaceutically dependent image representative of a period in which medical authority over women was more acceptable.

Variation in acceptance of medical authority has been detected, too, by Sefcovic (1996) in a study of the coverage of hysterectomy across a variety of US media, suggesting that different genres may be associated with variations in the encouragement of consumer assertiveness. Newspaper coverage was the most accepting of a medicalised perspective, frequently reporting new surgical procedures enthusiastically and underplaying the negative physical effects of these. Where negative effects were discussed, these focused on emotional and sexual dysfunctions perpetuating, in this author's judgement, 'traditional views of women as biologically predisposed to emotional and mental instability' (1996: 374). In general, newspapers failed to provide information putting into question the high rate of hysterectomy in America. On the other hand, magazines and, particularly, some books were more likely to portray women as knowledgeable consumers, and provided more information about both the pros and cons of hysterectomy.

MEN'S HEALTH

By contrast, studies of media representations of men's health are few and far between and have been done only in recent years, reflecting the growing interest in masculinity in the gender studies field. Some of these we have already touched on in this chapter: Dwight's study (1997) of male infertility in UK media and Jewitt's study (1997) of male sexuality in sexual health leaflets. In addition, there have been two studies of UK newspaper treatment of men's health issues (Coyle & Sykes, 1998; Lyons & Willatt, 1999), and work has been done by Clarke (1999b; Clarke & Robinson, 1999) on images of masculinity in coverage of male cancers in Canadian media. These reveal a complex mixture of media messages about traditional and newer forms of masculinity, reflecting the influence of earlier feminist critiques of present-day media messages.

In an analysis of a series of articles on male mental health appearing in the British upmarket *Independent* newspaper in 1996, Coyle and Sykes (1998) argue that these portrayed men as victims of social changes and pressures, chief amongst which are pressures from women to abandon traditional forms of masculine behaviour and to adopt a 'new man' approach, whose chief marker is the capacity to display and discuss emotions. Thus the danger of being male was constructed in one piece: 'If you are male, the chances are that it is actually putting your health at risk as you internalise your stress and anxiety instead of confronting and discussing your problems' (*Independent*, quoted by Coyle & Sykes, 1998: 269). At one level, this might be interpreted as another example of a particular feature of health 'scare' stories, in which ordinary 'objects' (in this case, being a man) suddenly appear to threaten health or safety. In another *Independent* piece, the line was taken that men were emotionally incompetent due to fear:

> Men are, I suspect, scared of discussing their feelings. The discussion itself is seen as a sign of weakness. The roots of this probably lie in the fact that such 'weakness', in a world where competitiveness and hardness are still seen as the ultimate in male attitudes, can and often does count against you. (the *Independent*, quoted by Coyle & Sykes, 1998: 270-1)

The modern way of life, no longer involving hunting and warfare, coupled with the lack of a legitimate role in maintaining domestic life, the *Independent* writers argued, placed men in an impossible position. The articles portrayed women as better off than men in their easy relationship with emotional life, and as at least equal to men in current conditions, if not more fortunate. On top of this, women were portrayed as insensitively placing men under pressure to perform sexually, subscribing to the 'myth' of the 'ever-ready' male, when in fact all they may want to do is relax after a 'full working day' or 'have time with the children' (quoted, 1998: 278). Coyle and Sykes conclude that these articles portray threats to traditional masculinity as health damaging, constructing the lot of the 'new man' as undesirable. Clearly, this is an attempt by the newspaper at reversal of a simple feminist oppression narrative. It is significant that it appeared in an upmarket publication, appealing to an educated readership well versed in such narratives and, presumably, judged ready for this understanding to be 'twitched' (Langer, 1998) to create a novel effect.

Lyons and Willatt (1999) present analysis of a similar phenomenon, a 'special feature' on men's health in a women's supplement attached to the UK paper the *Mail on Sunday,* a paper catering for a less-educated audience than the *Independent*, with a high proportion of female readers. Here, the focus was on how women could get their male partners to change their health-damaging behaviours. Like the *Independent*, the paper constructed men's health as being in a state of crisis arising from an inadequately fulfilled traditional masculinity. Health, however, in the *Mail* was confidently located as primarily a woman's concern, men being constructed as work-obsessed or focusing on higher things. In fact, this meant that men could also be shown as infantile and in need of women's care, contrasting with the traditional portrayal of women as childlike and dependent on masculine protection. Here we see a depiction that shares a great deal with the *Independent* pieces, in so far as women are portrayed as largely problem-free, and men as victims of modern social arrangements. But a more conservative 'solution' is offered by the *Mail*, as women are urged to take on traditional nurturing and caring roles in order to protect men's health.

In studies of North American print media coverage of prostate and testicular cancer, Clarke (1999b; Clarke & Robinson, 1999) found predominantly 'traditional' images of masculinity, although there were some signs of cracks in this façade. The threat to male sexual functioning constituted by prostate cancer (Clarke, 1999b), which can affect the capacity for erections, was a prominent feature of coverage, as were sporting and military metaphors in which men were urged to 'fight' or admired for 'fighting' the disease. There was also evidence of a 'gender war' (1999b: 67) in the oft-repeated theme that prostate cancer has a low profile, with few 'celebrity' victims willing to speak out about their experiences and little funding for prevention and awareness raising when compared with breast cancer. Testicular cancer coverage (Clarke & Robinson, 1999) contained some similar themes, in so far as the sexual symbolism of testicles contributed to a 'machismo' image for men, and the mixture of sporting prowess with illness experience was a significant feature. Men were portrayed as 'sexually active, athletic, competitive, interested in war and battles, concerned with finances and financial acumen, with cars and mechanics' (1999: 276).

Yet these authors also found many articles that, like the women's breast cancer pieces analysed in Chapter 8, discussed the importance of social support in going through the experience, one piece offering the address of a support group, others pointing out the importance of a supportive family. Coverage of prostate cancer, too, was found by Clarke (1999b) to highlight the importance of 'brotherhood' and 'fraternity' between men in preventing and experiencing the disease. These features (which Clarke & Robinson call 'modern possibilities' [1999: 276]) suggest that themes reflecting contemporary critiques about traditional masculinity have entered routine media health coverage.

PROFESSIONAL MEDIA: THE CASE OF DRUG ADVERTISEMENTS

The construction of gendered stereotypes in medical knowledge is a very large topic that extends beyond study of popular media. I do not propose to cover this vast field here, but confine this section to studies of advertisements in the specialist journals that serve health professions, since these studies share some of the methods that have been applied to mass media generally, and are revealing with regard to gender issues. In Chapter 3, Chapman's (1979) analysis of psychotropic drug advertisements in Australian medical magazines were shown to contain messages designed to appeal to male doctors' fantasies of wielding magical power over female patients. In a number of studies since then, this finding has been broadly repeated. Lupton (1993c), for example, found images of men as 'mechanical' and women as 'vulnerable' (1993c: 805) in the drug advertisements in an Australian medical weekly. However, some international variations have also been found. Lovdahl et al. (1999), for example, found that antidepressant advertisements in the *American Journal of Psychiatry* in 1995 depicted women as the chief recipients, contrasting with the medical journals of Scandinavian countries. Concentrating on these Scandinavian journals, Lovdahl and Riska (2000) found considerable variation between genders and over time. In 1975, for example, men were more frequently portrayed as recipients in Finnish and Danish medical journals; women in Norway and Sweden. Ten years later the pattern between countries was exactly reversed.

Leppard et al. (1993) analysed a large sample of advertisements from three US medical journals with a particular focus on cardiovascular treatments. Women in these adverts were generally younger than men, were shown with 'pleasant' rather than 'serious' facial expressions, and were less frequently portrayed as patients, an under-representation compared with the epidemiological prevalence of heart disease. These authors were concerned that this may lead to doctors taking women's complaints of heart symptoms less seriously than men's. Lusk (1999) is unusual in analysing advertisements in nursing journals, finding that images of patients in American nursing journals showed more male than female images, with a greater proportion of these involving critical or cardiac illness. Like Leppard, Lusk suggests that this may contribute to a perception that heart disease is a men's health problem.

NURSES

Understanding the media image of nurses is tied to understanding that of doctors, a topic that was explored in Chapter 7, particularly through the work of Turow (1989) on the role of television medical soaps. Turow, as well as other analysts of medical soaps (for example, Gerbner et al., 1981; McGlaughlin, 1975; Pearl et al., 1982), while largely concentrating on the doctor heroes of these dramas, has consistently pointed out the relative downplaying of the contribution of nurses to health care in such series. Nurses in general, according to these analysts, have been largely portrayed as handmaidens to doctors, with little focus on their independent contribution of professional care skills, and at worst depicted as sexual mascots or even as sadistic manipulators. These studies, though, do not provide an accurate picture of the contemporary media scene, which has seen some significant changes to the images of nursing. An analysis that is in some respects parallel to that of Turow, of US television drama focusing on nurses, has been provided by Kalisch et al. (1983), who, elsewhere, have also analysed film images of nursing (Kalisch & Kalisch, 1982). In the UK, a more recent major study of nursing images in a variety of media has been published (Hallam, 2000) and this is of use in showing recent shifts. This section draws on these and a number of other, more minor analyses to explore this profoundly gender-stereotyped topic.

Kalisch et al. (1983) survey all the American television dramas that had appeared up to then that featured an image of nursing, finding that these portrayals involved a 'consistent misrepresentation of reality' (1983: viii) that they judged to be damaging to the interests of nurses. This, of course, contrasts with the depiction of doctors, which, as we saw in Turow's (1989) analysis, was – at least in the early days – lauded by the medical profession for promoting a positive image of the profession. In the television dramas of the 1950s, Kalisch et al. found, nurses were rarely portrayed as having any technical competence or autonomous area of professional competence, nor was the profession shown as having internal lines of authority, the chief relationship being with doctors. Nurses were treated with sympathy and respect, being shown to be devoted, self-sacrificing and intuitive. Although prone to romance (often with doctors), nurses were not shown to be sexually promiscuous and in this, as well as other respects, they embodied the conventional images of ideal womanhood that were then prevalent. In the 1960s, with the phenomenal success of the *Dr Kildare* and *Ben Casey* shows, nurses were shown as rather powerless assistants to doctors, with little to offer in terms of patient care, largely being shown doing administrative or clerical tasks as a background 'prop'.

In the 1970s, a continuing downplaying of nurses' roles was evident in many series, and this was further emphasised with the emergence of female doctors in medical soaps. These characters needed to be distinguished as career-oriented women, different in this respect from traditional women, so that the image of nurses was subject to even further marginalisation. With the emergence of *MASH* in the 1970s, more comic images of nurses became popular. At first, these images were highly sexualised, but the picture of legitimate sexual harassment changed later on in the series, however, and nurses (embodied by the character of the chief nurse, Major Houlihan) came to be shown as professionally competent members of medical teams, albeit driven by a male-dominated medical agenda and rarely featuring as the chief players in plot lines. Kalisch et al. note that daytime television contained somewhat different images of nursing from prime-time, featuring more middle-aged nurses, who were accorded greater respect by other characters, in line with the different audience expectations of daytime viewers, who contained a high proportion of middle-aged women. In general, though, these authors regret the lack of a rounded professional image for nurses in both the prime-time and daytime television soaps they studied.

In their analysis of film images of nursing, Kalisch and Kalisch (1982) were able to go back further in time, noting that silent movies depicted nurses as saintly figures in dramas around the time of the First World War. The period before and during the Second War featured nurses in relatively respectable roles, following their profession as a calling and occasionally being the protagonists in adventurous plots. This was to change in the post-war period, when nursing was portrayed as little more than an interlude before marriage, with no opportunity for autonomous action or professional development. Nurses at this time were simply nonentities in the movies. Between 1960 and 1980 a more sinister development, from the point of view of the Kalisch, emerged: films like *Catch 22* and the original *MASH* film showed nurses as cold, manipulative and authoritarian. In *One Flew Over the Cuckoo's Nest* this was taken a step further in the depiction of the head nurse as an outright sadist. These negative images of nurses were repeated in a large number of more minor films.

In view of these depictions in popular mass media, it is of interest to consider any variations from this in the professional journals of doctors and nurses, using advertisements as a source of information about stereotypes. Lusk (2000) has analysed images of nursing in hospital administration magazines during the 1930s, 1940s and 1950s, finding that nurses were largely portrayed in roles subordinate to doctors and hospital administrators, as female, young and eager to please. The 1940s, however, saw an increase in portrayals of nurses performing more complex and autonomous activities, an image that was to decline again in the post-war period. This analysis, then, suggests broadly similar findings to that of the Kalisches' studies. Krantzler (1986), however, adopted the strategy of examining advertisements in doctors' and nurses' professional journals separately and discovered interesting variations. Very few advertisements featured doctors and nurses together, and a picture of separate professional development thus emerges. Doctors' journal advertisements (in the *Journal of the American Medical Association*) gradually moved away from a 1960s image of a white-coated male with stethoscope prescribing drugs towards an image of the doctor (now sometimes female) in a suit in a business role. In nursing journal advertisements (in the *American Journal of Nursing*) nurses increasingly came to be shown wearing white coat and stethoscope, as sometimes being male, and as part of a nursing hierarchy rather than subservient to doctors. A direct relationship with patients, an important symbol of professional identity, was commonly depicted in the nursing journal. It seems, then, that free of the oppressive presence of doctors on a more publicly available media stage, nurses' professional self-image has space to develop. The cost of this, though, is that images of democratically interprofessional health-care teamwork are unavailable.

Hallam's (2000) study suggests that contemporary media representations have moved on from this state of affairs, in part because of protests by nurses at demeaning media images. Nowadays, media portrayals of nursing are influenced by an 'equal opportunity' dynamic (2000: 188), in which multidisciplinary medical teams rather than individual doctors are depicted, with more women doctors, male nurses and ethnic diversity. In Hallam's view, though, 'the masculine vision of the professional ideal . . . is invariably sustained' in medical dramas (2000: 189), by which she means a stress on heroic rescue through the use of hi-tech methods in emergency situations where emotional control is paramount.

JUDGING THE MEDIA

It is evident to anyone reviewing the field of gender stereotypes that strong feelings about injustice imbue much media analysis. It also becomes clear that the urge to tell a story of oppression can lead to con-tradictions. For example, should the portrayal of women as emotionally expressive be condemned for the implication of irrationality that this may contain, or should it be celebrated as evidence of the particular skilfulness of women? Should confessional narratives of breast cancer be criticised as reminiscent of masculine heroic tales, or accepted as a sign of women's empowerment and wisdom? What does one make of highly sexualised, conventionally 'feminine' representations of the bodies of disabled women, who may themselves celebrate such visibility (Petersen, 1994)? Many media analysts seem to wish to make these overall judgements, but the urge to adjudicate may be premature. In this section, I shall assess the contribution of a variety of theorists and others in understanding how these issues of judgement may be approached. This discussion will then lead us back to some of the more general concerns about the relationships of audiences with media representations raised at the start of this book. It will become clear that, though few and far between, studies of audience responses to media messages are likely to be a way forward. These can be helpful in revealing variety in audience positions, the relevance of which for political agendas can then be assessed.

The problem of judgement, in the absence of evidence about audience readings, is highlighted by consideration of the contradictions contained in one author's account of the cultural context of cancer. This was writ-ten by Jackie Stacey (1997), in part to record her own experience of cancer, in part to present a feminist cultural analysis of the disease. Commenting on the phenomenon of published illness narratives, such as those I have described in Chapter 8 as 'pathographies', she observes that in such stories 'People who survive cancer are transformed from *feminised victim* to *masculinised hero* in the narrative retelling of individual triumph' (1997: 11, her italics). She feels that orthodox treatment is generally dominated by male doctors, who take over decisions, treating the situation as a battle against cancer cells. Alternative therapies can be understood as being in opposition to such dominance, allowing those with cancer to construct heroic narratives of resistance. At the same time there is a danger, according to Stacey, that these latter kinds of story can slip into masculine mode so that the whole experience is a rather delicate balancing act for women seeking to avoid the masculine and yet leave behind negative aspects of the feminine:

> While these new forms of self-knowledge also reproduce masculine notions of autonomy, mastery and self-determination and, to some extent, reinforce their privileged place in patriarchal culture, their centrality to alternative practices might also open up the rewards of such masculine preserves to female patients, enabling women to overcome some of the limitations of restrictive forms of femininity. (1997: 200)

In fact, the 'desire for mastery' (1997: 238) is a profoundly masculine urge, in Stacey's view, uniting both (masculine) 'modern science' and the 'self-health cultures of the 1990s'. Mystery, not knowing, not being in control, there being no ultimate purpose to the suffering caused by cancer: these perspectives are ruled out by the desire for mastery, as being, perhaps, 'feminine' matters. Stacey's cancer experience, then, was for her a political process in which judgements about gender stereotypes were never far away, apparently involving a continual need to categorise her own and others' responses as either 'masculine' or 'feminine'. While these judgements appear to have been subtle and context-sensitive, her cancer experience nevertheless seems to have been exceedingly burdened by this responsibility to make moral assessments. She then presents her struggles with these in book form, on the grounds that this will be enlightening to her readers. Thus her story, which is a compendium of judgements, allows Stacey herself to participate as a cancer hero by writing her own confessional book, which she ends with a passage that paradoxically criticises such narrative genres for promoting the

> familiar cliché, 'cancer was the best thing that ever happened to me'. According to this version we become wiser as we approach death . . . The so-called 'survivors' of cancer are . . . heroised for their confrontation with death, which is presumed to have enlightened them about how to live life. They are the bearers of knowledge. They have lived to tell the tale. (1997: 244–5)

Clearly, Stacey's position is profoundly contradictory (although it could be argued that some of the most interesting books have been written in the face of contradiction). Do we conclude that she has become a 'masculinised hero' by writing her book and presumably exploiting her position as a survivor bearing knowledge? Or, as Potts (2000) has argued in relation to cancer pathographies, do we conclude that she is telling a feminist moral tale that is a 'modification of the traditional masculine literary genre' (2000: 101) in aid of the collective empowerment of women? Such a call for judgement, it might be said, poses the problem in excessively crude terms, yet we have seen in this chapter that lesser media analysts of messages about gender and health continually confront readers with their stark verdicts.

To understand this problem of judgement, which applies to those who condemn media portrayals on grounds that lie outside the gender field as well – though for the moment it is helpful to exemplify the problems by the feminist example – it is necessary to look briefly at different moments in feminist theories of the media. Van Zoonen (1994) notes that liberal, radical and socialist feminist media analyses, while differing in certain respects, shared the view that the media acts as an instrument of oppressive social control, and saw the solution to this as lying in more 'realistic' depictions. Women who appeared to enjoy 'bad' media portrayals were judged to suffer from false consciousness. This analysis of early feminist perspectives is shared by McRobbie (1999), who notes the emergence of an alternative view based on the perception that women's 'pleasure' in viewing such sex-stereotyped shows as *Dallas* (see Ang, 1985), or reading traditional heterosexual romance fiction, can be viewed in more positive terms. Such indulgence does not necessarily mean that viewers and readers have bought into underlying ideologies of gender, but that these genres may provide pleasurable escape routes from an oppressive reality, or promote the development of supportive networks through shared topics of conversation, building a strong sense of female identity.

Associated with this is the view that early feminist analysis essentialised the 'feminine' and the 'masculine' and fixed the meaning of texts. In fact, gender is a social construction, and texts are open to a variety of readings. For one person a particular representation may be oppressive; for another, liberating; a quality that one person feels is 'masculine' (such as the heroic elements of a progress narrative of cancer) is for another person a feminist triumph. These ideas also tie in with the notion of resistant readings and variable decoding of encoded messages contained in Hall's (1980) legacy to media studies (discussed in Chapter 1). They help move the debate about media on from a realist 'lament' (Langer, 1998) about inaccuracy to a more complex understanding of the variable places media images may have in everyday life. Indeed, the mention of pleasure reminds us of the view that media experiences may involve enjoyment of the spectacular, including the opportunities for narcissistic self-reflection that this involves.

Catharine Lumby (1994) has pointed out the limitations of early feminist perspectives with particular force, regarding these as depending on a 'straw figure consumer of media . . . a misogynist male or a female dupe' (1994: 49). She commends later academic perspectives (for example, variable decoding) but feels that their implications have not been sufficiently taken on by many feminist media analysts, who persist in a prejudicial search for sexist imagery. Oppression narratives, Lumby feels, blind media analysts to what is going on in people's viewing habits and in media representations themselves. Maintaining that men watch evening current affairs programmes and women watch daytime soaps, for example, no longer holds up, according to viewing figures. In fact, news and current affairs programmes are themselves becoming more 'soapy'; women increasingly work in the day; newspapers are following the lead shown by television in collapsing traditional dichotomies between 'hard' and 'soft' news, between traditional male and female polarities, and between fact and fiction. Oppression narratives overlook the role of fantasy, irony and parody in today's media culture; Schwarzenneger and Madonna, for example, are not taken 'seriously' by audiences as if they represented ideally desirable images of masculinity or femininity. This means that

> many feminists have failed to grasp the contradictory, constantly shifting nature of contemporary mass media imagery or to realise that the mass media is not a stable platform for pushing political or moral values of any single persuasion. (1994: 53)

This attempt to break up simple readings, and to suggest a more complex relationship between audiences and media texts, returns us to themes raised in the early chapters of this book. Analysis of representations themselves is just the beginning if we are to understand the meanings of media health. The views of Lumby, McRobbie and Van Zoonen with regard to gender can be expanded to incorporate media health representations in general, since unitary readings of 'scares', 'villains', 'heroes' and the like are as much a matter of opinion as readings of masculinity or femininity. Studies of audience uses of and responses to media health imagery, and the relationship of these to everyday life so that media studies becomes a fully elaborated part of general investigations in the sociology of health and illness, are the way forward.

CONCLUSION

The overall story told in media health representations might be summarised as follows: life is full of danger, emanating from the environment,
harmful substances, malevolent bugs and, sometimes, bad people who
carry disease. We are all potential victims of both bad luck and bad
people, though children are particularly vulnerable. Fortunately, in
modern societies, we organise defence and rescue services, although
recently these have become less and less trustworthy. Sometimes, for
example, doctors are wonderful, but at other times they (and the tools
that they wield, such as drugs) can be a liability to health. In the end we
are on our own and it is up to us to tap the exceptional personal resources
that we all possess in order to overcome danger and disease. Media producers have noticed these heroic powers – which are exhibited in
profoundly gender-specific ways – in a way that other institutional representatives sometimes do not, so they are our allies and teachers. In fact,
they make us feel that we belong to a wider community of like-minded
souls, facing the same predicament. We can all take comfort from this.

This looks like a fairy story, and the unreality of this forms the major
part of health educators' complaints about the media treatment of health
topics. Although this book has shown that there could be more evidence,
and although it is clear that some people resist or diverge from dominant
messages, it is clearly the case that substantial sections of modern populations 'fall' for this tale and the inaccuracies and distortions that it
involves, even making their own contributions to it as confessional wit-
nesses if allowed. I do not support media producers who occasionally
defend their products on the grounds that active audience theory suggests
that people can freely distinguish fact from fiction. What evidence there is
shows that many people really do change their food-purchasing behaviour
in response to sensationalist scares and may fail to adjust to more realistic dangers that have not been covered in the media; many people (if not
all) do seem to soak up prejudices, copy unhealthy habits, and distrust
doctors and medicines unreasonably when media health stories encourage
these things. Thus, in describing the health educator's position on these
things as a 'lament', I do not want to convey that it is wrong to be
concerned about these things; the lament is simply somewhat limited in
its capacity to imagine other levels of response to media health stories.

The story of media health is, at another level, a mythologising of the
material life of the body in a modern world which, for all its advances in
comfort, cannot banish sickness and death from human experience. The
formation of community bonds, so that audiences are attracted to imagine

a shared sense of this human predicament, is an important role for media health representations and this seems to require a degree of 'inaccuracy'. Evoking fantasies of danger, encouraging experiments with trust and leaps of faith, and building up hopes in our personal strengths all play an important part in the stories that are told. These things are designed to work at an emotional level, drawing audiences into the fantasy. In this respect they are similar to the religious tales that once attracted and organised the imagination of the majority of people and shielded them from existential terrors. While it is clear that health promotion is a worthy goal for media analysts in this sphere, a sociologically informed analysis of media health and its audiences must attend to such broader concerns. This may in turn produce a fuller understanding of the problems of media health stories with which health educators are concerned.

References

Abercrombie, N. (1996). *Television and society.* Cambridge: Polity.

Abercrombie, N. & Longhurst, B. (1998). *Audiences: a sociological theory of performance and imagination.* London: Sage.

Alasuutari, P. (Ed.) (1999). *Rethinking the media audience.* London: Sage.

Albert, E. (1986). Illness and evidence: the response of the press to AIDS. In Feldman, D.A. & Johnson, T. (Eds), *The social dimensions of AIDS: method and theory.* New York: Praeger.

Allen, R. & Nairn, R.G. (1997). Media depictions of mental illness: an analysis of the use of dangerousness. *Australian and New Zealand Journal of Psychiatry, 31* (3), 375–81.

Allison, C., Roizen, J. & Olivier, P. (1997). The 1995 pill scare: women's perceptions of risk and sources of information. *British Journal of Family Planning, 23* (3), 79–82.

Altheide, D.L. & Michalowski, R.S. (1999). Fear in the news: a discourse of control. *Sociological Quarterly, 40* (3), 475–503.

Altman, D.G., Slater, M.D., Albright, C.L. & Maccoby, N. (1987). How an unhealthy product is sold: cigarette advertising in magazines, 1960–1985. *Journal of Communication, 37* (4), 95–106.

Amos, A. (1986). British women's magazines – a healthy read? In Leathar, D.S., Hastings, G.B., O'Reilly, K. & Davies, J.K. (Eds), *Health education and the media II.* Oxford: Pergamon Press. pp. 197–202.

Amos, A., Jacobson, B. & White, P. (1991). Cigarette advertising policy and coverage of smoking and health in British women's magazines. *Lancet, 12* (337), 93–6.

Anderson, B. (1991). *Imagined communities: reflections on the origin and spread of nationalism* (2nd ed.). London: Verso.

Anderson, R.C. & Larson, D.L. (1995). Reconstruction and augmentation patients' reaction to the media coverage of silicone gel-filled implants – anxiety evaluated. *Psychological Reports, 76* (3), Part 2: 1323–30.

Ang, I. (1985). *Watching Dallas: soap opera and the melodramatic imagination.* London: Methuen.

Angermeyer, M.C. & Matschinger, H. (1996). The effect of violent attacks by schizophrenic persons on the attitude of the public towards the mentally ill. *Social Science and Medicine, 43* (12), 1721–8.

Aronoff, C. (1974). Old age in prime time. *Journal of Communication, 24,* 86–7.

Arora, S., McJunkin, C., Wehrer, J. & Kuhn, P. (2000). Major factors influencing breastfeeding rates: mother's perception of father's attitude and milk supply. *Pediatrics, 106* (5), U50–4.

Auslander, G.K. & Gold, N. (1999). Media reports on disability: a binational comparison of types and causes of disability as reported in major newspapers. *Disability and Rehabilitation, 21* (9), 420–31.

Baker, A.J. (1986). The portrayal of AIDS in the media: an analysis of articles in the *New York Times*. In Feldman, D.A. & Johnson, T. (Eds), *The social dimension of AIDS: method and theory*. New York: Praeger.

Barnes, C., Mercer, G. & Shakespeare, T. (1999). *Exploring disability: a sociological introduction*. London: Routledge.

Barthes, R. (1975). *S/Z*. London: Cape.

Basil, M.D. (1996). Identification as a mediator of celebrity effects. *Journal of Broadcasting and Electronic Media, 40* (4), 478–95.

Bauman, Z. (1998). Postmodern religion. In Heelas, P., Martin, D. & Morris, P. (Eds), *Religion, modernity and postmodernity*. Oxford: Blackwell. pp. 55–78.

Beaulieu, A. & Lippman, A. (1995). 'Everything you need to know': how women's magazines structure prenatal diagnosis for women over 35. *Women and Health, 23* (3), 59–74.

Becker, E. (1973). *The denial of death*. New York: Free Press.

Becker, K. (1995). Media and the ritual process. *Media Culture and Society, 17* (4), 629–46.

Begg, N., Ramsay, M., White, J. & Bozoky, Z. (1998). Media dents confidence in MMR vaccine. *British Medical Journal, 316*, 561.

Beharrell, P. (1993). AIDS and the British press. In Glasgow University Media Group (Eds), *Getting the message: news, truth and power*. London: Routledge. pp. 210–49.

Bell, A. (1991). *The language of news media*. Oxford: Blackwell.

Bell, A. (1994). Media (mis)communication on the science of climate change. *Public Understanding of Science, 3*, 259–75.

Bell, V. (2002). The vigilant(e) parent and the paedophile: The News of the World campaign 2000 and the contemporary governmentality of child sex abuse. *Feminist Theory, 3* (1), 83–102.

Bell, R.A., Wilkes, M.S. & Kravitz, R.L. (1999). Advertisement-induced prescription drug requests – patients' anticipated reactions to a physician who refuses. *Journal of Family Practice, 48* (6), 446–52.

Benthall, J. (1993). *Disasters, relief and the media*. London and New York: I.B. Tauris.

Berger, P.L. (1973). *The social reality of religion*. Harmondsworth: Penguin. (First published in 1967 as *The sacred canopy*).

Berlin, F.S. & Malin, H.M. (1991). Media distortion of public's perception of recidivism and psychiatric rehabilitation. *American Journal of Psychiatry, 148* (11), 1572–6.

Berridge, V. (1991). AIDS, the media and health policy. *Health Education Journal, 50* (4), 179–85.

Best, J. (1987). Rhetoric in claims-making: constructing the missing children problem. *Social Problems, 34* (2), 101–21.

Best, J. (1988). Missing children, misleading statistics. *Public Interest, 92*, 84.

Black, M.E.A. (1995). What did popular women's magazines from 1929 to 1949 say about breast-cancer *Cancer Nursing, 18* (4), 270–7.

Blauner, R. (1966). Death and social structure. *Psychiatry, 29*, 378-94.

Borzekowski, D.L.G., Robinson, T.N. & Killen, J.D. (2000). Does the camera add

10 pounds? Media use, perceived importance of appearance, and weight concerns among teenage girls. *Journal of Adolescent Health, 26* (1), 36–41.

Botta, R.A. (1999). Television images and adolescent girls' body image disturbance. *Journal of Communication*, Spring, 22–49.

Boudioni, M., Mossman, J., Jones, A.L., Leydon, G. & McPherson, K. (1998). Celebrity's death from cancer resulted in increased calls to CancerBACUP. *British Medical Journal, 317,* 1016.

Bradby, H., Gabe, J. & Bury, M. (1995). 'Sexy docs' and 'busty blondes': press coverage of professional misconduct cases brought before the GMC. *Sociology of Health and Illness, 17* (4), 458–76.

Bratic, E. & Greenberg, R. (1979). An analysis of US newspaper coverage of cancer. In Hobbs, P. (Ed.), *Public education about cancer: recent research and current programmes.* Geneva: International Union Against Cancer. pp. 53–65.

Bray, A. (1994). The edible woman: reading/eating disorders and femininity. *Media Information Australia, 72,* 4–10.

Brookes, R. (1999). Newspapers and national identity: the BSE/CJD crisis and the British press. *Media Culture and Society, 21,* 247–63.

Brookes, R. (2000). Tabloidisation, media panics and mad cow disease. In Sparks, C. & Tulloch, J. (Eds), *Tabloid tales: global debates over media standards.* London: Rowman and Littlefield. pp. 195–209.

Brown, J.D. & Walsh-Childers, K. (1994). Effects of media on personal and public health. In Bryant, J. & Zillman, D. (Eds), *Media effects: advances in theory and research.* Hillsdale, NJ: Laurence Erlbaum. pp. 389–415.

Brown, J., Chapman, S. & Lupton, D. (1996). Infinitesimal risk as public health crisis: news media coverage of a doctor–patient HIV contact tracing investigation. *Social Science and Medicine, 43* (12), 1685–95.

Brown, P., Zavestoski, M., McCormick, S., Mandelbaum, J. & Luebke, T. (2001). Print media coverage of environmental causation of breast cancer. *Sociology of Health and Illness, 23* (6), 747–75.

Buckingham, D. (2000). *After the death of childhood: growing up in the age of electronic media.* Cambridge: Polity Press.

Bunton, R. (1997). Popular health, advanced liberalism and *Good Housekeeping* magazine. In Petersen, A. & Bunton, R. (Eds), *Foucault, health and medicine.* London: Routledge. pp. 223–48.

Burman, E. (1994). Poor children: charity appeals and ideologies of childhood. *Changes, 12* (1), 29–36.

Burman, E. (1996). Constructing and deconstructing childhood: images of children and charity appeals. In Haworth, J. (Ed.), *Psychological research: innovative methods and strategies.* London: Routledge. pp. 170–84.

Burman, E. (1999). Appealing and appalling children. *Psychoanalytic studies, 1* (3), 285–301.

Bury, M. & Gabe, J. (1994). Television and medicine: medical dominance or trial by media? In Gabe, J., Kelleher, D. & Williams, G. (Eds), *Challenging medicine.* London: Routledge. pp. 65–83.

Byrne, P. (2000). Some voices. *British Medical Journal, 321,* 770.

Cassata, M.B., Skill, T.D. & Boadu, S.O. (1979). In sickness and in health. *Journal of Communication, 29* (4), 73–80.

Cassata, M., Skill, T. & Boadu, S.O. (1983a). Life and death in the daytime television serial: a content analysis. In Cassata, M. & Skill, T. (Eds), *Life on daytime television: tuning-in American serial drama.* Norwood, NJ: Ablex. pp. 47–69.

Cassata, M., Anderson, P.A. & Skill, T. (1983b). Images of old age on daytime. In Cassata, M. & Skill, T. (Eds), *Life on daytime television: tuning-in American serial drama.* Norwood, NJ: Ablex. pp. 37–44.

Chapman, S. (1979). Advertising and psychotropic drugs: the place of myth in ideological reproduction. *Social Science and Medicine, 13A,* 751–64.

Chapman, S. (1989). The news on smoking: newspaper coverage of smoking and health in Australia, 1987–88. *American Journal of Public Health, 79* (10), 1419–21.

Chapman, S. (2001). Fear of frying: power lines and cancer. *British Medical Journal, 322,* 682.

Chapman, S. & Lupton, D. (1994a). *The fight for public health: principles and practice of media advocacy.* London: British Medical Journal Publishing Group.

Chapman, S. & Lupton, D. (1994b). Freaks, moral tales and medical marvels: health and medical stories on Australian television. *Media Information Australia, 72,* 94–103.

Chapman, S. & Wakefield, M. (2001). Tobacco control advocacy in Australia: reflections on 30 years of progress. *Health Education and Behaviour, 28* (3), 274–89.

Charteris-Black, J. (2000). A conceptual analysis of war metaphors in British newspaper sports reports. Unpublished typescript, English Language Institute, University of Surrey.

Check, W.A. (1987). Beyond the political model of reporting: nonspecific symptoms in media communication about AIDS. *Reviews of Infectious Diseases, 9* (5), 987–1000.

Cheek, J. (1997). Contextualising toxic shock syndrome. *Health, 1* (2), 183–204.

Chesterfield-Evans, A. & O'Connor, G. (1986). Billboard utilising graffitists against unhealthy promotions (B.U.G.A.U.P.) – its philosophy and rationale, and their application to health promotion. In Leathar, D.S., Hastings, G.B. & O'Reilly, K., Davies, J.K. (Eds), *Health education and the media II.* Oxford: Pergamon Press. pp. 241–4.

Chrisler, J.C. & Levy, K.B. (1990). The media construct a menstrual monster: a content analysis of PMS articles in the popular press. *Women and Health, 16* (2), 89–104.

Clarke, J. (1986). Cancer meanings in the media: implications for physicians. *Studies in Communications, 3,* 175–215.

Clarke, J.N. (1999a). Breast cancer in mass circulating magazines in the USA and Canada, 1974–1995. *Women and Health, 28* (4), 113–30.

Clarke, J.N. (1999b). Prostate cancer's hegemonic masculinity in select print mass media depictions (1974–1995). *Health Communication, 11* (1), 59–74.

Clarke, J. & Robinson, J. (1999). Testicular cancer: medicine and machismo in the media 1980–94. *Health, 3* (3), 263–82.

Collee, J. (1999). Medical fiction. *British Medical Journal, 318* (7189), 955–6.

Combs, B. & Slovic, P. (1979). Newspaper coverage of causes of death. *Journalism Quarterly, 56,* 837–43.

Condit, D.M. (1996). Media bias for reproductive technologies. In Parrott, R.L. & Condit, C.L. (Eds), *Evaluating women's health messages: a resource book.* Thousand Oaks, CA: Sage. pp. 341–55.

Conrad, P. (1996). *Media images, genetics and culture: potential impacts of reporting scientific findings on bioethics.* Boston, MA: Brandeis University.

Conrad, P. (1997). Public eyes and private genes. *Social Problems, 44* (2), 139–54.

Conrad, P. (1999). Uses of expertise: sources, quotes and voice in the reporting of genetics in the news. *Public Understanding of Science, 8,* 285–301.

Cooke, C., Daone, L. & Morris, G. (2000). *Stop press! How the press portrays disabled people.* London: Scope.

Coulter, L. (1996). The deviance of obesity: the fat lady sings. In Lester, D.M. (Ed.), *Images that injure: pictorial stereotypes in the media.* Westport, CT: Praeger. pp. 136–9.

Coward, R. (1989). *The whole truth: the myth about alternative health.* London: Faber.

Coyle, A. & Sykes, C. (1998). Troubled men and threatening women: the construction of crisis in male mental health. *Feminism and Psychology, 8* (3), 263–84.

Craib, I. (1994). *The importance of disappointment.* London: Routledge.

Crayford, T., Hooper, R. & Evans, S. (1997). Death rates of characters in soap operas on British television: is a government health warning required? *British Medical Journal, 315* (7123), 1649–52.

Cumberbatch, G. & Negrine, R. (1992). *Images of disability on television.* London: Routledge.

Cumberbatch, G., Gauntlett, S., Littlejohns, V., Stephenson, C. & Woods, S. (1998). *Older people on television.* London: BBC/Age Concern.

Dans, P.E. (2000). *Doctors in the movies: boil the water and just say Aah.* Bloomington, IL: Medi-Ed Press.

Dant, T. & Johnson, M. (1991). Growing old in the eyes of the media. In Franklin, B. & Parton, N. (Eds), *Social work, the media and public relations.* London: Routledge. pp. 169–82.

Darke, P. (1994). The Elephant Man: an analysis from a disabled perspective. *Disability and Society, 9* (3), 327–42.

Darling-Wolf, F. (1997). Framing the breast implant controversy: a feminist critique. *Journal of Communication Inquiry, 21* (1), 77–97.

Dayan, D. & Katz, E. (1992). *Media events.* Cambridge, MA.: Harvard University Press.

de Beauvoir, S. (1972). *The second sex.* Harmondsworth: Penguin (first published 1949).

Diamond, J. (1998). *C: because cowards get cancer too.* London: Vermilion.

Diefenbach, D.L. (1997). The portrayal of mental illness on prime-time television. *Journal of Community Psychology, 25* (3), 289–302.

Dietz, W.H. (1990). You are what you eat – what you eat is what you are. *Journal of Adolescent Health Care, 11* (1), 76–81.

Dietz, W.H. & Gortmaker, S.L. (1985). Do we fatten our children at the TV set? Television viewing and obesity in children and adolescents. *Pediatrics, 75* (5), 807–12.

Diller, L.H. (1996). The run on Ritalin: attention deficit disorder and stimulant treatment in the 1990s. *Hastings Center Report, 26* (2), 12–18.

Dingwall, R., Tanka, H. & Minamikata, S. (1991). Images of parenthood in the UK and Japan. *Sociology, 25* (3), 423–66.

Dixon-Woods, M. (2001). Writing wrongs? An analysis of published discourses about the use of patient information leaflets. *Social Science and Medicine, 52* (9), 1417–32.

Donaldson, J. (1981). The visibility and image of handicapped people on television. *Exceptional Children, 47* (6), 413–16.

Donaldson, L. & O'Brien, S. (1995). Press coverage of the Cleveland sexual abuse inquiry. *Journal of Public Health Medicine, 17* (1), 70–6.

Dovey, J. (2000). *Freakshow: first person media and factual television.* London and Sterling, VA: Pluto Press.

Dowson, S. (1991). Promoting positive images of people with learning difficulties: problems and strategies. In Franklin, B. & Parton, N. (Eds), *Social work, the media and public relations.* London: Routledge. pp. 157–68.

Driedger, S.M. & Eyles, J. (2001). Organochlorines and breast cancer: the uses of scientific evidence in claimsmaking. *Social Science and Medicine, 52* (10), 1589–1605.

Duncan, M.C. & Messner, M.A. (1998). The media image of sport and gender. In Wenner, L.A. (Ed.), *MediaSport.* London: Routledge. pp. 170–85.

Dunwoody, S. & Peters, H.P. (1992). Mass media coverage of technological and environmental risks: a survey of research in the United States and Germany. *Public Understanding of Science, 1,* 199–230.

Dwight, K. (1997). Sperm stories: romantic, entrepreneurial, and environmental narratives about treating male infertility. *Science as Culture, 6* (27), 246–76.

Eco, U. (1966). Narrative structure in Fleming. In del Buono, E. & Eco, U. (Eds), *The Bond affair.* London: MacDonald.

Eldridge, J. (1999). Risk, society and the media: now you see it, now you don't. In Philo, G. (Ed.), *Message received.* Harlow: Addison Wesley and Longman. pp. 106–27.

Elias, N. (1978). *The civilizing process. Volume I: The history of manners.* Oxford: Blackwell.

Elias, N. (1982). *The civilizing process. Volume II: State formation and civilization.* Oxford: Blackwell.

Elliott, T.R. & Byrd, E.K. (1982). Media and disability. *Rehabilitation Literature, 43* (11/12), 348–55.

Entwistle, V. (1995). Reporting research in medical journals and newspapers. *British Medical Journal, 310,* 920–3.

Entwistle, V. & Hancock-Beaulieu, M.M. (1992). Health and medical coverage in the UK national press. *Public Understanding of Science, 1,* 367–82.

Entwistle, V. & Sheldon, T. (1999). The picture of health? Media coverage of the health service. In Franklin, B. (Ed.), *Social policy, the media and misrepresentation.* London: Routledge. pp. 118–34.

Entwistle, V., Watt, I.S., Bradbury, R. & Pehl, L.J. (1996). Media coverage of the Child B case. *British Medical Journal, 312,* 1587–91.

Ferriman, A. (2001). Doctors find an ally. *British Medical Journal, 322,* 438.

Finzen, A., Wick, F., Alder, B. & Hoffmann-Richter, U. (1999). Minor tranquillizers in the printed media. *Psychiatrische Praxis, 26* (4), 194–8.

Fiske, J. (1987). *Television culture.* London: Methuen.

Fouts, G. & Burggraf, K. (2000). Television situation comedies: female weight, male negative comments, and audience reactions. *Sex Roles, 42* (9–10), 925–32.

Fowler, R. (1991). *Language in the news: discourse and ideology in the press.* London: Routledge.

Frank, A.W. (1995). *The wounded storyteller.* Chicago: University of Chicago Press.

Franklin, B. (1997). *Newszak and news media.* London: Arnold.

Franklin, B. (1999). *Social policy, the media and misrepresentation.* London: Routledge.

Franklin, B. & Parton, N. (1991). Media reporting of social work. In Franklin, B. & Parton, N. (Eds), *Social work, the media and public relations.* London: Routledge. pp. 2–19.

Franzosi, R. (1998). Narrative analysis, or why (and how) sociologists should be interested in narrative. *Annual Review of Sociology, 24,* 517–54.

Frayling, C. (2000). They're mad, bad and dangerous to know. *Times Higher Education Supplement,* 18 September , 18–19.

Freimuth, V.S., Greenberg, R.H., DeWitt, J. & Romano, R.M. (1984). Covering cancer: newspapers and the public interest. *Journal of Communication, 34,* 62–73.

Furedi, F. (1997). *Culture of fear: risk-taking and the morality of low expectation.* London and New York: Cassell.

Gabe, J. & Bury, M. (1988). Tranquillisers as a social problem. *Sociological Review, 32,* 524–46.

Gabe, J. & Bury, M. (1996). Halcyon nights: a sociological account of a medical controversy. *Sociology, 30* (3), 447–69.

Galtung, J. & Ruge, H.H. (1973). The structure of foreign news. *Journal of Peace Research, 2* (1), 64–91.

Gannon, L., Stevens, J. & Stecker, T. (1997). A content analysis of obstetrics and gynecology scholarship: implications for women's health. *Women and Health,* 26 (2), 41–55.

Gantz, W., Gartenberg, H. & Rainbow, C.K. (1980). Approaching invisibility: the portrayal of the elderly in magazine advertisements. *Journal of Communication, 30* (1), 56–60.

Garland, R. (1984). Images of health and medical science conveyed by television. *Journal of the Royal College of General Practitioners, 44,* 316–19.

Garner, A., Sterk, H.M. & Adams, S. (1998). Narrative analysis of sexual etiquette in teenage magazines. *Journal of Communication,* Autumn, 59–78.

Gerbner, G. (1978). Deviance and power: symbolic functions of 'drug abuse'. In Winick, C. (Ed.), *Deviance and mass media.* London: Sage. pp. 13–30.

Gerbner, G., Gross, L., Morgan, M. & Signorielli, N. (1981). Health and medicine on television. *New England Journal of Medicine, 305* (15), 901–4.

Gerbner, G., Gross, L., Signorielli, N. & Morgan, M. (1980). Aging with television: images on television drama and conceptions of social reality. *Journal of Communication, 30* (1), 37–47.

Gibb, H. & Holroyd, E. (1996). Images of old age in the Hong Kong print media. *Ageing and Society, 16* (2), 151–75.

Gibson, M.D. (1994). AIDS and the African press. *Media Culture and Society, 16,* 349–56.

Giddens, A. (1990). *The consequences of modernity.* Cambridge: Polity Press.

Giddens, A. (1991). *Modernity and self-identity: self and society in the late modern age.* Cambridge: Polity Press.

Giddens, A. (1992). *The transformation of intimacy.* Cambridge: Polity Press.

Gilman, S.L. (1988). *Disease and representation: images of illness from madness to AIDS.* Ithaca, NY: Cornell University Press.

Giroux, H.A. (1998). Nymphet fantasies: child beauty pageants and the politics of innocence. *Social Text, 16* 4(57), 31–53.

Glasgow University Media Group (1976). *More bad news.* London: Routledge and Kegan Paul.

Goffman, E. (1968). *Stigma: notes on the management of spoiled identity.* Harmondsworth: Pelican.

Gold, N. & Auslander, G. (1999). Newspaper coverage of people with disabilities in Canada and Israel: an international comparison. *Disability and Society, 14* (6), 709–31.

Goodman, N.W. (2001). Smear tests and seat belts. *British Medical Journal, 322* (7295), 1188.

Gordon, P.N., Williamson, S. & Lawler, P.G. (1998). As seen on TV: observational study of cardiopulmonary resuscitation in British television medical dramas. *British Medical Journal, 317*, 780–83.

Gough, D. (1996). The literature on child abuse and the media. *Child Abuse Review, 5*, 363–76.

Greenberg, B.S. & Woods, M.G. (1999). The soaps: their sex, gratifications, and outcomes. *Journal of Sex Research, 36* (3), 250–7.

Greenberg, R., Freimuth, V.S. & Bratic, R. (1979). Newspaper coverage of cancer. In D. Nimmo (Ed.), *Communication yearbook 3.* New Brunswick, NJ: Transaction Books. pp. 645–54.

Gulland, A. (2001). The media and GPs' day of action. *British Medical Journal.* Web-based data supplement at http://bmj.com/cgi/content/full/322/7295/DC1.

Gwyn, R. (1999). 'Killer bugs', 'silly buggers' and 'politically correct pals': competing discourses in health scare reporting. *Health, 3* (3), 335–45.

Hall, S. (1980) Encoding/decoding. In Hall, S. *Culture, media, language.* London: Hutchinson. pp. 128–38.

Hall, S., Critcher, C., Jefferson, T., Clarke, J. & Roberts, B. (1978). *Policing the crisis: mugging, the state, and law and order.* London: Macmillan.

Hallam, J. (2000). *Nursing the image: media, culture and professional identity.* London: Routledge.

Hammond, P.B. (1997). Reporting pill panic: a comparative analysis of media coverage of health scares about oral contraceptives. *British Journal of Family Planning, 23* (2), 62–6.

Hanlon, H., Farnsworth, J. & Murray, J. (1997). Ageing in American comic strips: 1972–1992. *Ageing and Society, 17* (3), 293–304.

Hanneman, G.J. & McEwen, W.J. (1976). The use and abuse of drugs: an analysis of mass media content. In Ostman, R.E. (Ed.), *Communication research and drug education. Vol III: International yearbooks of drug addiction and society.* London: Sage. pp. 65–87.

Harrison, D. (1992). The Terry Fox story and the popular media: a case study in ideology and illness. In Grenier, M. (Ed.), *Critical studies of Canadian mass media.* Toronto and Vancouver: Butterworths. pp. 13–28.

Harrison, K. (2000). The body electric: thin-ideal media and eating disorders in adolescents. *Journal of Communication, 50* (3), 119–43.

Harrison, K. & Cantor, J. (1997). The relationship between media consumption and eating disorders. *Journal of Communication, 47* (1), 40–67.

Hartley, J. (1987). Invisible fictions. *Textual Practice, 1* (2), 121–38.

Hawton, K., Simkin, S., Deeks, J., O'Connor, S., Keen, A., Altman, D.G., Philo,

G. & Bulstrode, C. (1999). Effects of a drug overdose in a television drama on presentations to hospital for self-poisoning: time series and questionnaire study. *British Medical Journal, 318* (7189), 972–7.

Henderson, A.M. (1999). Mixed messages about the meanings of breast-feeding representations in the Australian press and popular magazines. *Midwifery, 15* (1): 24–31.

Henderson, L. (1996). Selling suffering: mental illness and media values. In Philo, G. (Ed.), *The media and mental distress*. Harlow: Addison Wesley and Longman. pp. 18–36.

Henderson, L. (1999). Producing serious soaps. In Philo, G. (Ed.), *Message received*. Harlow: Addison Wesley and Longman. pp. 62–81.

Henderson, L. & Kitzinger, J. (1999). The human drama of genetics: 'hard' and 'soft' media representations of inherited breast cancer. *Sociology of Health and Illness, 21* (5), 560–78.

Henderson, L., Kitzinger, J. & Green, J. (2000). Representing infant feeding: content analysis of British media portrayals of bottle feeding and breast feeding. *British Medical Journal, 321*, 1196–8.

Herzlich, C. & Pierret, J. (1989). The construction of a social phenomenon: AIDS in the French press. *Social Science and Medicine, 29* (11), 1235–42.

Hill, A. (2000). Fearful and safe: audience response to British reality programming. *Television and New Media, 1* (2), 193–213.

Hoffmann-Richter, U., Wick, F., Alder, B. & Finzen, A. (1999). Neuroleptic drugs in the printed media. *Psychiatrische Praxis, 26* (4), 175–80.

Holzinger, A., Angermeyer, M.C. & Matschinger, H. (1998). What are your associations with the term schizophrenia? An inquiry concerning the social representation of schizophrenia. *Psychiatrische Praxis, 25* (1), 9–13.

Hunt, M.W. (1991). Being friendly and informal: reflected in nurses', terminally ill patients' and relatives' conversations at home. *Journal of Advanced Nursing, 16*, 929–38.

Hyler, S.E., Gabbard, G.O. & Schneider, I. (1991). Homicidal maniacs and narcissistic parasites: stigmatisation of mentally ill persons in the movies. *Hospital and Community Psychiatry, 42* (10), 1044–8.

Irwin, C.E. & Milstein, S.G. (1982). Predictors of tampon use in adolescence after media coverage of toxic shock syndrome. *Annals of Internal Medicine, 96* (2), 966–8.

Jackson, T. (2001). How the media report medical errors: blunders will never cease. *British Medical Journal, 322* (7285), 562.

Jacobs, R. (1996). Producing the news, producing the crisis: narrativity, television and news work. *Media, Culture and Society, 18* (3), 373–97.

James, A. & Jenks, C. (1996). Public perceptions of childhood criminality. *British Journal of Sociology, 47* (2), 315–31.

James, V. (1989). Emotional labour: skill and work in the social regulation of feelings. *Sociological Review, 37* (1), 15–42.

Jansen, S.C. & Sabo, D. (1994). The sport/war metaphor: hegemonic masculinity, the Persian Gulf War, and the new world order. *Sociology of Sport Journal, 11*, 1–17.

Jauchem, J. (1992). Epidemiologic studies of electric and magnetic fields and cancer – a case study of distortions by the media. *Journal of Clinical Epidemiology, 45* (10), 1137–42.

Jewitt, C. (1997). Images of men: male sexuality in sexual health leaflets and posters for young people. *Sociological Research Online, 2* (2). http://www.socresonline.org.uk/2/2/6.html.

Johnson, C.A. & Johnson, B.E. (1993). Medicine on British television: a content analysis. *Journal of Community Health, 18* (1), 25–35.

Johnson, J.D. (1997). Factors distinguishing regular readers of breast cancer information in magazines. *Women and Health, 26* (1), 7–27.

Jones, J.W. (1992). Discourses on and of AIDS in West Germany, 1986 to 1990. *Journal of the History of Sexuality, 2* (3), 439–68.

Kalbfleisch, P.H., Bonnell, K.H. & Harris, T.M. (1996). Media portrayals of women's menstrual health issues. In Parrott, R.L. & Condit, C.L. (Eds), *Evaluating women's health messages: a resource book.* Thousand Oaks, CA: Sage. pp. 279–92.

Kalisch, P.A. & Kalisch, B.J. (1982). The image of the nurse in motion pictures. *American Journal of Nursing, 82* (Spring), 605–11.

Kalisch, P.A., Kalisch, B.J. & Scobey, M. (1983). *Images of nurses on television.* New York: Springer.

Karpf, A. (1988). *Doctoring the media: the reporting of health and medicine.* London: Routledge.

Katzmarzk, P.T. & Davies, C. (2001). Thinness and body shape of *Playboy* centerfolds from 1978 to 1998. *International Journal of Obesity, 25* (4), 590–3.

Kaufert, P.A. & Lock, M. (1997). Medicalization of women's third age. *Journal of Psychosomatic Obstetrics and Gynecology, 18* (2), 81–6.

Kaufman, L. (1980). Prime-time nutrition. *Journal of Communication, 30* (Summer), 37–46.

Kennedy, G.E. & Bero, L.A. (1999). Print media coverage of research on passive smoking. *Tobacco Control, 8,* 254–60.

Kerson, T.S., Kerson, J.F. & Kerson, L.A. (2000). She can have a seizure maybe; then we can watch: the portrayal of epilepsy in film. *Social Work in Health Care, 30* (3), 95–110.

Kessler, L. (1989). Women's magazines' coverage of smoking related health hazards. *Journalism Quarterly, 66,* 316–23.

Kilgore, M. (1996). Magic, moralism and marginalization: media coverage of cervical, ovarian and uterine cancer. In Parrott, R.L. & Condit C.L. (Eds), *Evaluating women's health messages: a resource book.* Thousand Oaks, CA: Sage. pp. 249–60.

Kimball, P. (1994). *Downsizing the news: network cutbacks in the nation's capital.* Baltimore, MD: Johns Hopkins University Press.

King, D. (1990). 'Prostitutes as pariah in the age of AIDS': a content analysis of coverage of women prostitutes in the *New York Times* and the *Washington Post* September 1985–April 1988. *Women and Health, 16* (3/4), 155–76.

Kitzinger, J. (1988). Defending innocence: ideologies of childhood. *Feminist Review, 28* (January), 77–87.

Kitzinger, J. (1996). Media constructions of sexual abuse risks. *Child Abuse Review, 5* (5), 319–33.

Kitzinger, J. (1998). The gender-politics of news production: silenced voices and false memories. In Carter, C., Branston, G. & Allan, G. (Eds), *News, gender and power.* London: Routledge. pp. 186–203.

Kitzinger, J. (1999a). A sociology of media power: key issues in audience reception research. In Philo, G. (Ed.), *Message received*. Harlow: Addison Wesley and Longman. pp. 3–20.

Kitzinger, J. (1999b). The ultimate neighbour from hell? Stranger danger and the media framing of paedophiles. In Franklin, B. (Ed.), *Social policy, the media and misrepresentations*. London: Routledge. pp. 207–21.

Kitzinger, J. (2000). Media templates: patterns of association and the (re)construction of meaning over time. *Media Culture and Society, 22* (1), 61–84.

Kitzinger, J. & Miller, D. (1992). 'African AIDS': the media and audience beliefs. In Aggleton, P., Davies, P. & Hart, G. (Eds), *AIDS: rights, risks and reason*. London: Falmer Press. pp. 28–52.

Kitzinger, J. & Reilly, J. (1997). The rise and fall of risk reporting: media coverage of human genetics research, 'false memory syndrome' and 'mad cow disease'. *European Journal of Communication, 12* (3), 319–50.

Kitzinger, J. & Skidmore, P. (1995). Playing safe: media coverage of child sexual abuse prevention strategies. *Child Abuse Review, 4*, 47–56.

Klaidman, S. (1991). *Health in the headlines: the stories behind the stories*. New York: Oxford University Press.

Klapp, O.E. (1954). Heroes, villains and fools, as agents of social control. *American Sociological Review, 19* (1), 56–62.

Kleinman, A. (1988). *The illness narratives: suffering, healing and the human condition*. New York: Basic Books.

Kline, K.N. (1996). The drama of in utero drug exposure: fetus takes first billing. In Parrott, R.L. & Condit, C.L. (Eds), *Evaluating women's health messages: a resource book*. Thousand Oaks, CA: Sage. pp. 61–75.

Krantzler, N.J. (1986). Media images of physicians and nurses in the United States. *Social Science and Medicine, 22* (9), 933–52.

Kristiansen, C.M. (1983). Newspaper coverage of diseases and actual mortality statistics. *European Journal of Social Psychology, 13* (2), 193–4.

Kristiansen, C.M. & Harding, P.J. (1984). Mobilisation of health behaviour by the press in Britain. *Journalism Quarterly, 61* (2), 364–70, 398.

Kristiansen, C.M. & Harding, P.J. (1988). A comparison of the coverage of health issues by Britain's quality and popular press. *Social Behavior, 3* (1), 25–32.

Kubler-Ross, E. (1969). *On death and dying*. New York: Macmillan.

Labov, W. (1973). *Language in the inner city*. Philadelphia: University of Pennsylvania Press.

Lakoff, G. & Johnson, M. (1980). *Metaphors we live by*. Chicago: University of Chicago Press.

Langer, J. (1998). *Tabloid television: popular journalism and the 'other news'*. London: Routledge.

Lantz, P.M. & Booth, K.M. (1998). The social construction of the breast cancer epidemic. *Social Science and Medicine, 46* (7), 907–18.

Leask, J.A. & Chapman, S. (1998). 'An attempt to swindle nature': press anti-immunisation reportage 1993–1997. *Australian and New Zealand Journal of Public Health, 22* (1), 17–26.

Leathar, D.S., Hastings, G.B., O'Reilly, K., & Davies, J.K. (Eds) (1986). *Health education and the media II*. Oxford: Pergamon Press.

Leonhard-Spark, P.J. (1978). Obesity and the popular arts. In Winick, C. (Ed.), *Deviance and mass media*. Thousand Oaks, CA: Sage.

Leppard, W., Ogletree, S. & Wallen, E. (1993). Gender stereotyping in medical advertising – much ado about something. *Sex Roles, 29* (11–12), 829–38.

Lévi-Strauss, C. (1968). *Structural anthropology.* Harmondsworth: Penguin.

Lewis, J. (1991). *The ideological octopus.* London: Routledge.

Lichtenberg, J. & Maclean, D. (1991). The role of the media in risk communication. In Kasperson, R. & Stallne, P. (Eds), *Communicating risks to the public: international perspectives.* London: Kluwer Academic. pp. 157–73.

Lichtenstein, S., Slovic, P., Fischoff, B., Layman, M. & Combs, B. (1978). Judged frequency of lethal events. *Journal of Experimental Psychology: Human Learning and Memory, 4* (6), 551–78.

Lieberman, L. (1972). The changing ideology of socialization: toilet training, mass media, and society. *International Journal of Contemporary Sociology, 9* (4), 188–99.

Liebmann-Smith, J. & Rosen, S.L. (1978). The presentation of illness on television. In Winick, C. (Ed.), *Deviance and mass media.* London: Sage. pp. 79–93.

Livingstone, S. & Lunt, P. (1994). *Talk on television: audience participation and public debate.* London: Routledge.

Lloyd, G. & Norris, C. (1999). Including ADHD? *Disability and Society, 14* (4), 505–17.

Lorde, A. (1980). *The cancer journals.* San Francisco, CA: Spinsters Ink.

Lovdahl, U. & Riska, E. (2000). The construction of gender and mental health in Nordic psychotropic-drug advertising. *International Journal of Health Services, 30* (2), 387–406.

Lovdahl, U., Riska, A. & Riska, E. (1999). Gender display in Scandinavian and American advertising for antidepressants. *Scandinavian Journal of Public Health, 27* (4), 306–10.

Lowery, S.A. (1980). Soap and booze in the afternoon: an analysis of the portrayal of alcohol in daytime serials. *Journal of Studies on Alcohol, 41* (9), 829–38.

Lowry, D.T. & Towles, D.E. (1989). Soap opera portrayals of sex, contraception, and sexually transmitted diseases. *Journal of Communication, 39* (2): 76–83.

Luke, C. (1994). Childhood and parenting in popular culture. *Australian and New Zealand Journal of Sociology, 30* (3), 289–302.

Lumby, C. (1994). Feminism and the media: the biggest fantasy of all. *Media Information Australia, 72,* 49–54.

Lumley, K. (1998). 'Teeny Thugs in Blair's Sights': media portrayals of children in education and their policy implications. *Youth and Policy, 61* (Autumn), 1–11.

Lunin, L.F. (1987). Where does the public gets its health information? *Bulletin of the New York Academy of Medicine, 63,* 923–39.

Lupton, D. (1993a). AIDS risk and heterosexuality in the Australian press. *Discourse and Society, 4* (3), 307–28.

Lupton, D. (1993b). Back to Bedlam – Chelmsford and the press. *Australian and New Zealand Journal of Psychiatry, 27* (1), 140–8.

Lupton, D. (1993c). The construction of patienthood in medical advertising. *International Journal of Health Services, 23* (4), 805–19.

Lupton, D. (1994a). *Moral threats and dangerous desires: AIDS in the news media.* London: Taylor and Francis.

Lupton, D. (1994b). Femininity, responsibility, and the technological imperative: discourses on breast cancer in the Australian press. *International Journal of Health Services, 24* (1), 73–89.

Lupton, D. (1998a). Doctors in the news media: lay and medical audiences' responses. *Journal of Sociology, 34* (1), 35–48.

Lupton, D. (1998b). Medicine and health care in popular media. In Petersen, A. & Waddell, C. (Eds), *Health matters: a sociology of illness, prevention and care*. Buckingham: Open University Press.

Lupton, D. & Chapman, S. (1991). Death of a heart surgeon: some thoughts about press accounts of the murder of Victor Chang. *British Medical Journal, 303*, 1583–6.

Lupton, D. & McLean, J. (1998). Representing doctors: discourses and images in the Australian press. *Social Science and Medicine, 46* (8), 947–58.

Lusk, B. (1999). 'Patients' images in nursing magazine advertisements. *Advances in Nursing Science, 21* (3), 66–75.

Lusk, B. (2000). Pretty and powerless: nurses in advertisements, 1930–1950. *Research in Nursing and Health, 23* (3), 229–36.

Lyons, A.C. & Willatt, S. (1999). From suet pudding to superhero: representations of men's health for women. *Health, 3* (3), 283–302.

Makas, E. (1993). The portrayal of people with disabilities on television. In Berry, G.L. & Asanen, J.K. (Eds), *Children and television: images in a changing socio-cultural world*. Thousand Oaks, CA: Sage. pp. 255–68.

Manning, S. & Schneiderman, L.J. (1996). Miracles or limits: what message from the medical marketplace? *HEC Forum, 8* (2), 103–8.

Marino, C. & Gerlach, K.K. (1999). An analysis of breast cancer coverage in selected women's magazines, 1987–1995. *American Journal of Health Promotion, 13* (3), 163–70.

Martin, E. (1989). *The woman in the body: a cultural analysis of reproduction*. Buckingham: Open University Press.

Martinez, R., Johnson-Robledo, I., Ulsh, H.M. & Chrisler, J.C. (2000). Singing 'the baby blues': a content analysis of popular press articles about postpartum affective disturbances. *Women and Health, 31* (2–3), 37–56.

Martyn, C. (2000). Uncomfortable viewing. *British Medical Journal, 321*, 904.

Mazur, A. (1987). Putting radon on the public's risk agenda. *Science, Technology, and Human Values, 12* (3–4), 86–93.

McConatha, J.T., Schnell, F. & McKenna, A. (1999). Description of older adults as depicted in magazine advertisements. *Psychological Reports, 85* (3), 1051–6.

McGlaughlin, J. (1975). The doctor shows. *Journal of Communication, 25*, 182–4.

McKay, S. & Bonner, F. (1999). Telling stories: breast cancer pathographies in Australian women's magazines. *Women's Studies International Forum, 22* (5), 563–71.

McNaughton-Cassill, M.E. (2001). The news media and psychological distress. *Anxiety, Stress and Coping, 14* (2), 193–211.

McRobbie, A. (1999). *In the culture society*. London: Routledge.

Mercado-Martinez, F.H., Robles-Silva, L., Moreno-Leal, N. & Franco-Almazan, C. (2001). Inconsistent journalism: the coverage of chronic diseases in the Mexican press. *Journal of Health Communication, 6* (3), 235–47.

Miles, A. (1998). Radio and the commodification of natural medicine in Ecuador. *Social Science and Medicine, 47* (12), 2127–37.

Miller, D. (1995). Introducing the 'gay gene': media and scientific representations. *Public Understanding of Science, 4*, 269–84.

Miller, D., Kitzinger, J., Williams, K. & Beharrell, P. (1998). *The circuit of mass communication: media strategies, representation and audience reception in the AIDS crisis.* London: Sage.

Miller, D. & Reilly, J. (1995). Making an issue of food safety: the media, pressure groups and the public sphere. In Maurer, D. & Sobal, J. (Eds), *Eating agendas: food and nutrition as social problems.* New York: Aldine de Gruyter. pp. 305–36.

Miller, D.H. (1996). A matter of consequence: abortion rhetoric and media messages. In Parrott, R.L. & Condit, C.L. (Eds), *Evaluating women's health messages: a resource book.* Thousand Oaks, CA: Sage. pp. 33–48.

Miller, P.N., Miller, D.W., McKibbin, E.M. & Pettys, G.L. (1999). Stereotypes of the elderly in magazine advertisements 1956–1996. *International Journal of Aging and Human Development, 49* (4), 319–37.

Mirotznick, J. & Mosellie, B.M. (1986). Genital herpes and the mass media. *Journal of Popular Culture, 20,* 1–11.

Moller, D.W. (1996). *Confronting death: values, institutions and human mortality.* Oxford: Oxford University Press.

Moore, O. (1998). *PWA: Looking AIDS in the face.* London: Picador.

Moore, T.E. & Mae, R. (1987). Who dies and who cries: death and bereavement in children's literature. *Journal of Communication, 37* (4), 52–64.

Morley, D. (1980). *The Nationwide audience.* London: British Film Institute

Morley, D. (1986). *Family television: cultural power and domestic leisure.* London: Routledge.

Morrall, P.A. (2000). *Madness and murder.* London: Whurr.

Moyer, C.A., Vishnu, L.O. & Sonnad, S.S. (2001). Providing health information to women – the role of magazines. *International Journal of Technology Assessment in Health Care, 17* (1), 137–45.

Muncie, J. (1994). Exorcising demons: media, politics and criminal justice. In Franklin, B. (Ed.), *Social policy, the media and misrepresentation.* London: Routledge. pp. 174–89.

Murray, S. (1999). Eating disorders and criticism of cultural ideals. *European Eating Disorders Review, 7* (3), 204–12.

Naidoo, J. & Wills, J. (2000). *Health promotion: foundations for practice.* London: Baillière Tindall.

Nairn, R. (1999). Does the use of psychiatrists as sources of information improve media depictions of mental illness? A pilot study. *Australian and New Zealand Journal of Psychiatry, 33* (4), 583–9.

Nava, M. (1988). Cleveland and the press: outrage and anxiety in the reporting of child sexual abuse. *Feminist Review, 28* (Spring): 103–21.

Nelkin, D. (1995). *Selling science: how the press covers science and technology.* New York: W.H. Freeman.

Nelkin, D. & Lindee, M.S. (1995). *The DNA mystique: the gene as cultural icon.* New York: W.H. Freeman.

Noble, C. & Bell, P. (1992). Reproducing women's nature: media constructions of IVF and related issues. *Australian Journal of Social Issues, 27* (1), 17–30.

Nunnally, J.C. (1973). Mental illness: what the media present. In Cohen, S. & Young, J. (Eds), *The manufacture of news: social problems, deviance and the mass media.* Beverly Hills, CA: Sage.

O'Connor, S., Deeks, J.D., Hawton, K., Simkin, S., Keen, A., Altman, D.G.,

Philo, G. & Bulstrode, C. (1999). Effects of a drug overdose in a television drama on knowledge of specific dangers of self-poisoning: population based surveys. *British Medical Journal, 318* (7189), 978–9.

Olson, B. (1994). Sex and the soaps – a comparative content-analysis of health issues. *Journalism Quarterly, 71* (4), 840–50.

Owen, P.R. & Laurel-Seller, E. (2000). Weight and shape ideals: thin is dangerously in. *Journal of Applied Social Psychology, 30* (5), 979–90.

Pacl, P. (1998). The elderly as readers, listeners and viewers of mass media. *Sociologicky Casopis, 34* (3), 339–46.

Parkes, C.M. (1986). *Bereavement: studies of grief in adult life.* Harmondsworth: Penguin.

Pearl, D., Bouthilet, L. & Lazar, J. (1982). *Television and behavior: 10 years of scientific progress and implications for the 80s.* Washington, DC: US Government Printing Office.

Peters, H.P. (1995). The interaction of journalists and scientific experts: co-operation and conflict between two professional cultures. *Media, Culture and Society, 17* (1), 31–48.

Petersen, A. (1994). Governing images: media constructions of the 'normal', 'healthy' subject. *Media Information Australia, 72,* 32–40.

Petersen, A. (2001). Biofantasies: genetics and medicine in the print news media. *Social Science and Medicine, 52* (8), 1255–68.

Petersen, M. (1973). The visibility and image of older people on television. *Journalism Quarterly, 50,* 569–73.

Pfau, M., Mullen, L. & Garrow, K. (1995). The influence of television viewing on public perception of physicians. *Journal of Broadcasting, 39* (4), 441–58.

Pfund, N. & Hofstadter, L. (1981). Biomedical innovation and the press. *Journal of Communication, 31* (2), 138–54.

Philo, G. (Ed.) (1996). *Media and mental distress.* London: Longman.

Philo, G. (Ed.) (1999). *Message received: Glasgow media group research 1993–1998.* Harlow: Addison Wesley Longman.

Philo, G. & Secker, J. (1999). Media and mental health. In Franklin, B. (Ed.), *Social policy, the media and misrepresentation.* London: Routledge. pp. 135–45.

Philo G., Secker, J., Platt, S., Henderson, L., McGlaughlin, G. & Burnside, J. (1994). The impact of the mass media on public images of mental illness: media content and audience belief. *Health Education Journal, 53,* 271–81.

Picardie, R. (1998). *Before I say goodbye.* London: Penguin.

Pichert, J.W. & Hanson, S.L. (1983). Arthritis in the national TV news: 1971 to 1981. *Journal of Rheumatology, 10,* 323–5.

Pickering, M., Littlewood, J. & Walter, T. (1992). Beauty and the beast: sex and death in the tabloid press. In Field, D. (Ed.), *Death, gender and ethnicity.* London: Routledge. pp. 124–41.

Pini, P. (1995). Media wars. *Lancet, 346,* 1681–3.

Pinto, M.B. (2000). On the nature and properties of appeals used in direct-to-consumer advertising of prescription drugs. *Psychological Reports, 86* (2), 597–607.

Pitts, V. (1999). Body modification, self-mutilation and agency in media accounts of a subculture. *Body and Society, 5* (2–3), 291–303.

Platt, S. (1987). The aftermath of Angie's overdose: is soap (opera) damaging to your health? *British Medical Journal, 294*, 954–7.

Potter, J., Wetherell, M. & Chitty, A. (1991). Quantification rhetoric: cancer on television. *Discourse and Society, 3* (3), 333–65.

Potts, L.K. (2000). Publishing the personal: autobiographical narratives of breast cancer and the self. In Potts L.K. (Ed.), *Ideologies of breast cancer: feminist perspectives*. London: Macmillan. pp. 98–127.

Power, J.G. (1995). Media dependency, bubonic plague, and the social construction of the Chinese Other. *Journal of Communication Inquiry, 19* (1), 89–110.

Powers, A. (1999). Newspaper coverage of the breast implant controversy. *Women and Health, 30* (2), 83–98.

Prebish, C.S. (1993). *Religion and sport: the meeting of sacred and profane*. Westport, CT: Greenwood Press.

Press, N., Fishman, J.R. & Koenig, B. (2000). A collective fear, individualized risk: the social and cultural context of genetic testing for breast cancer. *Nursing Ethics, 7* (3), 237–49.

Propp, V.I. (1968). *Morphology of the folk tale*. Austin, TX: University of Texas Press.

Radford, T. (1996). Influence and power of the media. *Lancet, 347*, 1533–5.

Raymond, C.A. (1985). Risk in the press; conflicting journalistic ideologies. In Nelkin, D. (Ed.), *The language of risk*. Beverly Hills: Sage. pp. 97–133.

Reilly, J. (1999). 'Just another food scare?' Public understanding and the BSE crisis. In Philo, G. (Ed.), *Message received: Glasgow media group research 1993–1998*. Harlow: Addison Wesley Longman. pp. 128–45.

Reinharz, S. (1997). Enough already! The pervasiveness of warnings in everyday life. In Glassner, B. & Hertz, R. (Eds), *Qualitative sociology as everyday life*. Thousand Oaks, CA: Sage. pp. 31–40.

Roberts, R.E.L. (1997). Power/knowledge and discredited identities: media representations of herpes. *Sociological Quarterly, 38* (2), 265–84.

Robinson, I. (1990). Personal narratives, social careers and medical courses: analysing life trajectories in autobiographies of people with multiple sclerosis. *Social Science and Medicine, 30* (11), 1173–86.

Rolland, J.S. (1997). The meaning of disability and suffering: sociopolitical and ethical concerns. *Family Process, 36* (4), 437–40.

Rose, D. (1998). Television, madness and community care. *Journal of Community and Applied Social Psychology, 8* (3), 213–28.

Rose, N. (1989). *Governing the soul: the shaping of the private self*. London: Routledge.

Rosen, A. & Walter, G. (2000). Way out of tune: lessons from Shine and its exposé. *Australian and New Zealand Journal of Psychiatry, 34* (2), 237–44.

Ross, K. (1997). But where's me in it? Disability, broadcasting and the audience. *Media Culture and Society, 19* (4), 669–77.

Ross, K. (2000). Growing old invisibly: third agers and television. Unpublished research report for Carlton Television.

Roy, A. & Harwood, J. (1997). Underrepresented, positively portrayed: older adults in television commercials. *Journal of Applied Communication Research, 25* (1), 39–56.

Rutherford-Smith, R. (1979). Mythic elements in television news. *Journal of Communication, 29* (1), 75–82.

Sabo, D. & Jansen, S.C. (1998). Prometheus unbound: constructions of masculinity in the sports media. In Werner, L.A. (Ed.), *MediaSport*. London: Routledge. pp. 202–17.

Sacks, V. (1996). Women and AIDS: an analysis of media misrepresentations. *Social Science and Medicine, 42* (1), 59–73.

Safer, D.J. & Krager, J.M. (1992). Effect of a media blitz and a threatened lawsuit on stimulant treatment. *Journal of the American Medical Association, 268* (8), 1004–7.

Sampson, A. (1996). The crisis at the heart of our media. *British Journalism Review, 7* (3), 42–51.

Sapolsky, B.S. & Tabarlet, J.O. (1991). Sex in prime-time television – 1979 versus 1989. *Journal of Broadcasting and Electronic Media, 35* (4), 505–16.

Sarna, L. (1995). Lung cancer: the overlooked women's health priority. *Cancer Practice, 3* (1), 13–19.

Saywell, C., Henderson, L. & Beattie, L. (2000). Sexualised illness: the newsworthy body in media representations of breast cancer. In Potts, L.K. (Ed.), *Ideologies of breast cancer: feminist perspectives*. London: Macmillan. pp. 37–62.

Scheff, T. (1990). *Micro sociology, discourse, emotion and social structure*. Chicago: University of Chicago Press.

Schell, L.A. (1999). A content analysis of CBS's coverage of the 1996 Paralympic Games. *Adapted Physical Activity Quarterly, 16* (1), 27–47.

Schudson, M. (1989). The sociology of news production. *Media, Culture and Society, 11* (3), 263–82.

Seale, C.F. (1995a). Heroic death. *Sociology, 29* (4), 597–613.

Seale, C.F. (1995b). Stigma and normality. In Davey, B. & Seale, C.F. (Eds), *Experiencing and explaining disease*. Buckingham: Open University Press. pp. 11–26.

Seale, C.F. (1998). *Constructing death: the sociology of dying and bereavement*. Cambridge: Cambridge University Press.

Seale, C.F. (1999). *The quality of qualitative research*. London: Sage.

Seale, C.F. (2000). Changing patterns of death and dying. *Social Science and Medicine, 51* (6), 917–30.

Seale, C.F. (2001a). Sporting cancer: struggle language in news reports of people with cancer. *Sociology of Health and Illness, 23* (3), 308–29.

Seale, C.F. (2001b). Cancer in the news: religion, fate and justice in news stories about people with cancer. *Health, 5* (4), 445–60.

Seale, C.F. (2002). Cancer heroics: a study of news reports with particular reference to gender. *Sociology, 36* (1), 107–26.

Searight, H.R. & McLaren, A.L. (1998). Attention-deficit hyperactivity disorder: the medicalization of misbehavior. *Journal of Clinical Psychology in Medical Settings, 5* (4), 467–95.

Sefcovic, E.M.I. (1996). Hysterectomy: what the popular press said (1986–1992). In Parrott, R.L. & Condit, C.L. (Eds), *Evaluating women's health messages: a resource book*. Thousand Oaks, CA: Sage. pp. 370–81.

Shakespeare, T. (1994). Cultural representations of disabled people: dustbins for disavowal. *Disability and Society, 9* (3), 283–301.

Shakespeare, T. (1999). 'Losing the plot'? Medical and activist discourses of contemporary genetics and disability. *Sociology of Health and Illness, 21* (5), 669–88.

Shoebridge, A. & Steed, L. (1999). Discourse about menopause in selected print media. *Australian and New Zealand Journal of Public Health, 23* (5), 475–81.

Shoemaker, P.J., Wanta, W. & Leggett, D. (1989). Drug coverage and public opinion, 1972–1986. In Shoemaker, P. (Ed.), *Communication campaigns about drugs: government, media and the public.* Hillsdale, NJ: Lawrence Erlbaum Associates. pp. 67–80.

Signorielli, N. (1989). The stigma of mental illness on television. *Journal of Broadcasting and Electronic Media, 3,* 325–31.

Signorielli, N. (1993). *Mass media images and impact on health.* Westport, CT: Greenwood Press.

Signorielli, N. & Bacue, A. (1999). Recognition and respect: a content analysis of prime-time television characters across three decades. *Sex Roles, 40* (7–8), 527–44.

Signorielli, N. & Staples, J. (1997). Television and children's conceptions of nutrition. *Health Communication, 9* (4), 289–301.

Silverman, D. (1998). *Harvey Sacks: social science and conversation analysis.* Cambridge: Polity.

Silverstein, B., Perdue, L., Peterson, B. & Kelly, E. (1986). The role of the mass media in promoting a thin standard of bodily attractiveness for women. *Sex Roles, 14* (9/10), 519–32.

Silverstone, R. (1994). *Television and everyday life,* London: Routledge.

Singer, E. (1990). A question of accuracy: how journalists and scientists report research on hazards. *Journal of Communication, 40* (4), 102–16.

Singer, E. & Endreny, P. (1987). Reporting hazards: their benefits and costs. *Journal of Communication, 37* (3), 10–26.

Skidmore, P. (1998). Gender and the agenda: news reporting of child sexual abuse. In Carter, C., Branston, G. & Allan, G. (Eds), *News, gender and power.* London: Routledge. pp. 204–18.

Smith, M.E.G. (1992). The Burzynski controversy in the United States and in Canada: a comparative case study in the sociology of alternative medicine. *Canadian Journal of Sociology/Cahiers Canadiens de Sociologie, 17* (2), 133–60.

Smythe, T.C. (1996). Growing old in commercials: a joke not shared. In Lester, D.M. (Ed.), *Images that injure: pictorial stereotypes in the media.* Westport, CT: Praeger. pp. 113–16.

Sommerland, E.A. & Robbins, A. (1997). Healthy alliances and social action broadcasting: assessment of a local radio project. *Health Education Journal, 56,* 51–63.

Sontag, S. (1991). *Illness as metaphor.* London: Penguin (first published in 1978).

Spanier, B.P. (2000). What made Ellen (and Anne) gay? Feminist critique of popular and scientific beliefs. In Marchessault, J. & Sawchuk, K. (Eds), *Wild science: reading feminism, medicine and the media.* London: Routledge. pp. 80–101.

Sparks, C. & Tulloch, J. (Eds) (2000). *Tabloid tales: global debates over media standards.* London: Rowman and Littlefield.

Sparks, R. (1992). *Television and the drama of crime: moral tales and the place of crime in public life.* Buckingham: Open University Press.

Stacey, J. (1997). *Teratologies: a cultural study of cancer.* London: Routledge.

Stack, S. (1987). Celebrities and suicide: a taxonomy and analysis 1948–1983. *American Sociological Review, 52* (June), 401–12.

Stallings, R. (1990). Media discourse and the social construction of risk. *Social Problems, 37* (1), 80–95.

Stepney, R. (1996). The concept of addiction: its use and abuse in the media and science. *Human Psychopharmacology–Clinical and Experimental, 11,* S15–S20.

Thurber, J. (1948). Onward and upward with the arts: soapland. *The New Yorker,* 29 May: 30–3.

Todorov, T. (1977). *The poetics of prose.* Oxford: Blackwell.

Tones, K. & Tilford, S. (Eds) (1994). *Health education: effectiveness, efficiency and equity.* London: Chapman Hall.

Torrey, E.F. (1994). Violent behavior by individuals with serious mental illness. *Hospital and Community Psychiatry, 45* (7), 653–62.

Trujillo, N. (1993). Interpreting November 22nd: a critical ethnography of an assassination site. *Quarterly Journal of Speech, 79* (4), 447–66.

Tsaliki, L. (1995). The media and the construction of an 'imagined community': the role of media events on Greek television. *European Journal of Communication, 10* (3): 345–70.

Tuckett, D., Boulton, M., Olson, C. & Williams, A. (1985). *Meetings between experts: an approach to sharing ideas in medical consultations.* London: Tavistock.

Tulloch, J. (1995). From grim reaper to cheery condom: images of aging and death in Australian AIDS education campaigns. In Featherstone, M. & Wernick, A. (Eds), *Images of aging: cultural representations of later life.* London: Routledge. pp. 263–79.

Tulloch, J. & Lupton, D. (1997). *Television, AIDS and risk: a cultural studies approach to health communication.* St Leonards, New South Wales: Allen and Unwin.

Turner, B.S. (1992). *Regulating bodies: essays in medical sociology.* London: Routledge.

Turow, J. (1989). *Playing doctor: television, storytelling, and medical power.* Oxford and New York: Oxford University Press.

Turow, J. (1996). Television entertainment and the US health-care debate. *Lancet, 347,* 1240–3.

Uusitalo, L. Ovaskainen, M.L. & Prattala, R. (2000). Antioxidants in the Finnish press: a battlefield of alternative and conventional medicine. *Health Promotion International, 15* (1), 71–8.

Van de Berg, L.R. (1998). The sports hero meets mediated celebrityhood. In Wenner, L.A. (Ed.), *MediaSport.* London: Routledge. pp. 134–53.

Van der Wardt, E.M., Taal, E., Rasker, J.J. & Wiegman, O. (1999). Media coverage of chronic diseases in the Netherlands. *Seminars in Arthritis and Rheumatism, 28* (5), 333–41.

Van Trigt, A.M., de Jong-van den Berg, L.T., Haaijer-Ruskamp, F.M., Willems, J. & Tromp, T.F. (1994). Medical journalists and expert sources on medicines. *Public Understanding of Science, 3,* 309–21.

Van Trigt, A.M., de Jong-van den Berg, L.T., Voogt, L.M., Willems, J., Tromp, T.F. & Haaijer-Ruskamp, F.M. (1995). Setting the agenda: does the medical literature set the agenda for articles about medicines in the newspapers? *Social Science and Medicine, 41* (6), 893–9.

Van Zoonen, L. (1994). *Feminist media studies*. London: Sage.

Viser, V. (1997). Mode of address, emotion, and stylistics: images of children in American magazine advertising, 1940–1950. *Communication Research, 24* (1), 83–101.

Wahl, O.F. (1992). Mass media images of mental illness – a review of the literature. *Journal of Community Psychology, 20* (4), 343–52.

Wahl, O.F. & Lefkowits, J.A. (1989). Impact of a television film on attitudes towards mental illness. *American Journal of Community Psychology, 17* (4), 521–8.

Walkerdine, V. (1997). *Daddy's girl: young girls and popular culture*. Cambridge, MA.: Harvard University Press.

Wallack, L. (1994). Media advocacy: a strategy for empowering people and communities. *Journal of Public Health Policy, 2*, 420–36.

Walter, T. (1991). The mourning after Hillsborough. *Sociological Review, 39* (3), 599–625.

Walter, T. (1994). *The revival of death*. London: Routledge.

Walter, T., Littlewood, J. & Pickering, M. (1995). Death in the news: the public invigilation of private emotion. *Sociology, 29* (4), 579–96.

Ward, L.M. (1995). Talking about sex – common themes about sexuality in the prime-time television programs children and adolescents view most. *Journal of Youth and Adolescence, 24* (15), 595–615.

Warner, K.E. (1985). Cigarette advertising and media coverage of smoking and health. *New England Journal of Medicine, 312* (6), 384–8.

Warner, K.E., Goldenhar, L.M. & McLaughlin, C.G. (1992). Cigarette advertising and magazine coverage of the hazards of smoking. *New England Journal of Medicine, 326* (5), 305–9.

Wartenberg, D. & Greenberg, M. (1992). Epidemiology, the press and the EMF controversy. *Public Understanding of Science, 1*, 383–94.

Wasserman, I.M., Stack, S. & Reeves, J.L. (1994). Suicide and the media: the *New York Times*'s presentation of front-page suicide stories between 1910 and 1920. *Journal of Communication, 44* (2), 64–83.

Watney, S. (1997). *Policing desire: pornography, AIDS and the media*. (3rd ed.) London: Cassell.

Watson, M.S., Trasciatti, M.A. & King, C.P. (1996). Our bodies, our risk: dilemmas in contraceptive information. In Parrott, R.L. & Condit, C.L. (Eds), *Evaluating women's health messages: a resource book*. Thousand Oaks, CA: Sage. pp. 95–108.

Way, W.L. (1983). Food-related behaviours on prime-time television. *Journal of Nutrition Education, 15* (3), 105–9.

Weldon, R.A. (2001). An 'urban legend' of global proportion: an analysis of non-fiction accounts of the Ebola virus. *Journal of Health Communication, 6* (3), 281–94.

Wellings, K. (1986). Help or hype: an analysis of media coverage of the 1983 'pill scare'. In Leathar, D.S., Hastings, G.B., O'Reilly, K. & Davies, J.K. (Eds), *Health education and the media II*. Oxford: Pergamon Press. pp. 109–16.

Wellings, K. (1988). Perceptions of risk: media treatment of AIDS. In Aggleton, P. & Homans, H. (Eds), *Social aspects of AIDS*. London: Falmer Press. pp. 83–105.

Weston, L.C. & Ruggiero, J.A. (1986). The popular approach to women's health issues: a content analysis of women's magazines in the 1970s. *Women and Health, 10* (4), 47–62.

Westwood, B. & Westwood, G. (1999). Assessment of newspaper reporting of public health and the medical model: a methodological case study. *Health Promotion International, 14* (1), 53–64.

Whelan, E.M., Sheridan, M.J., Meister, K.A. & Mosher, B.A. (1981). Analysis of coverage of tobacco hazards in women's magazines. *Journal of Public Health Policy,* March: 28–35.

Whiteman, M.K., Cui, Y.D., Flaws, J.A., Langenberg, P. & Bush, T.L. (2001). Media coverage of women's health issues: is there a bias in the reporting of an association between hormone replacement therapy and breast cancer? *Journal of Women's Health and Gender-Based Medicine, 10* (6), 571–7.

Wigand, R.T. (1994). Health information dissemination in the information age: media, messages and roles. *Communications, 19* (2/3), 209–22.

Wilkins, L. (1996). The blind in the media: a vision of stereotypes in action. In Lester, D.M. (Ed.), *Images that injure: pictorial stereotypes in the media.* Westport, CT: Praeger. pp. 127–34.

Williams, K. (1999). Dying of ignorance? Journalists, news sources and the media reporting of HIV/AIDS. In Franklin, B. (Ed.), *Social policy, the media and misrepresentation.* London: Routledge. pp. 69–85.

Wilson, C., Nairn, R., Coverdale, J. & Panapa, A. (1999). Constructing mental illness as dangerous: a pilot study. *Australian and New Zealand Journal of Psychiatry, 33* (2), 240–7.

Wilson, C., Nairn, R., Coverdale, J. & Panapa, A. (2000). How mental illness is portrayed in children's television – a prospective study. *British Journal of Psychiatry, 176,* 440–3.

Winick, C. (1978). Mental illness and psychiatrists in movies. In Winick, C. (Ed.), *Deviance and mass media.* London: Sage. pp. 45–77.

Winick, C. & Winick, M.P. (1976). Drug education and the content of mass media dealing with 'dangerous drugs' and alcohol. In Ostman, R.E. (Ed.), *Communication research and drug education. Vol III: International yearbooks of drug addiction and society.* Thousand Oaks, CA: Sage. pp. 15–37.

Wiseman, C.V., Gray, J.J., Mosimann J.E. & Ahrens, A.H. (1992). Cultural expectations of thinness in women – an update. *International Journal of Eating Disorders, 11* (1), 85–9.

Wolf, J.H. (2000). The social and medical construction of lactation pathology. *Women and Health, 30* (3), 93–110.

Yamey, G. (2001). You can always pop a pill. *British Medical Journal, 322,* 804.

Zillmann, D. (2000). Influence of unrestrained access to erotica on adolescents' and young adults' dispositions toward sexuality. *Journal of Adolescent Health, 27* (2), 41–4.

Ziporyn, T. (1988). *Disease in the popular American press: the case of diphtheria, typhoid fever and syphilis. 1870–1920.* New York: Greenwood Press.

Index